HARD TIMES
CATALOG
FOR
YOUTH MINISTRY

HARD TIMES CATALOG FOR YOUTH MINISTRY

HARD TIMES
CATALOG
FOR
YOUTH MINISTRY

COMPILED BY
MARILYN & DENNIS BENSON

group
BOOKS
P.O. BOX 481, LOVELAND, CO 80539

CREDITS

**HARD TIMES CATALOG
FOR YOUTH MINISTRY**

Designed by
Laurel Watson

ILLUSTRATION

Jean Curtiss—58, 111, 127, 142, 151, 191, 204,
214, 223
Laurel Watson—covers, 35, 51, 52, 57, 58, 59, 60,
68, 69, 70, 75, 79, 83, 91, 97, 102, 105, 109, 112,
114, 115, 124, 125, 127, 138, 139, 143, 145, 152,
154, 155, 173, 177, 181, 183, 184, 185, 190, 206,
212, 213, 218, 219, 221, 299, 235, 236, 239, 243,
253, 262

PHOTOGRAPHY

Church World Service—174
Paul Conklin—71, 87, 128, 240
Ron Engh—179
Michael Goldberg—192, 198
Grand Canyon Youth Expeditions, Inc.—146
GROUP Workcamps—164, 165
Institute for Creative Living—147
Dick Kezlan—226
Mass Media—189
Anne Merrifield—286 (Costumes by Harriet
Woodcock)
Octavio Noda—23
Gary Rehn—222, 227
Rising Hope—200
Schwinn—230
Thom Schultz—32, 38, 40, 43, 45, 50, 53, 56, 61,
62, 64, 66, 69, 70, 74, 75, 76, 85, 89, 93, 95, 106,
108, 110, 112, 113, 115, 116, 117, 120, 123, 129,
131, 132, 133, 134, 135, 136, 137, 142, 144, 156,
161, 166, 168, 169, 176, 178, 180, 183, 186, 207,
208, 215, 216, 217, 218, 221, 224, 225, 228, 232,
234, 238, 239 241, 242, 248, 250, 254, 261, 265
Ben Smith—199
Lee Sparks—81, 108, 128, 135, 149, 154, 245
David S. Strickler—26, 54, 61, 84, 98, 101, 108,
123, 126, 130, 144, 148, 150, 158, 181, 182, 237,
247
Bob Taylor—49, 73, 140
Jim Whitmer—20, 24, 27, 31, 82, 184
World Vision—167, 169, 170

DEDICATION

To Amy and Jill—
daughters, friends,
colleagues in ministry—
who give us love
and creativity.

CONTENTS

HARD TIMES

RIDING THE RAILS

We will never relive the depression. At least, the hard times of our present and future will be different. Times have changed from the bubbly 60s and the consumptive lifestyle of the 70s. More people are discovering a lack of "fat" in budgets and wallets.

You may feel this more completely than the young people you serve. In fact, you are probably better prepared for a change in the times than the youth in your group. They have been media-conditioned to desire the things of the affluent society just as these times are passing away forever. You have the good fortune to be able to build upon the hard times history of your parents and grandparents. You know that they have made it through the trials of the past and this legacy will enable you to adjust. The youth of this age haven't experienced the courage which the older generation passes on. These fathers and mothers in the faith have faced moments of suffering, pain, fear and poverty while being sustained by their faith in Jesus Christ. This faithfulness is an assurance for us.

Youth ministry in this new age means that you will be a spiritual hobo as you face this important ministry. You may have to "ride the rails" as you work in a climate of limited budgets and deficient backing for that trip or youth project.

Hard times can be good times

However, we are convinced that this shift to leaner times is also a great blessing. We have spent more than a decade within a community of sharing folks who have sought new teaching and programming ideas by using existing resources. They have found that the hard times mindset has become good times for youth and adults. We are sharing the youth ministry programming designs which have resulted from the creative recycling of this hard times mentality.

The Hard Times Catalog is not just another book of ideas

This book will swallow you and draw you into a wondrous world of possibility. This collection of material is not just another book of ideas. We have gathered the harvest from hundreds of people in many parts of the world. They willingly shared their hunches and risks. They so love their young people and are so committed to their faith in Jesus Christ that they will risk almost anything to bring the two together.

You may read items which sound familiar and seem to have been inspired from something else you have read. We have not knowingly included anything in this book which originated from any other source. Yet, it may have happened that the inspiration of the contributor's idea has not been credited. It has been unintentional. There is another reason why a sense of creativity linkage may appear in these fine contributions from our folk. We believe that the creative process is not a solo effort. Creativity is the capacity to order fragments of experience into a new meaningful whole. The painter does not make up colors for his or her canvas, nor does the musician invent musical notes. It is the creative use of existing components which gives life to the fresh painting or the new song. This means that every creative person must draw upon the legacy of the created order and those who have come before.

Fold, spindle, mutilate: These ideas are for you to use

We hope you will reshape the hard times items we share with you throughout this book. Make them your own. Only you know how something will work with your young people. You are not stealing from others. You are just building upon that which has been passed on by the communion of saints.

We also know that you will use your wisdom as you deal with these youth ministry designs. In many cases, we are able to share only a brief outline of how something was utilized. As you fill in the blank spots to fit your program needs, use your common sense in terms of safety and practicality. However, don't underrate your youth. Almost any young person will try new and unusual ideas if they are presented within a context of love and acceptance. If your youth know you as a risking adult, they will accept your model. We are convinced that when we stand in judgment before God, we will be forgiven for risking and failing in our work with youth. However, it will be hard to explain why we have made the gospel boring and lifeless. If you are comfortable in your youth programming, check yourself. The gospel you serve is not comfortable. It is a life experience which demands growth and change. The methods we use must be consistent with our content.

We are interested in your adventure with this book. Do write with your stories. We would also like to have your probes and dreams with hard times items. Drop us a note (P.O. Box 12811, Pittsburgh, PA 15241). We publish a newsletter (**Recycle**) which shares ongoing hard times possibilities contributed by an extensive worldwide community.

We wish you well on this journey. Our times are hard and there will be many challenges in your ministry with youth. However, it is God who leads us on this trek. The hard times will also be good times, very good times.

Dennis C. Benson
Marilyn J. Benson

HOBO STEW

HOW TO USE THIS BOOK

This book is not a random collection of ideas. It is also not an ordered curriculum for youth ministry. Yet, the **Hard Times Catalog** features the possibilities of both models. It can be an amazing resource in the hands of a sensitive youth worker. Here are some clues about using the book to serve you creatively.

First, begin your journey outside the pages of this book. Spend some time with the front cover. What feeling do you get from the design? What does the cover make you think about? Based on the cover, what do you think the ideas inside the book will be like?

Now, open the book to pages 284-285. Two pages of contributing authors! When's the last time you saw so much credit given to so many folks? Our ministry family extends to people all over the world. Run down the list of contributors. How many do you know? You will probably run across a couple people you have met at a conference or at a nearby church. Perhaps you are one of them. Great!

Next, read "Riding the Rails" on pages 8 and 9. This will enable you to get inside our kind of communication. While you're thinking about the book, take a look at "Toolbox" on page 69 and "Youth Ministry Philosophy" on page 25. These two columns appear regularly throughout the book and will help you sharpen your skills and attitudes toward your ministry.

Spend a little time with each of the major sections (Education/Learning, page 18; Fellowship/Community, page 118; Outreach/Mission, page 162; Worship/Celebration, page 196). You might want to "spirit scan" the sections. This term comes from the good folk who read the Bible "where the Spirit moves them." Just make four stabs at each section. Make random selections and read the complete two-page spread.

After you've completed this four-way scan of the sections, turn to pages 275-283. We call the index the "Junk Yard Sorter." You'll find the index helpful in directing your attention to just the right ideas to meet your needs. Pick out three items which may have a bearing on some project or teaching occasion facing you. Follow the references. Write down aspects of any items which attract you. Don't worry about how you are going to use the idea. You will notice that almost every idea is cross referenced. This is a good way to stumble across ideas which just may open up to something unexpected for your group, class or sermon. Don't be afraid to write down a number of ideas. These reports are not answers to your prob-

lems. They are simply sparks which may flame your ideas into a fuller blaze of possibility. You are supposed to alter and change the ideas to fit your needs.

Whether you're planning one session or an entire course of study, you'll not want to miss "How to Design Group Sessions Using the **Hard Times Catalog**" on pages 12-17. This practical section takes you through a creative planning process.

We'd like to end our deluxe tour through the **Hard Times Catalog** by meeting one last time with you on pages 286-287. We are a family: You, us, and the thousands of fellow trekkers who travel the ministry road. Join us as we journey this road together.

How To Design Group Sessions Using

Whether you plan one meeting or a series of sessions for your group, **Hard Times Catalog** is a treasure chest of ideas for you!

While **Hard Times Catalog** isn't a book of step-by-step session outlines, it has unlimited possibilities for youth ministry programming. Whether you rely on this book as the basis of your planning or use it to enrich your existing curriculum, you need to follow a systematic planning process in developing effective sessions.

The following process is one method of planning unique and creative sessions. The lefthand column describes that process. The handwritten copy lets you look over Marilyn's shoulder as she plans specific sessions using that process. Across the page from these sections is a worksheet for you to use in planning your own creative session.

THE CREATIVE PLANNING PROCESS

Thinking About It

You've agreed to teach a six week course. How do you get it all together? You'd like a teaching partner. You're going to create your own curriculum with the help of the **Hard Times Catalog.** You've got a few ideas, but nothing that would be a six-week course. How do you put your ideas together with materials, space, time, people, etc. to come up with the best for your youth?

The Group

Why has this class/group been formed? Do they have a common interest? Or, are they the same age, in the same grade in the public school? Has this group been together previously? What have they done together? How has it worked out?

As individuals, who are these youth? Focus on persons. With whom do they have intense relationships? With whom do they have long, ongoing friendships? What heroes, idols or respected people do they mention? With which other group members do they relate the least? What do they listen to or watch? What are their leisure time activities? How do they feel about school?

These are all questions to which you may not have definite answers. However, even the process of speculating about the answers will be helpful to you in focusing on the particular youth in your group. Finding out the answers may help you get to know your group better.

Looking Over Marilyn's Shoulder

"Would you do something with the seventh grade Sunday morning class? They just don't seem interested in anything." Okay. I accepted the challenge. Asked for a partner – I'd enjoy working with another person. But, will call on others for help if I need it (Greg, high schooler, music is his thing; Mrs. Thomas, librarian, she really likes kids; Bob's dad, great in photography).

Most of their parents are active in church. I'm not so certain that the kids want to be here on Sunday morning, but that's the time for their class. They are all in seventh grade in a middle school system, but they're not all in the same local school.

Interests:

boys–boys	radio – music
girls–boys	records – whats popular
siblings	friends, music lessons
parents	sports, hobbies
teachers	heroes; stars –
other adults	movie, rock, sports

I'd like to know how close I am in my guesses. Possible use of cassette recorder to get to know the kids better. Check index for ideas.

THE HARD TIMES CATALOG ①

After you've read the corresponding paragraphs on the opposite page, work through the following worksheet. Let your mind wander over different possibilities. Jot your thoughts here.

Two Creative Planning Ideas

1. Want an exciting planning experience? Get your partners, adults and young people, together. Borrow or buy enough copies of this book for each person to have a copy. Then have each person work through this planning process independently. Compare notes once everyone is finished. Then plan the session(s) together.

2. Give this book to interested young people in your group or class. Have them look through the book and list 10 ideas for their group/class. Then plan the sessions together using this planning process.

SESSION PLANNING WORKSHEET

Thinking About It

What age group are you teaching? Who's helping you as a partner in the planning process? *(If you have no partners, write the names of people you might like as partners.)*

The Group

What's the purpose of your group/class?

_____

_____

What interests do they share?

_____

_____

What do your young people have in common? (school? age? past experiences, etc.)

_____

_____

If your group/class has been together before, what positive or negative events have they experienced together?

_____

_____

List the names of the people in your group in the following blanks. Then complete the series of questions for each name.

NAME	Closest friends?	Best friend?	Heroes/respected adults?	Hobbies/Leisure activities?	Feelings about school?	Feelings about God?

THE CREATIVE PLANNING PROCESS

What Do We Do?

Let's move now to the kinds of things the group may study or do together. Again, there are a variety of processes you might want to use in order to come up with some ideas:

1. Brainstorming—get all those thoughts "on the board" whether they seem workable or not.
2. Take your cue from the seasons, or liturgical year or from something in the contemporary world.
3. Include the group/class in a brainstorming session.
4. Work on an area of interest that you as an enabler are especially excited about!

1. Drugs, pollution, world hunger, who am I, what's a Christian?

2. The course starts in the fall. Election year; Halloween; thanksgiving.

3. Responses from seventh grade class: "I dunno," "Why're you asking us?" With a little more thought: drugs, football, sex, school, the Bible.

4. I think I've got it! General title, "My Brother's/Sister's Keeper?" Will cover some of my ideas and some of theirs: who am I?, drugs, Bible, world hunger, pollution, sex. Used concordance — Genesis 4:9; Matthew 25:31-46; Luke 10:25-37.

Selecting a Few

Hopefully, you have now compiled a list of possible areas of interest (content). Look over each suggestion and consider the following:

1. Is this adaptable to the age level of the group?
2. Can we make some headway with this subject in the time available?
3. Are the teachers enthused about this subject?
4. Can we design some experiences for sharing this enthusiasm?

Select from your list those with the most positive responses.

One topic per week works out well. I'll need some help on some of them. Especially excited about world hunger. It's current, relevant, a learning experience for all of us. Will need more information. We already feel badly about starving children. What can we do about it?

Drugs — maybe it's not drugs anymore, but booze. Could be a touchy subject with parents. Ask some parents for help on this one.

Writing Objectives

You will want to suggest reactions you hope to have as you study/learn together. The following are some possible behaviors: understand, comprehend, believe, feel, act. Write statements of what you hope to see happen in terms of the individual, the content, and the behavior. Be specific. Write as many objectives as you need.

Try to put these objectives into some order. Is there a natural sequence? Is there a unifying idea found in several of them? Could a couple of them be combined?

1. To understand the world hunger problem.

2. To relate the world problem to our own position as Christians (Bible).

3. To discover ways of helping my brother/sister as a Christian.

4. To discover differences between how I respond as a Christian and how the U.S. responds to the world hunger problem.

THE HARD TIMES CATALOG ②

What Do We Do?

Use one or more of the following processes to come up with programming ideas:

● Brainstorming. List everything that comes into your mind that you could do with your group. Nothing is too dumb or crazy.

● What seasonal events (Christmas, Easter, school opening) are coming up that you could build special sessions around?

● What's happening in your church that you could build into a session? (Good Friday, missions week, special emphases)

● What are a few common needs, issues and questions among the group members? List them and prioritize them.

● What areas would you especially like to develop for or with the group?

Compile an exhaustive list of all ideas conjured up by the preceding questions.

When's a time you can get with the group/class and get their input? How will you go about getting information from your young people?

Selecting a Few

Choose six ideas from the list you just made and write them in the blanks below. Then answer the questions about each idea.

IDEAS	Is this adaptable to the age level of the group?	Can we make some headway with this subject in the time available?	Are the teachers enthused about this subject?	Can we design some experiences for sharing this enthusiasm?

After completing the preceding box, which ideas have the most positive response?

Writing Objectives

What reactions do you expect from your young people in these session(s)?

Write statements of what you hope to see happen in terms of what you want your young people to learn.

Now, write statements in terms of what you want to see happen as a result of your session(s).

Finally, write statements in terms of behaviors you'd like to see in your young people as a result of your session(s).

Of the statements (objectives) you've just written, list them in a natural sequence.

Are there any objectives you need to rewrite, combine or toss?

THE CREATIVE PLANNING PROCESS

Choosing Experiences

Based on your objectives (what you hope to study/learn together), choose experiences that can enable learning to happen.

At this point you will want to think again about your particular group. Are there some kinds of activities they most enjoy?

Learning experiences can take many forms: lecture, simulation games, discussion, crafts, media, role play, dialogue, etc. The particular form chosen should be related to the objective, the interests and abilities of the group, the time and space, and the materials and leadership available.

We've got plenty of space, but not lots of time (60 minutes). Would love to find a simulation game. I think seventh graders could really get involved in a game situation.

This age is definitely not sedentary. They learn best by doing. Keep this in mind when considering experiences. Have strong feelings about wanting both learners and enablers to be involved in experience together. Feel that a real important aspect of class is relationship with peers and adults.

Experiences involving the learning of new skills at the same time as working on content objectives would be great. Use of media, cassettes, slides, etc. seems to fit this age group! Try to fit in interviewing skills.

Hard Times Catalog

The sharing of experiences is what **Hard Times Catalog** is all about. Other people have shared with us the "good times" they have had together. Keep in mind that their particular experience worked for them because of their unique hopes and youth. You can draw upon their experiences and adapt them to meet your hopes and your youth.

Start going through the index, jotting down items related to general theme; found self focusing more on hunger and "Who am I" objectives. Checked out some listings immediately, left others for later.

Revising

It will probably be necessary to go back and rework some of your objectives. You may find that you have tried to do too much —then eliminate some of your objectives. Then put the experiences into the order in which you would like to use them.

There were so many ideas here that we must consider. Could expand on world hunger and "who am I" objectives and use the other topics at a later time. New ideas were sparked by reading the experiences of others. Will need to change things to meet our situation.

Evaluating

This step in the process of developing a curriculum is often left out. It is good for the enablers (and learners, too) to have some time of evaluation about the experiences. Were your hunches right about the kinds of things your youth would enjoy doing together? Were you able to pinpoint the realization of some aspects of your objectives? Evaluation can be informal: "How did you feel about the experience?" Or, evaluation can be more structured, actually checking out each objective to see if the goals of the experience were accomplished.

Realizations about things came rapidly, especially when playing the game. Not all questions raised were answered; not all problems resolved; but that's the process of learning. Several objectives were fulfilled; others may need some more time. Enablers and seventh graders felt good about new relationships.

THE HARD TIMES CATALOG ③

Choosing Experiences

What activities or experiences do your young people seem to enjoy most?

What are possible learning experiences available for your group/class (i.e., role plays, discussions, films, skits, worksheets, etc.)?

Hard Times Catalog

What items from the index relate to the general ideas and learning experiences you have chosen? Read through the entries themselves and determine ways each catalog entry can be modified to fit your situation.

Revising

Take another look at the objectives you wrote earlier. Have you tried to do too much? If so, which objectives should you eliminate? Revise? Once you've reworked your objectives, write them here:

Looking at those objectives, list learning experiences in the order you'd like to use them.

Evaluating

Two or three different ways you can evaluate this course are:

1. Did the course meet the objectives?

3. Which learning experiences were most effective? least effective?

2. What things would you have changed?

4. What have you learned from this teaching experience that might benefit future sessions?

EDUCATION
LEARNING

Christians can always learn more about their faith. Yet learning is especially powerful with young Christians. How do you get across the "facts" of the faith while commanding the interest of the young? A high school student stopped a younger Dennis after one of his first Sunday school classes. "Benson, baby, you make it painless Christianity," he said. Dennis didn't know whether he should be flattered or filled with despair. Your role as enabler or teacher in youth ministry will leave you in that tension.

There are three kinds of educational demands placed on youth by the church. The adults want them to know the basics about the faith. Secondly, the church wants them prepared for a more complete role in the body. The confession of faith or confirmation process is usually handled by the clergy. The third area of education is that of equipping them for the practical aspects of being a Christian as teenagers.

There are many designs which will help you in this section. It is often wise to work out a series of sessions on a particular theme. You can then ask the youth to make a commitment for a certain number of weeks. This will help you overcome one of the greatest difficulties in teaching youth: continuity. Use the indices and cluster the ideas for a general theme. Follow the guidelines in the "How to Design Group Sessions Using the **Hard Times Catalog**" (page 12).

Remember that the models for learning which come to the students from their daily school experiences are not very creative. When you try these "Hard Times" approaches, the youth may be uncertain at first. They are not accustomed to sharing how they think and feel. The formal educational experiences tend to deal with only portions of the young person. Christ teaches to risk ourselves in order to reach others for him. The following ideas will help you to lead youth as they learn the greatest life-shaping force ever revealed to humanity.

1. TRY TO REMEMBER . . .

Our youth leaders met to "relive" their younger years. This exercise of a guided reflection was helpful for them in getting back into some of the feelings they had as teenagers. Remembering their own youth made understanding some of today's youth concerns considerably easier.

I. This is an opportunity to reflect on feelings about youth and youth ministry. Using pencil and paper, each person should number from one to seven. The leader reads the following incomplete sentences, allowing time for answers to each incomplete sentence.

   1. The thing I *like* most about young people is . . .
   2. The thing I *dislike* most about young people is . . .
   3. The thing which *scares me* most about young people is . . .
   4. The reason I took the job as advisor was . . . (Urge them NOT to respond "Because I was asked.")
   5. The thing I have most to offer as advisor is . . .
   6. The personal needs of mine which are met by being an advisor are . . .
   7. At this, or another, workshop I'd like to learn . . .

II. Sharing (about 30 minutes)

   Participants gather in groups of three. Preferably they will not have known each other before. They should briefly share their answers to numbers one through six.

   For about five minutes, have the whole group share responses to number seven, including those which came to mind in their groups of three. These responses should be written on newsprint, so all can see. The leader(s) should respond to these hopes/expectations for number seven. Identify which of the hopes/needs will be worked on.

III. Guided reflection (about 10 minutes)

   Encourage people to get in a relaxed position (but not one that induces sleep), e.g. sitting without legs crossed, lying on the floor, perhaps shoes off. Invite participants to close their eyes.

   The leader reads the following:

   Let's spend a few minutes going back to when you were 15 years old. Remember the town in which you lived. Take your time as you wander back through the years. Think about the school you attended when you were 15. Remember the outside of the building?

   You are leaving school. How do you get home? You are walking toward your house. What does the place look like? Is it a place you like? You're going in the door now . . . who is home? What feeling do you have about coming home? You put down the things you brought home from school.

   You decide to have a snack. You realize that your favorite snack is there. You go and get it. As you eat, you look around. What do you see? Do you see things which are especially important to you? Are there things you use a lot? Now pay attention to other senses. What does the place smell like? What do you hear around the neighborhood? Do you like or dislike the things you hear?

   Now you decide to go sit on your bed. Where is it? Do you share your room? Look around the room and pay attention to the furniture. Look at the walls. What are the things which make this your

continued

TRY TO REMEMBER . . .

place? What would you like to do to change the room? Is your room a safe place to be? Do you spend a lot of time in your room? What do you like to do in your room? Who would you think about inviting to your room?

IV. Written reflections (about 10 minutes)

The leader brings participants out of the guided reflection by saying something like: Our memories of being 15 are vivid. The visions and feelings have rushed in upon us, and bathed us in their glow. Now it is time for us to return to this time, and this place. When you are ready slowly open your eyes. We need not rush, so take your time and roll over, or do what is necessary to get ready to use your pencil and paper. Please write brief answers to a few questions:

1. What's school like for you? Do you like it? Is it pleasant? Do you want to go regularly?
2. Are you popular?
3. What do you like to do at school?
4. What frightens you about school?
5. How are your grades?
6. Who are your friends?
7. How many do you have?
8. Who's your best friend?
9. What are your favorite activities?
10. What kind of hobbies, sports or recreational activities do you like?
11. Other than parents, who are the significant people in your life?
12. Are any of them older? Do you look up to them? What do they do for you? Do you do anything for them?
13. What thoughts, feelings, pressures do you have about sexuality?

Now I want you to quickly write short answers. As preparation, please number from one to nine on your page. Now I want you to jot down the first word or phrase which comes to mind. Use only one word or phrase.

Remember, answer as if you were 15.

1. Church
2. God
3. Confirmation
4. Youth group
5. Minister
6. Jesus
7. Who's the president now?
8. What significant historical events are taking place?
9. What's important to you now, at age 15?

V. Sharing the reflections (30 minutes)

The leader asks participants to share thoughts and feelings generated by the written reflections with the whole group. Responses to the following questions should be written on newsprint or a blackboard so all can see.

1. As you thought back, and recalled your thoughts and feelings as a 15-year-old, did anything surprise you?
2. What were your special thoughts about your room?
3. How did you react to school?
4. What did you remember about friends or significant adults?
5. Are there young people who seem to be going through some of the same struggles you went through? Can you share an example?
6. Does it help to know something about 15-year-olds when working with young people? How?
7. Keeping today's exercise in mind, what are some things our youth ministry should do?

John Rawlinson
Oakland, California

2. THE FUTURE GAME

Our youth leaders met together to do some long-range planning for our summer camp. In order to get the group into a dreaming mode, I introduced the Future Game.

Passing around a bowl of jelly beans, I told the adult leaders that I had been fortunate enough to obtain a special "future" pill. I urged them all to eat the pill and allow it to work on them. I played some futuristic music (not too difficult to find), and passed out "future files." I had gathered short articles on the future by famous futurists (i.e. Alvin Toffler). After reading through the articles and spending some time thinking about and getting into the mode of the early 21st century, the group was asked to share and discuss what the world of the 2000s was going to be like.

We moved on then to the possible challenges the church will face in the early 2000s. What might be the "pinch points" the faith community may be feeling? The group was then ready to deal with the dreams of the camping ministry today. Remembering to keep the future benefit of the church helped us plan for youth ministry today.

Elly Fleming
Pittsburgh, Pennsylvania

See also 1) TRY TO REMEMBER . . ., 7) PLANNING STRATEGY, 32) CARING, 71) 2083, 122) MID-WINTER SUMMER CAMP

3. TEN YOUTH MINISTRY CONCERNS

Youth ministry demands intentional and creative planning, implementation, and experiencing. Alive and joy-filled happenings capture the attention and bring significant meaning to youth. The church's youth ministry must speak to the contemporary youth culture. To speak effectively, those responsible for youth ministry should consider at least 10 concerns.

1. **Room environment**—A room for youth to call their own is a necessity. A room's size, availability, privacy and warmth contribute to a sense of having a place to do youth ministry.

2. **Celebration**—Youth ministry is celebration. The experience of the gospel is a joyful experience. We need to create opportunities for celebrating our relationships with each other and with God.

3. **Community building**—Youth ministry means relationships. We care about each other. Through being sensitive to the problems, needs, hopes and dreams of each other member, we develop a sense of trust. The goal is to experience the love of the gospel within and between persons.

4. **Leadership**—Training, ability, commitment, preparation and caring are all necessary ingredients for youth and adults charged with youth ministry leadership. Goals, calendaring, purposes and directions are helpful in ministering to youth.

5. **Christ encounter**—Youth ministry means encountering and experiencing the living Christ. What does it mean to be a Christian? What does the Christian faith ask of me? How does Christ Jesus touch my life? What am I doing with my life? Where am I going? Young people crave the answers to these questions.

6. **Mission awareness**—Our world is full of need. People are hurting. Hunger, violence, injustice, hatred and retardation are some of the problems of our world. How does youth ministry respond?

7. **Resources**—Resources are people, the environment, films, books, poems, music and on and on. Resources bring youth ministry alive by igniting creativity within people.

8. **Visual environment**—Rooms and places for youth ministry are important; so are the colors, shapes, symbols, and sounds. Banners, posters, lights, paint, chairs, pillows and rugs—all contribute to the youth ministry experience.

9. **Partnership**—Are youth and adults open with each other? Are youth and adults really working together?

10. **Purpose**—Why youth ministry? Where is the group going? What do you, as a youth leader, want to do and be?

Wesley Taylor
Oregon City, Oregon

See also 4) WHAT'S A LEADER?, 6) PLANNING SKILLS, 7) PLANNING STRATEGY, 53) RESOURCE CONSUMER TIPS, 93) SMALL GROUPS, 96) BIG QUESTIONS, 108) A FIVE-PART MEETING DESIGN, 164) WORSHIP ENVIRONMENT, 165) WORSHIP TASK FORCE

4. WHAT'S A LEADER?

"Much of my first four years of teaching was phony because I was afraid to let the kids get to know me. I never allowed myself to love the kids. The turning point came when I finally realized I didn't have to be a know-it-all. People talk about being equal with kids. It's not a question of equality; it's one of sharing."

Ann

When the teacher to the left decided to be herself, her style of leadership changed. She started by assessing her incorrect leadership style.

What's your style of leadership? One author suggests that there are five styles: telling, selling, consulting, joining and delegating. Other words used to describe leadership styles include autocrat, benevolent, dictator, laissez-faire, directive, nondirective, etc. Even though these styles have validity in different situations, it seems there are as many leadership styles as there are people. So, what kind of a leader are you?

The following items describe aspects of leadership behavior. Respond to each item according to the way you would be most likely to act if you were the leader of a group. Circle whether you would be likely to behave in the described way frequently (F), occasionally (O), seldom (S).

In Functioning as a Leader in a Group . . .

F O S 1. I would most likely act as the mouthpiece of the group.

F O S 2. I would permit the members to use their own judgment in solving problems.

F O S 3. I would needle members for greater effort.

F O S 4. I would try out my ideas in the group.

F O S 5. I would let the members do the work the way they think best.

F O S 6. I would be able to tolerate postponement and uncertainty and failure.

F O S 7. I would turn the members loose on a job, and let them go to it.

F O S 8. I would settle conflicts when they occur in the group.

F O S 9. I would be reluctant to allow the members too much freedom of action.

F O S 10. I would decide what shall be done and how it shall be done.

F O S 11. I would assign group members to particular tasks.

F O S 12. I would trust the group members to exercise good judgment.

F O S 13. I would persuade the group that my ideas are to their advantage.

F O S 14. I would permit the group to set its own pace.

continued

WHAT'S A LEADER?

Dilemmas of Leadership

Our basic dilemma may be a discrepancy between what we believe to be right and desirable and what we do in practice. Maybe we express this dilemma in the form of two questions: How democratic can I be? How authoritarian must I be?

We also face a series of dilemmas:

● We have a tradition of competing, but we must be cooperative.

● We are under pressure to get the job done—to be efficient, but we believe all points of view must be heard.

● We are pushed for time, but we want participative decision making and this takes time.

● We see opportunities for quick results in one-man decisions, but we believe shared responsibility makes for better and longer lasting solutions (and we believe in educational process).

We can look at these dilemmas in terms of a continuum developed by Warren Schmidt and Robert Tannenbaum of California.

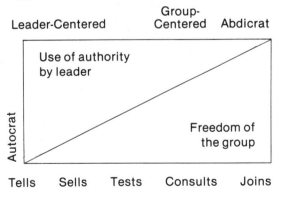

Leader-Centered — Group-Centered — Abdicrat

Use of authority by leader

Autocrat

Freedom of the group

Tells   Sells   Tests   Consults   Joins

If we extend the continuum at either extreme we get autocracy or abdication. The autocrat violates our traditional values and our self-image as people who are open and sensitive. The abdicrat is irresponsible and violates concepts of leadership which get work done.

How do I decide where I stand on the continuum?

Take a look at these factors:

A. Forces in me, including my motives and needs and my assumptions about people (colleagues, subordinates, superiors, peers).

I would have to look at my:

● value system
● confidence in the group
● assumptions about people
● leadership inclinations
● feelings of security—and my "tolerance for ambiguity"
● motives as related to my own needs I am satisfying

B. Forces in the group, including my understanding of members' needs, motives, perceptions.

I would have to look at their:

● needs for independence or dependence
● readiness to assume responsibility
● tolerance for ambiguity
● interest in the problem
● understanding of goals—and their role in formulating them
● knowledge, experience and skill in the particular task
● expectations

I'd also want to understand the effect on the group of my own assumptions about them, their motives, their needs.

C. Forces in the situation.

I would have to look at the:

● type of organization
● effectiveness of the group
● pressure of time
● consequences of action
● the perception I have and the group has of the task

Two Leadership Styles

Every time a group or a class does something, someone has helped it to happen. That person is usually called a leader or it is said that a person "gave leadership" to a particular situation.

There are at least two concepts of leadership. There is the *specific leader*, the person who is elected president and is expected to lead. In the church the pastor, the board member, the church school teacher are all in specific leadership roles. When most people think of leadership, they think of these kinds of leaders.

Yet, there is also a second type of leadership. It can be illustrated in this way. A group is trying to make a decision. They are confused and Sam helps the group see the different choices they face. He mentions them one by one. He lists them. (That's a leadership role.) Then Jane says, "Let's each list the choices in order from best to worst as each of us sees them." (And that's leadership, too.) They make individual lists, and it appears that most people name choice X either first or second. George sees that and says, "Choice X is the one most of us favor. Let's do it." (That, too, is leadership.)

Some call that kind of leadership "participant leadership." It means that each person in the group understands that everybody in the group has the responsibility of assuming leadership when appropriate.

(*Appropriate* might mean they have the necessary information; they think they know a way to do what needs to be done; they are willing to take a risk and suggest an idea, etc.)

Creative "participant leadership" involves:

- helping to establish "ground rules" which show respect for all persons and points of view based upon the dignity of the human individual.
- asking questions that point up differences and get all angles out in the open.
- making suggestions. A great power of Jesus' ministry was his belief that personalities could be led by the leaven of suggestions.
- reminding the group that all human judg-

ments stand under the judgment of God.
- helping all to see that fellowship deepens and grows out of the experience of facing up to differences and problems.
- appreciating the issues and restating points of view.
- taking initiative in suggesting that more facts may be needed for decision and action.
- marveling at the way things work out.
- being absolutely honest, sincere and perceptive.
- having a sense of humor.

Creative "participant leadership" will probably not involve:

- knowing it all. Be honest, share what you know, but don't be afraid to say "I don't know".
- becoming impatient. If you become impatient, admit it.
- pressing. Whatever seems proper, suggest it or raise a question. Youth feel enough pressure from society, school, etc. Make opportunities available, call for commitment, but do not press.
- arguing. Differ, yes. State the position as cheerfully as possible.
- being devious and clever. Be direct as possible; debate over differing points of view and methodology can stand in the way of action and growth.
- interrupting. Let ideas be expressed and then build one upon another.
- educating people by instructing them. Good program, planned activities, speakers, arranged visits and conferences are essential to the success of any group; however, education and learning grow out of mutual sharing.
- being worried, harassed or alarmed when youth or people let you down.
- defending self.
- being noble.

continued

WHAT'S A LEADER?

Leadership Roles in a Group or Class

When a group or class is involved in doing something and all want to help or participate, there are certain roles or parts that must be played:

- Initiator
- Information seeker
- Information giver
- Clarifier
- Summarizer
- Consensus checker
- Coordinator

At different times in a group or class effort different persons must assume those roles if everybody is to share in leadership.

No one plays one role. Early in the conversation a person may offer information. Later, the same person may be the summarizer. See how it works: If you can initiate, you do. If not, someone else will. You do your part later. That's participant leadership.

But, that's not all there is to it! If a group is to work well together, the members must be concerned about each other. Caring brings up other sets of roles:

- The encourager
- The gate keeper
- The standard setter
- The follower
- The feeling expressor
- The mediator
- The tension reliever

You may summarize the decision of the group and say "I think we feel pretty good about that decision." So, you are a summarizer and a feeling expressor. In playing the two roles you gave leadership and helped the group accomplish its goals.

Virgil Nelson
Santa Paula, California

See also 1) TRY TO REMEMBER . . . , 5) BIBLICAL LEADERSHIP, 6) PLANNING SKILLS, 7) PLANNING STRATEGY, 16) BRICKS, 35) STAY FRESH . . . , 53) RESOURCE CONSUMER TIPS, 62) THE AVERAGE KID, 72) CREATIVE CONJURING, 83) BEING THERE, 93) SMALL GROUPS, 94) YOUTH LEADERS AND RELATIONSHIPS, 95) LEADER SUPPORT, 96) BIG QUESTIONS, 97) TRANSPARENCY, 100) DEAR TEACHER, 124) YOUNG PEOPLE AS LEADERS

5. BIBLICAL LEADERSHIP

We were leading a camp for our youth advisors. We presented the profile of three biblical leaders: Moses, Jeremiah, and Peter. The adult youth leaders were then asked to read these accounts of leadership and to do four things:

1. Underline the words or phrases that describe the leadership skills of that leader.
2. Circle one or two most important leadership attributes.
3. Draw arrows pointing to those skills which are part of their leadership style.
4. Check things they would like to make a part of their leadership style.

The participants then shared their results in small groups.

Grant and Wendy Nichol, Melbourne, Australia

See also 4) WHAT'S A LEADER?, 83) BEING THERE, 96) BIG QUESTIONS, 97) TRANSPARENCY

6. PLANNING SKILLS

When I am talking to youth advisors who may be at the beginning of their ministry, I start by talking about their ideas and goals. It is important to utilize their hunches and dreams. From there, I go to what I call "survival skills." These are the skills of planning ahead with youth who are the leaders. It is important to build on the things they want to see happen.

For instance, recently I was working with two people who were just thrown into a youth group situation. They wanted to take the kids on a retreat. We started with this single idea and started planning for such an event. We outlined the flow of the retreat and the kinds of resources which could be used. I tried to affirm the kinds of things they wanted to see happen. It was hard for a couple of adults who had been thrown into that kind of situation to feel they were accomplishing anything. This is particularly hard when they come together with 20 young people who only want to have fun.

Obid Hofland
New Haven, Connecticut

See also 1) TRY TO REMEMBER, 3) TEN YOUTH MINISTRY CONCERNS, 4) WHAT'S A LEADER?, 7) PLANNING STRATEGY, 52) RETREAT FEEDBACK, 95) LEADER SUPPORT, 96) BIG QUESTIONS

7. PLANNING STRATEGY

A youth leader once said to me, "We don't plan, we just get together and do what seems right."

My reaction was that "not planning is one form of planning." It is a type of planning that has great potential for failure.

Planning is an important aspect of youth ministry. Planning, however, does not guarantee success. It does increase the probability of meeting most needs and expectations. Four guidelines increase good planning and decrease headaches:

1. Don't plan too far ahead. Plan for a three-month period. Plan what you will *definitely* do in the current month, *probably* do next month and *anticipate* doing the month after next. As you move through this month, take time to consider those things you said you'd probably do next month. If they are still sensible, make them definite.

2. Keep your planning flexible. Allow for the possibility of change, revision or replacement. Good planning makes change and responsiveness possible. Without planning, it's impossible to be flexible.

3. Involve the entire group in planning. If the adult advisors or the youth officers do all the planning and *announce* the plans to the total group, you're in trouble. The entire group needs to be involved in planning. The group members must be helped to identify their needs, asked for activity suggestions

4. Continually evaluate the things you do. Determine whether you achieved the group's goals for a program, activity, project, etc. It's helpful to write out a reason that indicates why you're doing what you're doing. What changes have taken place? What needs have been met? Which new needs or concerns should be met? This helps you go beyond concluding "that everybody had a good time" as an evaluation of what you've done.

Let's try some planning. There are a lot of ways to plan. The following exercises offer some planning tools.

continued

PLANNING STRATEGY

PLANNING FOR YOUTH MINISTRY

(This tool helps you identify symptoms, needs and actions.)

SYMPTOMS	NEEDS	ACTIONS		
List six things that you see as you observe and listen to your group/class.	What do the symptoms mean?	What are some things you might do in response to the needs?		
			Definite	Possible
1.		Month 1		
2.				
3.		Month 2		
4.				
5.		Month 3		
6.				

ESTABLISHING GOALS IN YOUTH MINISTRY
(This tool helps you move from idea to action.)

1. *Brainstorm your concerns and needs*
   List anything on anyone's mind—no arguments, no debate; all concerns are acceptable.

2. *Refine your needs*
   Select the specific needs you can respond to in light of resources (time, personnel, money, etc.).

3. *Formulate your goal*
   The goal is your response to the need, what you intend to do about it. A goal is a clear, concise statement of intended outcome that will meet the needs.
   A goal is:
   Behavioral: Change is anticipated.
   Specific: It is not a general statement.
   Achievable: It can be done.
   Limited: It doesn't take in the whole world.
   To develop goals:
   a. Look at the needs.
   b. Brainstorm ideas about the entire area of life to which the need relates. Do not discuss specific suggestions at this point. Merely list as many things as possible which could be part of the goal and could relate to implementation of the goal.
   c. Identify the ideas presented which seem to represent workable goals.

d. Rewrite the idea into a clear sentence of intended outcome.
   e. Ask:
      1) Will the goal really reduce the problem?
      2) Can I picture myself working on the goal?

4. *Design your strategy*
   Develop a statement of what you intend to do to move toward the achievement of the goal.
   a. *Who* initiates the action?
   b. *Who* receives the action? For whom is it intended?
   c. *What* is the time span? *When?*
   d. *What* kind of action is planned? What do you intend to do?

5. *Develop your tactics*
   Work out the details necessary to implement the strategy. How do you get the job done?

6. *Evaluate*
   a. Has change taken place? Have needs been met?
   b. Has the problem been reduced?
   c. What new concerns have been generated by this action with which we need to deal?
   d. What needs can you now identify?

continued

PLANNING STRATEGY

AN INVENTORY OF YOUTH NEEDS
First Any Church
Anytown, U.S.A.

(This tool should be utilized as a confidential resource by the teacher for planning purposes. An inventory should be done for each person in the group, class, or other youth ministry effort.)

Name of young person _____ Date_____

1. Respond to the question in each box on the left. Do the work and then read it over carefully, seeing it as a whole.

2. Now respond to the questions in the boxes at the right in light of your comments in the left-hand boxes.

What friendship and peer group relationships does this person have?	What one thing do you think needs to occur in this person's life *now* to enhance relationships?
What is the person's self-image?	What kind of steps should you take to: ● reinforce positive behavior? ● help the person to deal with negative behavior?
What are the main concerns and attitudes that you have heard this person express in the last two to three months? (personal, social, regarding faith, etc.)	Identify what you think is this person's chief concern and suggest at least two specific ways you can respond.
Where is this person in understanding the Christian lifestyle?	What should happen in the group to foster this person's Christian growth?

PROBLEM SOLVING THROUGH PLANNING

(This tool helps you work through problems.)

A. List
1. The problem right now is _____
2. The way I would like the situation to be is _____

B. List forces working *for* solving	B. List forces working *against* solving.

1.
    2.
    3.
    4.
    5.
 Go back and underline the most important or powerful force.
	1.
	    2.
	    3.
	    4.
	    5.
	 Go back and underline the most important or powerful force.

C. For the most important force list possible action steps you might plan to increase that force.
    1.
    2.
    3.
    4.
    5.
	C. For the most important force list possible action steps you might plan to reduce or eliminate that force.
	    1.
	    2.
	    3.
	    4.
	    5.

D. Review the action steps; underline the more promising and list resources available for each.	D. Review the action steps; underline the more promising and list resources available for each.

EVALUATION AND FUTURE REFERENCE

(This tool helps to encourage feedback from members.)

1. Was the program worth your effort to attend? Why?

2. What was the most helpful?

3. Are there areas which you would like to develop in more detail?

4. Would this program be helpful for another group? Would you help to organize it?

Virgil Nelson, Santa Paula, California

See also 3) TEN YOUTH MINISTRY CONCERNS, 4) WHAT'S A LEADER?, 6) PLANNING SKILLS, 8) RECRUITING TEACHERS, 93) SMALL GROUPS, 126) YOUTH MEMBERS FIRST, 165) WORSHIP TASK FORCE, 166) GETTING THE WORD OUT

8. RECRUITING TEACHERS

Ease the trauma of recruiting skilled teachers and leaders by following a systematic approach.

"Bill, I'm desperate. We need a teacher for a class of 7th graders. I have called a dozen different people and each one has given me an excuse. Some are too busy, you know, club work, P.T.A., overtime. Others said they are not qualified or don't know enough about the Bible. Still others say they can't cope with teenagers. Bill, will you help me? If you can't teach these kids all year, will you take them until I can find someone else?"

Does this sound familiar? The question frequently asked by pastors and church leaders: "How do you effectively recruit volunteer workers in the church?"

In circumstances where recruiting or enlistment is a problem, consider several things before contacting candidates.

Too often, enlistment responsibility falls upon one person. The restraint of time usually dictates that contacts be made by telephone, generally the least profitable method. Effective recruiting requires time for planning and executing.

My experience has shown that it is best to involve several persons in the enlistment process. In some situations a special team is formed for this specific purpose. Those responsible for Christian education may serve as the recruiting team. Or, the team may be the officers of the department in which the vacancy exists.

The "enlistment team" should review the biblical basis for an enlistment strategy.

The Apostle Paul did not become an effective "ambassador" for Christ until his confrontation on the Damascus road. Immediately afterward, Jesus gave Paul his marching orders. Paul asked, "Who are you, Lord?" And he said, "I am Jesus, whom you are persecuting; but arise and enter the city, and you will be told what you are to do" (Acts 9:5-6).

Later, when writing to the Christians in Rome, Paul left little doubt about what is expected of committed disciples of Christ. Romans 12:12: "I appeal to you therefore, brethren, by the mercies of God, to present your bodies as a living sacrifice, holy and acceptable to God, which is your spiritual worship. Do not be conformed to the world but be transformed by the renewal of your mind, that you may prove what is the will of God, what is good and acceptable and perfect."

Again consider that God has designed each of us to fit into his divine plans and summons us to answer his call. In selecting candidates for the Lord's service it is well to remember that he uses ordinary and sometimes unlikely persons, by our standards, to do his work. 1 Corinthians 1:26-27: "For consider your call, brethren; not many of you were wise according to worldly standards, not many were powerful, not many were of noble birth; but God chose what is foolish in the world to shame the wise; God chose what is weak in the world to shame the strong."

Fortified with the biblical understanding that Christ expects his disciples to participate in the work of his church, we are ready to begin the process of searching for the person whom the Lord wants to fill the vacancy we have in hand.

First, we secure a written description of what is expected of someone filling this position. A variety of guidelines are available for preparing job descriptions. Descriptions will generally not be longer than one page and contain what is expected of a person in the job, in both general and specific terms. It should mention the title of the person and to whom the person is directly responsible.

Commitment to Christ, availability and dependability are expected.

Now we are ready to prepare a list of people who seem to meet the job and personnel requirements. Names may be selected from personal knowledge of the team members, from other knowledgeable members of the church, or perhaps the church maintains a skills inventory of members. After the initial list is made, the next step is to review the list and rank order the names, from the most to the least qualified. We are now ready to make personal contacts following the order of ranking until acceptance is obtained.

Select a two-person team to interview the prospects. One of the two persons on the team should be the person to whom the candidate will be directly responsible. The other team member should know the candidate personally. Phone the prospect and set a date, time and place to discuss the possibilities of matching the person to the needs of the church.

At the interview, after introductions and all are comfortably seated, the purpose of the visit is explained. Read the job description together and make verbal additions or elaborations as needed. Invite questions from the candidate. After the candidate understands the task, ask to carefully consider your request and give you an answer within a specified time, perhaps one week. Conclude the interview with prayer for the Holy Spirit's leading in the decision.

If the candidate declines the offer, repeat the process with successive names until one accepts. Do not be discouraged by the amount of time consumed. The reward is in the quality and performance of workers recruited by this strategy.

Willard McCown
Pittsburgh, Pennsylvania

See also 6) PLANNING SKILLS, 7) PLANNING STRATEGY, 35) STAY FRESH, 83) BEING THERE, 94) YOUTH LEADERS AND RELATIONSHIPS, 134) OLDER FOLKS IN YOUTH MINISTRY, 198) THE CALL

9. BIBLE EXPLORATIONS

We have been enjoying our work on Bible study. Youth really relate to a kind of biblical probing which draws them into the text. Here is my structured thinking on creative Bible study with youth.

NOTIONS RELATED TO CREATIVE BIBLE STUDY

Problem: Sometimes the Word seems dry and dusty like walking through a desert.

New notion: The Word isn't dusty and dry but our approach may be.

Problem: Sometimes we start out with a lot of zip but somehow our zip gets zapped.

New notion: We need a motivational factor that will sustain.

Problem: Sometimes our study doesn't seem to fit the needs of people with whom we study.

New notion: No one is creative alone. We need many eyes to develop insight.

Problem: Sometimes we believe the only effective personal study of the Bible is what's done alone.

New notion: We need the support and wisdom of fellow Bible students.

Problem: Sometimes we think that there are two kinds of truth—pagan truth and Christian truth.

New notion: There are all kinds of truth, and all truth belongs to God.

Problem: Sometimes we study the Bible to get "spiritual."

New notion: Spirituality is not a cozy feeling. It is a result of following Jesus.

Problem: Sometimes we study the Bible to get simple answers to complex problems.

New notion: We need a sense of perspective —learning for now and later.

Problem: Sometimes we think we know the answers before we even open the Bible.

New notion: We need to ask more questions and offer fewer answers. This keeps us learning.

Problem: Sometimes we think we can find all the answers in the Bible.

New notion: God didn't write the Bible as an encyclopedia of answers on life's questions. The Bible was written to help us work to discover the answers.

HOW TO DO CREATIVE BIBLE STUDY

Assume you are seated in an easy chair in front of your best friend (one who accepts you as you are, not for what you will be). Now begin to share with your friend your deepest concerns about life (injustice, attitudes, people, struggles, whatever). Now that you've shared these with your best friend, think about the following:

God is a *person*—not truth as an idea. He loves you and accepts you (Romans 5:8). Ask him your questions about these concerns. Try formulating them in complete sentences so that you and the Lord are aware of what you are asking specifically.

Another method of getting *into* your study is to listen to other persons' stories. Ask them about their feelings toward your concern on cassette tape. Then develop a series of questions you'd like to ask the Lord on behalf of this person who has shared his or her story with you. Isolate the verbs or action words in your questions or concerns. See if they fall into similar themes.

Look up these word themes in a concordance noting the definitions given. Try to set them in context. What realities or insights flashed through your mind as you were looking these words up? Write them down before they get away.

Now, bring the personal study and share it with the group. Follow this six-step process:

1. Share concerns. What concerns do we share in common?

2. What circumstances in life gave rise to your concern? Focus on the situation but clearly define the issue in life.

3. Share your combined insight with each other.

4. Formulate specific plans of action based on the insight of the group and personal study.

5. Support each other's goals (plan of action) in prayer often between meeting times.

6. Check up on each other throughout the time before the next Bible study.

A SECOND CREATIVE METHOD FOR BIBLE STUDY

Preparation for the Leader

1. Read the passage and look for the following:
   - Action words—verbs
   - Relationship words—usually nouns or modifying words
   - Images and metaphors, such as "The Word is a lamp unto my feet" or "The Word of God is a two-edged sword."

2. Visualize the passage in your mind. What kinds of ideas does this image suggest? Do this little free association exercise:

   Look in your wallet. You may find a telephone credit card. Think of all the things associated with the telephone. Soon you'll have a list like distance, wire, operators, numbers, dials, connections, computers, calling, messages, money. This then can be converted into relational ideas (i.e. distance = proximity of people—how close they are; wire = connections—what do they have in common?; numbers = ways to establish communication, etc.)

This simple exercise can help us to visualize ideas in scripture. For example, "being diligent to preserve the unity of the Spirit in the bond of peace" (Ephesians 4:3). You could take any of the words like "preserve" or "unity" or "bond" and do some free association. "Preserve" equals protection, keep from spoiling, maintain, conserve, store, refrigerate, freeze, support, save, rescue, guard or defend. "Unity" equals one, inseparable, singleness, individuality, harmony, concurrence, isolation, seclusion, identity. "Bond" equals cement, connected, union, accord, sympathy, guaranty, pledge, shackle, junction, relation.

From these associations, decide which ideas best express what the writer of the passage was saying according to the context. For instance, when Paul instructed

continued

BIBLE EXPLORATIONS

the Ephesians to "preserve the unity," was he saying to refrigerate it, freeze it, store it or keep it from spoiling, or support and save it? It doesn't take long to see what he wanted. Paul wanted them to rescue unity as if it were sinking in the waters of tension.

3. Create a group simulation experience. Now that you have begun to see the images, approach the idea of building a simulation so that the group will experience the meaning of this passage.

Simulation means to create a similar situation. To do this we might have to visualize positive and negative. For example, if we are to preserve unity, make a list of ideas that destroy unity (the negative): elitism (I'm better than you are, or I'm more informed than you are); fragmentation (I believe women should wear dresses, or I believe slacks are more modest), separation (you are always giving in, you're so liberal, our church takes a firm stand); exclusion (why don't you attend a church of your denomination, you're not in your element.)

It seems there is a wall between people. So why not build a "wall" with the group.

For the Group

1. Let's take some chairs and boxes and build a wall. We'll put the boxes on chairs so that people can't see each other (since that's what happens in disagreements anyway). Leave room at both ends of the wall so that people can walk from one side to the other, and then have the group members take "stands" on various controversial issues (e.g., gay rights). Pros on this side, cons on that side; if unsure, stand at the end.

When the groups have formed, dialogue with each other on the reasons "why" they are standing where they are. Be sure to include those standing in the "unsure" zone. Do this on several issues (abortion,

marijuana, premarital sex). Each issue should take about five minutes.

2. Now come together and read Ephesians 4:1-3 (printed on sheets of paper). Ask the group to:
   a. Read the text to get the feel of it.
   b. Find the key words and circle them.
   c. Divide this passage (outline, breakdown).
   d. Find the "Big Idea" or pivot point of the text.
   e. Underline nouns and pronouns.

3. Divide into small groups. Discuss these questions:
   1. What images do you see in the passage?
   2. What is this passage saying to you?

Now let's see if we can go back to our wall. Let's find a way to tear down our wall and symbolize our unity and oneness in spite of differences. After the wall is broken down, informally share your feelings and insights as a result of this experience.

Randall R. Scheer
Sterling, Kansas

See also 10) BIBLE WHO, WHAT AND WHERE, 12) DISCOVERY BIBLE STUDY, 13) HOW WE GOT OUR BIBLE GAME, 14) JURY BIBLE STUDY, 20) STORY TELLING, 72) CREATIVE CONJURING, 78) LORD'S PRAYER DANDELIONS, 81) REDACTION IN ACTION, 138) OBJECT-IVE REFLECTIONS, 133) PROGRESSIVE DINNERS, 167) CLOWNING, 176) COMMON OBJECT MEDITATIONS

10. BIBLE WHO, WHAT AND WHERE

The "Bible Who, What and Where" game helps put the competitive spirit to work for learning the Bible's content. The format is very much like the old "Who, What and Where" television game except that this is a team game.

Organize the young people into three teams. The game may be played with as few as three or as many as 30 players. If you have more than 30 persons, you should divide into two or more games. You may even want to divide with fewer than 30. Four or five persons per team is an ideal number. However, you should always have three teams per game in order to keep participation lively.

After the teams have been chosen, give each team a stack of 10 large cards with a multiple of five on each card (i.e. 5, 10, 15, 20 . . .). The number should be written large enough that it may be seen easily by the leader. Each group is also given a "Who" card, a "What" card, and a "Where" card. Each team should choose one person as its leader.

The rules: "I will offer you three questions in a Bible category. For example, the first category is **Jesus.** The three questions are a Who question, a What question, and a Where question. Each team begins the game with 50 points. You must decide how many of your 50 points you want to risk on the question, and which question you (your group) will attempt to answer.

"But first you need to know the odds on each question. In this category the odds are: Even on the Who, Two-for-one on the What, and Three-for-one on the Where. This means that if you choose the Who question for, say, 30 points, you will add 30 points to your 50 if you answer it correctly. If you miss it, you lose 30 points. If you risk 30 on the What question, you earn 60 points with a correct answer, or you lose 30 with a wrong answer. If you risk 30 on the Where question, you gain 90 with a correct answer, or you lose 30 with a wrong answer.

"But remember, the odds also tell you how difficult the question is. And remember that you cannot risk more points than you have at any time.

"Now, with the leader of your group, decide which question you want to bid on and how many points you want to risk. All bidding is always in increments of five."

Allow about 30 seconds for the decision, then ask each team to hold up two cards— one identifying the question they want to answer, and the other the number of points they choose to risk. The cards should be raised simultaneously by all teams.

If two teams choose the same question, the one bidding the most points gets that

continued

43

WHO, WHAT AND WHERE

question. The other team then can risk any number of their points up to the amount of their bid on the unbid question. If all three bid for the same question, the group bidding the greatest amount gets the question, the second highest bidder gets first choice of the other two questions, and the lowest bidder gets the remaining question. Again, if all bid for the same question, and the lower two tie, these two re-bid secretly, as above, for the remaining two questions.

If two or three of the groups bid the same amount for the same question (and this is the highest amount bid for that question), a "bid-off" takes place. A group may raise its bid in increments of five until one group drops out, or until they have bid all their points. The group losing the bid-off may risk any number of their points up to their original bid on the unclaimed question. If there are two "bid-off" losers, they should re-bid on the two remaining questions. If bid-offs occur often, alternate first bids among the groups involved.

When all bidding is determined in a given category, ask the questions one at a time in the order "Who," "What," and "Where." You may prefer to alter the order, with highest bid questions asked first or last—as you choose. But be consistent.

Scoring may be kept on a blackboard or newsprint. Each group begins with 50 points and points are added or subtracted as questions are answered or missed. If a group loses all its points, at that time add 10 points to all three groups, so that all groups continue to play throughout the game. Bids of "0" are not allowed.

The game may be played for any period of time or until you run out of categories. However, the last question on any occasion is an "open bid" question. In this special bid the bidding is the same, except that after selecting a category the group may bid (in increments of five) any amount of the points they have at that time in the game. This number is written on a blank card. After this opening bid the game proceeds as above.

Here are a few sample questions:

Odds

Jesus

Who (even): Who presided at the trial of Jesus and pronounced the verdict?

What (2-1): What did Jesus tell the crowd to do to the woman caught in adultery?

Where (3-1): Where did Jesus walk on the water (what body of water)?

Genesis

Who (2-1): Who was the oldest man to ever live, according to Genesis?

What (even): What happened to Lot's wife?

Where (2-1): Where did God tell Abraham to go?

Acts

Who (2-1): Who was the first Christian martyr?

What (4-1): What caused the split between Paul and Barnabas?

Where (even): Where did Paul's conversion take place?

Moses

Who (2-1): Who was Moses' brother who acted as his spokesman on many occasions?

What (2-1): What happened that finally made the Egyptians let the Israelites leave Egypt?

Where (even): Where did Moses receive the Ten Commandments?

Revelation

Who (even): Who wrote the Book of Revelation?

What (3-1): What was the author doing when the vision came to him?

Where (2-1): Where did the vision take place?

Jesse J. Sowell, Jr.
Fort Worth, Texas

See also 9) BIBLE EXPLORATIONS, 13) HOW-WE-GOT-OUR-BIBLE GAME

11. COMIC STRIPS AND THE BIBLE

I love comic strips and political cartoons. I use them frequently with my group in Bible studies and discussions.

Give each student a comic strip which has had the words in the conversation balloon removed. (I paste balloons over the words.) If we study a biblical passage, students are asked to rewrite the passage, then write in new dialogue in the conversation balloons. If we discuss an ethical or moral question, the comic strip characters are used to suggest the student's opinion about the subject.

An opaque projector makes it easy for the group to see the new creations. Discussion usually follows spontaneously from the use of this enjoyable medium.

Charlann Blodgett, Dubuque, Iowa

See also 9) BIBLE EXPLORATIONS, 12) DISCOVERY BIBLE STUDY, 79) HAPPINESS IS . . ., 81) REDACTION IN ACTION

12. DISCOVERY BIBLE STUDY

Leading young people into the Bible is more effective than trying to drill the Bible into them. There are a lot of young people who are serious Bible students who simply enjoy getting together and reading scripture.

Most of the young people I know, however, are not that interested in really digging into the Bible. It is usually a small minority who are willing to risk that kind of commitment. The majority are committed Christians, but  they are also committed to being together and having fellowship. Discovery Bible study works on relationships, building community and relating the scriptures to their own experience.

The unique thing about my Bible study is that it is an active learning experience. It starts with an activity which leads into the theme of the Bible study.

For example, I may use a top-40 song with good lyrics to start the study. I let them listen to it and discuss issues raised by the song. We then go into the Bible and explore the ways real love is the answer. We then bring the problems and the promises of the Bible together in our discussion. We use the chorus of the song at the close of the session as a litany.

Dean Dammann, Tustin, California

See also 9) BIBLE EXPLORATIONS, 11) COMIC STRIPS AND THE BIBLE, 15) WONDERS, 17) EN-COUNTER BIBLE CHARACTERS, 19) ZACCHAEUS AND HIS FEELINGS, 34) NEIGHBORS AND FRIENDS, 61) DISCIPLESHIP, 72) CREATIVE CONJURING, 82) LEMONS, 187) POP MUSIC POSSIBILI-TIES, 193) ROOTED IN WORSHIP

13. HOW-WE-GOT-OUR-BIBLE GAME

This is a game I made to help my confirmation class learn the history of the Bible.

They found it fun to play, and learned from it.

The Story of Our Bible

This game is played with any number of students, each taking turns throwing a single die, moving a marker, and following instructions. The first to complete the course (a correct number is required to land on the finish) is the "winner" of the game, although winning and losing should be secondary to learning from it. Whenever a correct answer is given to a question where a student has landed, he or she may advance one space. No penalty is given for incorrect answers.

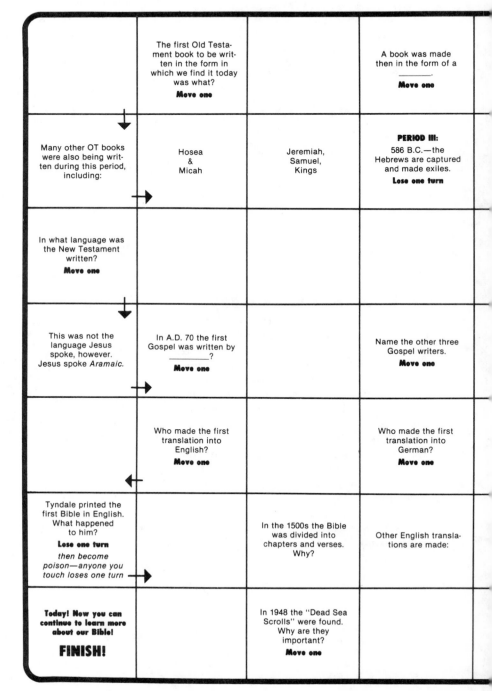

	The first Old Testament book to be written in the form in which we find it today was what? **Move one**		A book was made then in the form of a _____. **Move one**	
	Many other OT books were also being written during this period, including:	Hosea & Micah	Jeremiah, Samuel, Kings	**PERIOD III:** 586 B.C.—the Hebrews are captured and made exiles. **Lose one turn**
In what language was the New Testament written? **Move one**				
	This was not the language Jesus spoke, however. Jesus spoke *Aramaic*.	In A.D. 70 the first Gospel was written by _____? **Move one**		Name the other three Gospel writers. **Move one**
		Who made the first translation into English? **Move one**		Who made the first translation into German? **Move one**
	Tyndale printed the first Bible in English. What happened to him? **Lose one turn** *then become poison—anyone you touch loses one turn*		In the 1500s the Bible was divided into chapters and verses. Why?	Other English translations are made:
	Today! Now you can continue to learn more about our Bible! **FINISH!**		In 1948 the "Dead Sea Scrolls" were found. Why are they important? **Move one**	

START HERE	PERIOD I: 3,000 years ago. (No Bible) The Hebrews are wanderers.	Stories repeated from father to son, mother to daughter			First attempts at writing:
		songs	stories	sayings	
Stories were first written on animal skins and on papyrus.	DRHPHSMSDRLHT What does this tell us about that language? **Move one**	Stories were first written down in what language? *(the Old Testament language)* **Move one for correct answer**	PERIOD II: The Hebrews are now in Palestine (1000-586 B.C.)	On the first paper which was called what? **Move forward one for correct answer**	On Stone **Lose one turn** (trying to carry a stone book)
Books of *Hope* are written including:	Ezekiel	Isaiah *(ch. 40-55)*	PERIOD IV: 536 B.C.—the Hebrews are freed and return home. **Take one extra turn**	Work on the Old Testament continues, including:	Chronicles, Ezra, Nehemiah
There are 13 letters of Paul in the New Testament. Move up to three extra spaces by naming some of his other letters.	In A.D. 50 Paul wrote a letter—the first book of the New Testament to be written. What was it? **Move one**	The life, death, and resurrection of Jesus.	PERIOD V: New Testament Times	Esther and Daniel are the last Old Testament books to be written.	Final Old Testament books being written.
	Who wrote the book of Acts? **Move one**		PERIOD VI: *(Early Christian times)* Choosing the books of the Bible	About A.D. 100 The final decision is made on the ____ books of the Old Testament.	About A.D. 400 The final decision is made on the ____ books of the New Testament.
PERIOD VIII: Recent and modern times	Who made the first translation of the Bible into Latin? **Move one**		Who copied Bibles by hand? **Move one**	PERIOD VII: The Dark or Middle Ages *(about A.D.400 to 1200)*	Those books which "just missed" being included were put in the Apocrypha.
1611 The King James Version	1885 The Revised Version	1952 The Revised Standard Version	**STOP HERE!** Roll the die and move one space for each number on it	*PLUS* one extra space for each additional modern Bible translation you can name (up to *nine* total spaces)	
	Today, besides English, the Bible has been translated into more than 1000 languages				

continued

HOW-WE-GOT-OUR-BIBLE GAME

ANSWERS

Period I: The first paper was papyrus.

Period II: •The Old Testament language was Hebrew.

•"DRHPHSMSDRLHT" translates "The Lord is my Shepherd." This demonstrates three things about Hebrew: 1. It had no vowels. 2. There were no spaces between words. 3. It was written from right to left. One, two, or all three points may be required to equal a correct answer.

•Books were made in the form of a *scroll.*

•The first Old Testament book was *Amos.*

Period III: No questions

Period IV: No questions

Period V: •The first book of the New Testament was *1 Thessalonians.*

•The New Testament was written in *Greek.*

•The first Gospel was *Mark,* followed by Matthew, Luke, John.

•*Luke* wrote Acts.

Period VI: There are 39 books in the Old Testament and 27 books in the New Testament. These are not "advancement" questions unless you choose to make them so.

Period VII: •*Monks* copied the Bible by hand.

•*Jerome* translated the Bible into Latin.

Period VIII: •*Luther* translated the Bible into German.

•John *Wycliffe* translated the Bible into English.

•William Tyndale *printed* the first English Bible. For doing this he was driven from England, hunted throughout Europe, and finally caught and put to death. Good discussion might come about among the students at this point as to why there might have been such a terrible reaction to what we now consider a very good act on Tyndale's part. Whoever lands here misses a turn, but from then on causes anyone else to miss a turn whenever they land on the same space.

•The Bible was divided into chapters and verses for easier reference. This may also create discussion and, again, is not an advancement question unless you want it to be.

•All players must stop at the STOP HERE! sign. If the player had extra steps on his die, he may immediately roll again. If not, he must wait until his next turn. Here he rolls one die, as always. If he rolls a 4 he moves that many spaces, then names as many modern Bible translations as he knows (other than those already named on the board). In this case, the player may move from one to five additional spaces, depending on how many he knows.

•The "Dead Sea Scrolls" are important because of the old Bible manuscripts they contained. Just as other such archaeological discoveries, they show us that the hand of God is still at work today, helping us to learn more about the Bible. Discussion may be developed with this as a starting point with the students.

Harold Steindam
Upper Sandusky, Ohio

See also 9) BIBLE EXPLORATIONS, 10) BIBLE WHO, WHAT AND WHERE, 55) STUDENT/PARENT CONFIRMATION, 81) REDACTION IN ACTION, 193) ROOTED IN WORSHIP

14. JURY BIBLE STUDY

The jury method of Bible study can be used with some of the longer stories in the Bible. It's ideal with stories that are somewhat unfamiliar to the group. (Even if your kids grew up in church, chances are they still lack Bible knowledge.)

The following is the story of Joseph (Genesis 37-50); it works well with groups as young as junior high.

If you have a group larger than eight, divide them into two or more groups, having no more than six to eight per group. They are to think of themselves as a jury, even choosing a jury foreman.

Tell in your own words the first part of Joseph's story: the favorite son, his "air of superiority," and so forth (Genesis 37:1-17). In your jury groups discuss these questions: 1. What do you think of this kind of situation? 2. How would you as outsiders help in such a situation? For the second question, think of three different solutions and then agree on one of the solutions. Report this to the total group. Allow 15-20 minutes.

Relate Joseph's older brothers' solution: selling Joseph into slavery and telling his father, Jacob, that an animal had killed and eaten his favorite son (Genesis 37:18-36). Ask the jury groups to determine: 1. Whether

continued

JURY BIBLE STUDY

this was a good solution. 2. How Jacob may have felt when he was told of his son's "death." (Ask them how they would have felt if they had been in Jacob's sandals.) 3. Are any contemporary events that are similar to that of the brothers' plot? How do we deal with our own brothers/sisters we think are favorites? After 15 minutes, have the groups report their findings.

Relate what happened to Joseph: his rise to power and his brothers' visits to buy grain from him (Genesis 39-45:1-3). In jury groups discuss the following: 1. What would you do if you were Joseph? Again think of three different solutions and come up with a consensus on one of these. 2. How do you think the brothers felt when they found out who this ruler was? Have a general reporting after 10 minutes.

Relate Joseph's solution (Genesis 45:4-15). What do the jury groups think of this solution? Discuss ways in which brothers and sisters can forgive each other while still maintaining justice. Allow 10 minutes. Finally ask them to think about their own family situations. In the light of this story how might they handle their quarrels and hassles?

I used this jury study of Joseph with 30 junior highs one night and 40 senior highs another night. I was amazed at how much more the junior highs identified with Joseph. The senior highs were much more vindictive, especially the boys. Because they didn't know the story as well, junior highs also threw themselves into the study more intensely than did the seniors.

This method works well with the stories of David (Saul and Jonathan, and Bathsheba and Nathan). It also works well with the Prodigal Son.

Henry Sawatzky
Chatham, New Jersey

See also 9) BIBLE EXPLORATIONS, 17) ENCOUNTER BIBLE CHARACTERS, 18) THE PRODIGAL DAUGHTER/SON, 20) STORYTELLING, 33) OPINION LINE-UP, 50) GUILTY, 93) SMALL GROUPS, 214) THE LOST SON

15. WONDERS

I like to use this Bible study with youth when we are in beautiful natural settings. I call it, "I Wonder About the Wonders I See." I start out by having everyone in the group make a little pin hole viewer. This viewer is created by putting a small hole in a piece of paper the size of a business card. As they look at their surroundings through this limited perspective, I encourage them to see the "pieces" of creation in detail. I lead them in the reading of Psalm 85 as they come to appreciate God's creation. We then share the things which call forth praise from us. This kind of Bible study combines their experience with the blessings of scripture.

Dean Dammann
Tustin, California

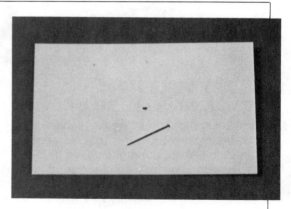

See also 12) DISCOVERY BIBLE STUDY, 42) CAMP PRODUCTIONS, 43) BLUE TASSELS, 71) 2083, 72) CREATIVE CONJURING, 78) LORD'S PRAYER DANDELIONS, 82) LEMONS, 164) WORSHIP ENVIRONMENT, 193) ROOTED IN WORSHIP, 194) ON THIS ROCK

16. BRICKS

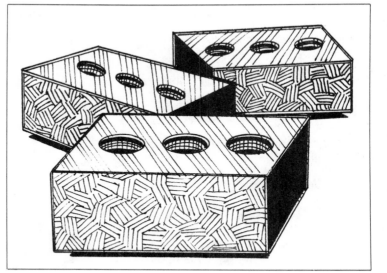

Nehemiah is an exciting book. Here is a simulation developed from the reading of Nehemiah 3 and 4, where the wall of Jerusalem was rebuilt once the people learned to cooperate.

1. **Goal:** We sought to demonstrate the need for cooperation between individuals if a large task is to be accomplished.

2. **Materials:**
- Building blocks ("bricks")—10 for each player. We used unused quart-size milk cartons made obsolete when the local dairy went to the metric system.
- Series of questions or statements about relationships with others.

3. **Process:**
- Divide people into several teams.
- Each group has the task of building a wall between two marked points.
- Each round consists of all players answering for themselves a question (or responding to a statement), then placing a brick on the wall. If the answer is a positive one, a brick is laid lengthwise; if negative, brick is laid endwise. Hence, a negative response means less distance covered in building the wall between two points.
- The game ends when all questions have been answered by all players. The "winning" team is the one which has covered the greatest distance.

4. **Reflection:**
I can calmly help someone who is facing a crisis.

I try not to give "advice" to others who are in trouble.
I don't mind helping people who aren't "my kind."
I accept as true what other people tell me.
I listen attentively to what other people say.
I finish what I say I'll do for someone else.
I'm tactful in helping other people.
I try to understand the feelings of others.
I keep to myself what I'm told in confidence.
I'm tolerant of those with different view-points.
I'm sensitive to the needs of others.
I'm honest and sincere with others.

5. **Options:**
If there are space limits, bricks can be laid in two or more layers. If this is done, then negative answers, necessitating end-wise laying of the brick, need propping up by other bricks. (That is, negative responses "use up" some positive responses, without any "progress" being made.)

6. **Debriefing:**
a. How did you feel when the need to be absolutely honest clashed with the responsibility to help the group complete its assignment?
b. How did you feel when you had to prop

continued

BRICKS

up another player's brick, or when you were propped up by another?

c. Were there any pressures on you to conform?

d. How true of life is:
   1. the clash between the individual and the group?
   2. "propping up" anti-social behavior of someone else?

Some players expressed strong surprise when someone wanted to give a negative response. One team found that the negative responses were turned into strengths because the propping up served to reinforce that section of the wall.

Leigh Wilson
Shepparton, Australia

See also 4) WHAT'S A LEADER?, 9) BIBLE EXPLORATIONS, 32) CARING, 36) PUT-DOWN WEDGE, 37) THE WALL, 38) GOSSIP BLOCKS, 76) TEA TIME, 95) LEADER SUPPORT, 97) TRANSPARENCY, 98) PROBLEM SHARING, 100) DEAR TEACHER,

17. ENCOUNTER BIBLE CHARACTERS

I have been exploring what I call Encounter Bible Studies. The group members pick a biblical character which they dislike or find puzzling. They are then asked to put a chair in front of themselves and talk with the imagined character, switching back and forth between chairs.

For example, one person at such a meeting picked Esau for being such a loser in his dealing with Jacob. This youth was projecting his own "doormat" tendencies on Esau. After having such a dialogue, the person was asked to sit in the chair and take the character's role. After defending the biblical person, another change was made back to the critic's chair.

After the dialogue, each person thinks about the experience. These questions might be pursued:

● "What bugs you about the character in the Bible?"

● "Who reminds you of this character?"

Then each member dialogues through the use of the chair with that person.

Finally, the young people focus on similarities between themselves and the biblical character. This is done again by having dialogue with oneself, again using the chair.

John Scherer, Spokane, Washington

See also 12) DISCOVERY BIBLE STUDY, 14) JURY BIBLE STUDY, 18) THE PRODIGAL DAUGHTER/SON, 19) ZACCHAEUS AND HIS FEELINGS, 39) SHORT PEOPLE, 40) GOOD SAMARITAN MIME, 58) PARENT/YOUTH ENCOUNTER, 169) LOAVES AND FISHES, 190) A.D. 81, 207) PARTICIPATORY CHRISTMAS PAGEANT, 211) GOOD FRIDAY SACRED DANCE, 218) GOIN' TO NINEVAH, 219) JESUS MEETS THE ELDERS

18. THE PRODIGAL DAUGHTER/SON

We did a fascinating session with our senior high group to explore sex-role expectations and stereotypes. I had rewritten the Parable of the Prodigal Son into two contemporary versions. One of the new stories featured a mother and her two daughters as the main characters; the other story was rewritten into a contemporary mode, but it retained the same main characters as the original—a father and his two sons.

The group was divided into two smaller groups—each part taking one of the stories to focus on. Each group listened to their version and then talked about each character and listed impressions of each character. (It was most important in rewriting the story to remain faithful to the concepts presented in the biblical account.)

We were all quite surprised! The group which discussed the qualities of the female characters had thought of the mother as being divorced and poor (although this was never mentioned in the rewritten version). The father in the other version turned out to be a successful businessman.

Joy Edwards
Kingston, Rhode Island

See also 14) JURY BIBLE STUDY, 17) ENCOUNTER BIBLE CHARACTERS, 33) OPINION LINE-UP, 128) COMPUTER DATING NIGHT, 213) THE FIFTH GOSPEL, 214) THE LOST SON

19. ZACCHAEUS AND HIS FEELINGS

Our junior high youth always enjoy games. This game provided an opportunity for delving into a discussion about our own feelings as well as providing a focus on the study of Zacchaeus (Luke 19:1-10).

The objectives of "Zacchaeus and His Feelings" are to explore the range of human emotions and to observe the effects of Jesus Christ on these emotions.

The following materials are needed:
● 3 x 5 cards, each containing a "feeling word," e.g. love, anger, guilt, jealousy, anxiety, repentance, forgiveness, acceptance. Each young person can make a set of these cards.
● copies of Today's English Version of the New Testament
● sheets of paper.

After each student completes the set of cards, have them arrange the set in order from the "worst" feeling to the "best." Read the story of Zacchaeus in Luke 19:1-10. After each verse, each student chooses a feeling experienced by Zacchaeus and writes it on a piece of paper numbered one through ten. The numbers on the paper correspond to the verses in Luke 19:1-10.

Now, compare the feelings on the cards to Zacchaeus' feelings on the paper. Both the cards and Zacchaeus' feelings should change from the "negative" to the "positive." Discuss the reasons for the change in Zacchaeus (and the crowd toward Jesus). Discuss situations in which Jesus transforms our own negative emotions into positive ones.

Leigh Wilson
Shepparton, Australia

See also 17) ENCOUNTER BIBLE CHARACTERS, 39) SHORT PEOPLE

20. STORYTELLING

We have found that a well-told story is one of the most powerful ways to reach our youth with whatever thoughts, emotions or ideas we have in mind. Here are some of the guidelines that we found most helpful in preparing ourselves for telling stories.

● What is the value of the story in Christian education?

The story is a picture presented to the mind's eye to stir the interest and feeling of the hearer. Listeners are unconsciously learning to evaluate and are establishing life standards. Stories from the Bible become real to young persons. They see themselves in the story. They learn to see Christ as the way to truth, humility and kindness.

● What should be the specific aim in telling a story?

In Christian work, one is not justified in telling a story to entertain or to fill time. Only one specific aim should exist for each story, such as encouraging a decision for Christ; inspiring consecration to service; provoking worship; correcting wrong conduct; creating interest in people of other lands and the church's mission to them.

What is the basic construction of a good story?

A good story has a good beginning. The good beginning rouses interest. It introduces the characters, the setting and the time. It gives some idea of the kind of characters or the problem of the story.

A good story is well developed. It moves in an orderly way with smooth transitions. Each picture adds to the interest of the next until all culminate in a climax. The development of the story must intensify the conflict; the effort of two forces to overcome each other must arouse the sympathy of the hearers.

A good story has a climax. The climax is the revealing of the secret, the moment of discovery. Every part of the story preceding has built up to this high point. The climax must be expressed in simple, carefully chosen language, and must sound spontaneous—and that takes practice.

A good story has a satisfactory ending. The ending of the story must leave the mind at rest. It should be as brief as possible, rounding out the tale by telling what happened to the characters, etc. Some stories end satisfactorily with the climax.

● What background preparation does the storyteller need?

A good storyteller needs to study the best of many types of stories. He needs to study the background of stories, their context in the Bible, geography, customs, modes of dress, life, history, etc. She needs to study nature to let the sunshine, the running brook, the rain, the birds, the wind pour into the story. He needs to practice observing and describing in fine details everyday events.

List the main points of the story on a story pattern chart, as below.

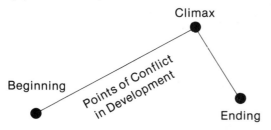

● **How should the specific story be prepared?**

Choose a story which is worthy of Christ, of your best work. Read the story through for enjoyment. Reread and analyze, noting each incident in its order. List the incidents on paper; fix them in your mind. Visualize the story—see each incident clearly. (Myer Pearlman's advice for telling the story so that it lives is to know it; see it; feel it.) Obtain background material for the specific story. Determine the conflict and climax so you can make them clear. Practice the story; tell it to an imaginary audience. Do not memorize the words; rather tell what you see. Criticize your telling; practice voice changes aloud. Mark any quotations to be read from the Bible so you will find them quickly; practice with them for smooth entry. Lengthen or shorten your story as needed so the story can be filled with details.

● **How should the story be told?**

The story should be told with sincerity and naturalness. It should be told with no unnecessary gestures. It should be told without rushing. Think as you go along. It should be told with dialogue where possible. Change your pitch and tone of voice to fit characters.

● **How is the truth of the story applied?**

Repetition can be used to emphasize the words which convey the truth. Contrast will sharpen the good by showing it against the bad, the light against the dark, etc. Strengthened teaching sentences will make the parts containing the lesson more forcible. Your sincere attitude will teach; it will make the truth of the story convincing. Concentrate on the aim of the story. A very short appeal for decision, for action of the will, will be all that is needed if the truth has been woven strongly into the fiber of the story.

● **What types of stories might be used with youth?**

Junior highs learn from stories dealing with attainment and idealism; heroes who have principle, self-mastery, and triumph over hardship, suffering and sacrifice; realistic situations; adventure—action, even romantic settings; biographies of men and women who have given their lives in service to humanity.

Senior highs learn from stories of vocation (missionary stories, careers of Christian heroes); courtship, romance (which show the highest meaning of love, clean manhood and womanhood, the Christian home); challenge—to thinking, to provoke argument, to evaluate own conduct; realistic situations and the solving of problems; biography as well as idealistic and symbolic stories.

● **Where may I find good stories?**

The Bible contains the greatest stories in all literature. It holds stories for every age level. Biography is one of the greatest sources of inspiration literature. Actual Christians have lived lives that exceed fiction. Christian magazine and Sunday school paper stories may be clipped and filed for later use.

Stories especially equipped with visual aids may be very effective if the story is properly prepared. Stories can come from your own experience or from observation—suggested by pictures in magazines, scenes and incidents of everyday life, nature study articles, narrative poems, accounts of holiday observances.

Edith Armstrong and Sylvia Lee
Springfield, Missouri

See also 9) BIBLE EXPLORATIONS, 14) JURY BIBLE STUDY, 21) ECHO PANTOMIMES, 207) PARTICIPATORY CHRISTMAS PAGEANT, 208) CHRISTMAS STORIES, 213) THE FIFTH GOSPEL

21. ECHO PANTOMIMES

Echo pantomime is one of the more popular activities with our group. Echo pantomime is an activity in which the group repeats everything the leader says and does. You can use this with Bible reading, songs, poems or whatever. Just try it.

● Some points to remember:

1. Lines must be short and easy to remember.

2. Words must be clear.

3. Write down what you'll say and do.

4. The viewpoint does not change . . . you are always just one person speaking. The other side of the conversation is assumed, but not spoken.

5. In your notes, include simple directions for arms, legs or posture.

6. Practice it a couple times.

● Some planning tips:

1. Who is your character?

2. What is the situation?

3. What points do you want to bring out about this situation?

4. What is the climax?

5. What is the conclusion?

Robert W. Havens
Rochester, Minnesota

See also 20) STORYTELLING, 38) GOSSIP BLOCKS, 213) THE FIFTH GOSPEL

22. FILM CRITICISM

For many years, I have enjoyed using film as a means of education, personal growth and theological probing. I find that many fine commercial movies open up opportunities for Christian thought. To get beyond "I liked it" or "It stunk," the following process will help a group evaluate a film.

Movie Art Form Conversations

Introduction

The church always has used the art form of its culture. Good art is reflective of reality and helps us see the really real. Discuss art through a trilogue (you, I, the art form) and not by asking what the artist means. Look at the art form through the eye glasses of the person of faith. Then ask these questions:

What was said, shown?

Through the use of objective questions, a sharing takes place which allows us to see if we all saw the same thing. Discuss:

● scenes
● sets
● minor characters
● props
● dialogue
● music

What were the feelings?

Through the use of reflective questions we are enabled to get more in touch with ourselves. Discuss:

● symbols
● where did you feel emotion?
● who did you like, dislike?
● what was your mood at the end of the movie?
● where did you see emotion?
● with which character did you identify?

23. DISCUSSION BASICS

A major misconception in youth ministry is that a lot of talk equals a discussion. It doesn't. We may talk a lot, but we don't always say very much. We don't go beyond the surface level. We don't get to the core of the problem. This happens because we have not established a comfortable environment for the group members.

If you have a group of 20 people and six or seven carry the whole discussion, then something is wrong. The second clue to trouble is the presence of much talk, but little depth of emotion or content. You may have a lot of people using clowning or other masking techniques to hide feelings. Another clue is that the group is not getting to the

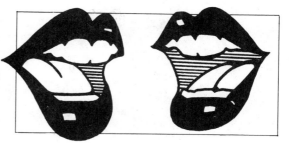

core of the topic. This means that the atmosphere has not been prepared.

The first way to overcome this situation is to help the youth get acquainted. This goes for groups which have been in existence for a long time. Each member of the group needs to know the other members of the group. This means more than names. Listening to another person's ideas and feelings is a valuable get-acquainted exercise.

The second way to develop good discussion is to create trust. We need to feel good about our relationships before sharing personal aspects of our lives.

Listening skills are also important for good discussion. When do we listen and when do we speak?

We need to look at the masks or defense techniques which hide our contribution to the group. We don't need to remove our masks. Just being aware of them will help the situation.

The last way to improve discussion is to help the members of the group move beyond the surface level. Ask the people to clarify, justify, compare and contrast.

If you do these kinds of things, your discussions will move along much more quickly. Discussions will move from the surface to a deeper level. I believe you will have more exciting discussion experiences.

John Bushman
Lawrence, Kansas

What was it about?

Through the use of interpretive questions, a major thrust or impact can be encountered. Discuss:
- retitle the film
- give a one sentence description
- what happened in the next scene *after* the movie ended?
- what did the main character face?
- what were the possibilities of the film's outcome?

Where do you see verbal Christian symbols?
- Where did you see the activity of God, event of the Christ?
- What point in the film was compared with "sin" (clue: may be in seeing separation)?
- Where did you see the "Resurrected Life"?
- What similarities with Bible stories?

William E. Burdick
Pittsburgh, Pennsylvania

See also 53) RESOURCE CONSUMER TIPS, 73) MEDIA PROBING, 80) TV WISDOM, 187) POP MUSIC POSSIBILITIES (apply same critical tools for music)

See also 24) SPINNING TOP, 25) THE HOT SEAT, 33) OPINION LINE-UP, 49) ALL NIGHT TALK, 54) CHEAP ROLE PLAYS, 60) SEX EDUCATION, 70) LEARNING CENTERS, 93) SMALL GROUPS, 97) TRANSPARENCY, 98) PROBLEM SHARING, 99) SELF AWARENESS, 109) ROOM DYNAMICS

24. SPINNING TOP

Some of the senior high students and I were exploring the concept of "creed" one Sunday morning in church school. The students wrote their own statements of belief. We compared these with the creeds of the church. There was some difficulty getting discussion going. To help the youth further develop their thinking about beliefs I used a child's toy top. Students spun the top and had to tell about their relationships with God before it stopped spinning. The thoughts seemed to flow more easily as they focused on the spinning top.

Dr. Christopher Schooley
New Albany, Indiana

See also 23) DISCUSSION BASICS, 25) THE HOT SEAT, 33) OPINION LINE-UP, 54) CHEAP ROLE PLAYS, 75) A SPOONFUL OF HONEY

25. THE HOT SEAT

We have put to use that old concept of the "hot seat" in our youth meetings. Once a month we invite a person (we like to think of them as being somewhat unusual for the typical youth group meeting) to be our guest in the "hot seat." We have developed a particular style of conversation with this guest. Questions and dialogue are in order, much like a press conference. Both the youth and the guests enjoy the good exchange of ideas, thoughts, and feelings.

Warren Keating, Phoenix, Arizona

See also 23) DISCUSSION BASICS, 60) SEX EDUCATION

26. FLIGHT 108

I have used variations of this simulation game, "Flight #108," with several different kinds of groups—overnight lock-ins at church, evening youth groups, etc. The version I describe below was used in a retreat but can be easily adapted to other settings.

Prior to the weekend, 10 people were asked a simple question: "If a plane were about to crash with only five parachutes aboard, should you receive one of the parachutes?" "Why?" The respondent included a little boy eating an ice cream cone, a mounted policeman, retired people, single people, students. These people were interviewed on cassette tape and were photographed on color slide film.

The group's makeup was as follows: 17 junior high students, four senior high students, four adult counselors. One of the counselors was aware of what was about to take place. The four senior high students were given the honor of acting as the crew of a regular flight. The junior high students and the other counselors were passengers.

Twenty-three seats were set up as they would be arranged in an airplane. Each seat was numbered and each passenger was given a seat number at random. As the passengers entered the room, each person was escorted to his/her seat by a stewardess who welcomed them to Flight 108. After all were seated, the stewardess gave the normal safety instructions, and the pilot gave the normal welcome.

The lead counselor then asked each person to assume the identity of someone else for the duration of the flight. A wide range of passengers emerged: Betty Ford, Mickey Mantle, a CIA hit man, a rich minister, a poor minister, the Six Million Dollar Man, a retarded child, a professional football player. It is important that each person is unique. This will eliminate a popularity contest. Each person is told to react during the flight as they feel the personality they are portraying would react.

A projector screen was pulled down. We played a movie we checked out from the public library. The projector was suddenly turned off. The pilot shouted, "May Day, May Day!!" He informed the control tower that the plane had suffered a mid-air collision.

The lead counselor then informed everyone that there were only five parachutes aboard the plane. Each person was asked why the character he or she was portraying should have a parachute. Each person then gave a response which varied from greed to a desire that someone else get the parachute.

Each crew member chose a passenger to receive a parachute. They had to give reasons for their choices. (Any article can be used to represent the parachutes.) The lead counselor gave out the last parachute.

continued

FLIGHT 108

After all the parachutes were passed out, recipients were given the opportunity to give their parachutes to someone else. If they elected to give up their parachutes (they all did), they had to state why they felt the other people were more deserving.

When the final parachute owners were established, they were told some of the problems had been corrected and that a safe landing was possible. All five immediately gave up their parachutes; however, five other people took them. Those five then left the plane; and the others were told that the plane crashed with no survivors. The participants became totally involved, uncovering many values.

We then split into small discussion groups. Using the slides and taped interviews gathered before the weekend, each group picked five survivors.

The props needed for the above games are:

1. Blackboard or chart paper to record identity of each player.

2. Anything available to represent parachutes, i.e., pillows, pieces of wood.

3. Chair for each passenger (random seating is also very effective).

4. Projection screen (a brief movie can be shown before "collision" if available).

5. A camera and tape recorder are required for the interview portion.

An interesting variation to Flight 108 is to have the young people interview 10 people on-the-street *after* playing the simulation game.

Ken Scarborough
Wilmington, Delaware

See also 46) HAVES AND HAVE NOTS, 49) ALL-NIGHT TALK, 54) CHEAP ROLE PLAYS, 174) YOUTH AND SOCIAL ISSUES

27. OVER THE RAINBOW

We held a New Year's resolution youth event on the theme, "What's at the End of Your Rainbow?" The event was held during the Christmas break, just before the beginning of the New Year. A New Year's Eve party would also be a good setting for this idea.

The kids painted a wall-sized rainbow and constructed a pot of gold. After a goal-setting exercise (short- and long-term goals) they wrote themselves letters and put them in the "pot of gold." The covenant of the rainbow (Genesis 9:12-17) was read and shared.

Between Palm Sunday and Easter I mailed the letters to the youth. They remembered our time together, read their letters, and assessed the progress they had made toward their rainbow resolutions.

William R. Pennock, Addison, New York

See also 28) DEAR ME, 29) A STEP AHEAD, 41) SENIORITIS, 100) DEAR TEACHER, 116) GROUP BANNER, 156) REACH

28. DEAR ME,

Some people think letter writing is a lost art. We recaptured the joy of writing and reading letters at one of our group meetings.

We discussed a variety of letters: Philemon, Emily Dickinson's "Letter to the World" and Dietrich Bonhoeffer's *Letters From Prison*. After discussing this variety of letters, all members received sheets

of paper and envelopes to write letters to themselves. These letters were filed away and mailed to the youth at the end of the school year. The letters contained reflections about how they felt and where they were in their relationship with God. It was a sobering, reflective evening.

John and Bobbie Rankin
California, Pennsylvania

See also 27) OVER THE RAINBOW, 87) STICKY FLAPS, 100) DEAR TEACHER, 156) REACH

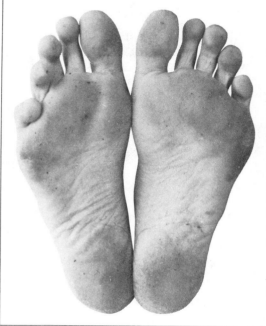

29. A STEP AHEAD

The theme of our senior high retreat, held during the break between Christmas and New Year's Day, was "Putting Your Right Foot Forward in the New Year." This theme was developed by having participants make name tags in the shape of their own feet. During the retreat our Bible study focused on passages and concepts that dealt with the theme of "getting started on your best foot." It is amazing how much there is in biblical materials that can be used with this theme (for instance, John 13:4-16; 1 Timothy 5:10). We even concluded our retreat with a worship service in which we featured footwashing.

Monica Brown
Hyattsville, Maryland

See also 27) OVER THE RAINBOW, 176) COMMON OBJECT MEDITATIONS (SHOES)

30. BEING HANDICAPPED

My work has led me to a great interest with those who face special physical and mental challenges. I have developed the following instrument for use with youth.

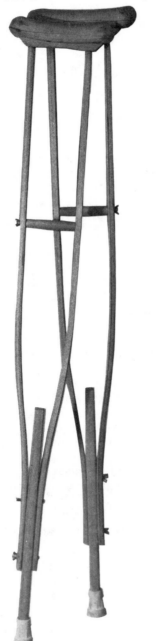

TAKE TIME TO FEEL

(An Experience in Experiencing)

You are destined to be developmentally disabled. You have a real advantage today, because you can choose the disability you would prefer. After choosing your disability, answer the following questions in light of the disability you choose in question 1.

1. Choose the disability you would rather have:
   - ☐ A. mentally retarded at birth, i.e., Down's syndrome, PKU, hydrocephalus, etc.
   - ☐ B. mentally retarded due to child abuse, neglect, environment, etc.
   - ☐ C. cerebral palsy
   - ☐ D. epilepsy (severe seizures)
   - ☐ E. mentally retarded and blind
   - ☐ F. autistic
   - ☐ G. mentally retarded and physically handicapped
   - ☐ H. mentally retarded and deaf
   - ☐ I. other (specify) _____

2. Briefly describe your disability: _____

3. What level do you function at?
   - ☐ A. borderline normal
   - ☐ B. mildly retarded
   - ☐ C. moderately retarded
   - ☐ D. severely retarded
   - ☐ E. profoundly retarded
   - ☐ F. severe physical impairment

4. What is your I.Q.?
   - ☐ A. 0-20
   - ☐ B. 21-35
   - ☐ C. 36-52
   - ☐ D. 53-75
   - ☐ E. 76-90

5. Your age:_____

6. Where do you live?
   - ☐ A. group home
   - ☐ B. with parents

☐C. institution
☐D. nursing home
☐E. foster home
☐F. independently

7. How do you occupy your time?
   ☐A. activity center
   ☐B. workshop
   ☐C. classroom
   ☐D. institutional ward
   ☐E. same room at home all day
   ☐F. competitive employment
   ☐G. whatever I want—but at home
   ☐H. other (specify) _____

8. How does your family feel about your disability?
   ☐A. pretend it doesn't exist
   ☐B. want me out of my home
   ☐C. help me to grow and develop
   ☐D. full of self-blame
   ☐E. indifference
   ☐F. expect too little of me
   ☐G. expect too much of me
   ☐H. other (explain) _____

9. Do they respect your: (check if answer is yes)
   ☐A. rights?
   ☐B. privacy?
   ☐C. opinions?
   ☐D. right to risk?
   ☐E. desire for independence, etc.?

10. How many friends do you have?
    ☐A. one
    ☐B. a few
    ☐C. none
    ☐D. no chance to make any
    ☐E. no one wants to be my friend

11. Do your friends: (check if answer is yes)
    ☐A. respect your rights?
    ☐B. ask your opinion?
    ☐C. do things with you?
    ☐D. help you make other friends?
    ☐E. come to visit you?
    ☐F. share their feelings with you?

12. Do you get along with your peers: (check if answer is yes)

☐A. in the classroom?
☐B. at work?
☐C. socially?
☐D. in the institution?
☐E. never?
☐F. no chance to find out

13. When are you involved in decisions about your life? (check if answer is yes)
    ☐A. at home
    ☐B. at school
    ☐C. with friends
    ☐D. with doctors
    ☐E. in employment situations
    ☐F. other (specify) _____
    ☐G. never

14. What do you dream about?
    ☐A. friends
    ☐B. college
    ☐C. job
    ☐D. nice clothes
    ☐E. your own home
    ☐F. marriage
    ☐G. being like other people
    ☐H. taking a trip
    ☐I. other (specify) _____
    ☐J. having your own family

15. Does your handicap keep you from communicating with others? _____Yes _____No

16. Do you always have to watch from the sidelines? _____Yes _____No

17. Briefly describe how a youth group could make your life better: _____
_____

18. Briefly describe what you'd like to see change in the community to make your life better:_____
_____

Wesley Taylor
Oregon City, Oregon

See also 31) HANDICAPPED RETREAT, 32) CAR-ING, 34) NEIGHBORS AND FRIENDS, 45) TOUCH OUR MISSION, 54) CHEAP ROLE PLAYS, 174) YOUTH AND SOCIAL ISSUES, 177) LIVING WATER

31. HANDICAPPED RETREAT

We designed a retreat for about 50 junior high youth to help them appreciate and respect the handicapped. We started by using relational and group building activities. Then we raised the young people's awareness level regarding persons with handicaps. Proceeding through the weekend in a series of activities, studies and discussions, we went from "awareness," to "exploring," to "responding" and finally to "doing something about it."

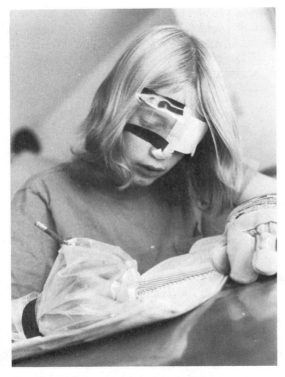

Creative learning sessions can help your young people to experience what it's like to be handicapped.

Awareness activities:

1. We viewed and discussed the film, "Who are the DeBolts and Where Did They Get Nineteen Kids?" (available from Pyramid Films, Box 1048, Santa Monica, CA 90406). You could skip this activity if your budget is tight.

Exploring activities:

1. We divided into groups of six and brainstormed how much everyone knew about disabilities and handicaps, including those related to aging and mentally/emotionally ill persons. Each small group shared its list of specific disabilities with the entire group. Of all the disabilities listed, we chose six disabilities which we assigned to each group. We used those disabilities in later activities (see activity 4 under this heading and activity 1 under "Responding" activities.)

2. After discussing different disabilities, the entire group defined the term "handicapped." We used that definition throughout the retreat.

3. We divided into small groups and read about the blind man who was healed (John 9:1-7) and about Jesus at a Pharisee's house (Luke 14:1-14). Each group role-played one of the passages, emphasizing the Christian attitude toward those with disabilities and how they related to God's kingdom.

4. Using a variety of props to simulate disabilities, we had each person in the group of six take one of the following disabilities and live through some normal living experiences (e.g., eating, playing a game, walking up and down steps, getting in and out of a car). We used the following props and disabilities:

DISABILITY	PROP
Blindness	blind folds
Partial deafness	ear plugs with tape and ear muffs
Speech impairment	hospital tape over mouth covered with surgeon's mask
Loss of limbs	legs tied together with rope or tape and using crutches
Aging	hospital glasses with vaseline smeared on the lenses, plus gloves
Ambulatory	short rope tied to legs making it impossible to take big steps

At the end of this three-hour segment, we discussed what these experiences meant and how everyone felt about being handicapped.

Responding activities:

1. We divided everyone who had the same handicaps into the same group. (See activity #4 under "Exploring Activities.") For instance, all the blind people met together, all the deaf people met together and so on. Then everyone described how they felt and thought as they experienced their handicap.

2. The director of a special school described his work with mentally retarded persons.

3. The entire group listed various ways people respond to persons with handicaps.

4. I handed out a questionnaire which asked the young people to determine how they'd react to certain types of handicaps, how they felt about older persons, how much they knew about certain handicaps. We later used the questionnaires as a springboard for discussion.

What Are You Going to Do About It Activities:

1. We listed as many disabled or handicapped person's names as we could and described some of the barriers each had to live with. We also discussed how each of those disabilities would affect us.

2. We divided into small groups and discussed how each person might become involved with disabled/handicapped persons and what the church could do to help.

FIRST CHURCH ASSOCIATION

Because God loved me through Christ just as I am, I will try to, in the next six (6) weeks to . . .

_____

_____

_____

for a handicapped or disabled person I know.

SIGNED _____

DATE _____

3. We used a commitment sheet (above) that asked everyone to commit themselves to a specific action or response within the next six weeks. Each person wrote his/her name and address on an envelope. We mailed the sealed envelopes the next week to remind the young people of their commitments.

Larry K. Waltz
Philadelphia, Pennsylvania

See also 30) BEING HANDICAPPED, 32) CARING, 45) TOUCH OUR MISSION, 52) RETREAT FEEDBACK, 74) YOUTH AND SOCIAL ISSUES, 115) RETREAT CHECKLIST, 177) LIVING WATER

32. CARING

For a session in a Sunday school series on caring, I used a little acting to make a point.

I set up a desk with telephone and books. On Sunday morning I entered the room and sat down grumbling about life in general. For 25 minutes I spoke to myself about a personal crisis without giving any details other than that I needed some help. I then tried to phone someone, letting the phone ring up to 10 times. There was no answer. I tried again and again. The calls were interspersed with attempts at Bible reading (no comfort there) and prayer (that didn't work). I once left the room determined to end it all. That was unsuccessful also.

Finally, I "telephoned" some members of the class. "Surely Wilma should be home, or maybe Ken." Still there was no answer to the ringing of the telephone. In desperation I left the room with 15 minutes left in the class period. I had decided that I would not go back into the room. Before I got very far down the hall, the entire class came out. I asked what they were doing. "We came to find you," one said. What followed was one of the better discussions on caring our class ever shared.

Another class responded differently. One of the members, after about 25 minutes, did answer the telephone (having none, he mimed it). He talked with me, keeping the lines of communication open. He then offered to meet for coffee and conversation.

Dave Kaiser, Outlook, Saskatchewan

See also 34) NEIGHBORS AND FRIENDS, 54) CHEAP ROLE PLAYS, 83) BEING THERE, 89) PHONE-A-THON, 98) PROBLEM SHARING, 119) BALL OF ENERGY, 146) DOWN-AND-OUTS

33. OPINION LINE-UP

In our junior high group we tried discussing several sensitive issues. The group was reluctant to talk about them. To protect each person's privacy, I asked the junior highs to line up facing the wall. I then asked a series of questions concerning drinking, drugs, dating, etc. After each inquiry I asked each person to signal behind herself/himself with one finger for *yes,* two fingers for *maybe,* and three fingers for *no.* We then talked about these issues, and I had a much better idea about where the group as a whole stood on different things.

Karen Walisch, South Bend, Indiana

See also 14) JURY BIBLE STUDY, 18) THE PRODIGAL DAUGHTER/SON, 23) DISCUSSION BASICS, 24) SPINNING TOP, 49) ALL-NIGHT TALK, 100) DEAR TEACHER,

34. NEIGHBORS AND FRIENDS

We have found that one of the continuing areas of discussion among our youth is friendship. This study enabled us to probe the biblical understanding of friendship and how to be better friends.

Neighbors and Friends

1. Read Matthew 10:5; Acts 8:25; John 4:7-9
   A. Who were the Samaritans?
   B. What was their relationship with the Jews?
   C. What would the attitude of a Jew toward a Samaritan most likely have been?

2. In a few words describe the main characters in the The Good Samaritan (Luke 10:29-37):
   A. Robbers—
   B. Priest—
   C. Lawyer—
   D. Levite—
   E. Samaritan—
   F. Innkeeper—

3. Do people you know ever act like any of the characters in the story? Make a few notes about people who do or explain why you think there is no comparison.

4. Which of the characters in the story behaved like you behave most often? Explain.

5. If you translate "neighbor" as "friend," what does this passage teach about friendship?

6. Think about being a friend. Then jot down some ways you could be a better friend to people you know.

Earl R. Eckhart
Bloomfield Hills, Michigan

See also 12) DISCOVERY BIBLE STUDY, 30) BEING HANDICAPPED, 32) CARING, 36) PUTDOWN WEDGE, 39) SHORT PEOPLE, 40) GOOD SAMARITAN MIME, 82) LEMONS, 98) PROBLEM SHARING, 216) THE GOOD SAMARITAN

35. STAY FRESH: WORK WITH YOUTH

My wife and I have learned more from our three children than we have ever taught them. Young people keep me in touch with the world as it is today. I tell my wife often that if I didn't have youth to work with, I would be climbing the walls. I see progress, challenge, rewards, excitement, and thrills as I help them to develop their abilities. Without them I probably would be dull and boring.

The traditional is often the easiest way. The traditional is so comfortable. You know where you are and how you fit in. You are tempted to live out your life doing the same thing forever because it is tradition. You can sit back and while away precious time.

To be innovative means you have to think, to reach out, to experiment, to create. You have to try things. And for all the innovations that don't work, the ones that do are worth the effort.

This thought is my personal proverb: Never settle for the comfortable. I love the mystery of the new adventures around the next bend. That's why I love to paddle a canoe down rivers. As I paddle along I never know what is around the bend. It's exciting to anticipate new trees, currents and other canoe enthusiasts.

I love the innovative type of life and work with youth because I never know what the next day is going to bring. Canoeing through life's bends and currents keeps me on edge, ready to face fresh and exciting adventures.

Walter Horsley
Pittsburgh, Pennsylvania

See also 1) TRY TO REMEMBER, 4) WHAT'S A LEADER?, 83) BEING THERE, 86) KARATE CHOP, 97) TRANSPARENCY, 121) PHYSICAL RISK, 136) THE WOOD CARVER'S GIFT

36. PUTDOWN WEDGE

For some time I had been concerned about the destructive putdowns which were occurring in our youth group. I wanted to do some gut-level talking about the situation, but I wasn't quite sure the group would buy into this approach.

One day while splitting logs for my fireplace a wild idea hit me. The following Sunday evening I brought a large log, a wedge, and a big sledgehammer to our meeting. The kids were puzzled, of course.

When I started to drive the wedge into the log, the deafening smash of metal with metal won everyone's attention. As I pounded the wedge, I compared log splitting to cuts and putdowns we drive into others. Each impact of the sledge drove that wedge deeper and deeper into the wood, just as each putdown drives an invisible wedge deeper and deeper into someone. Finally, with a re- sounding blow I split the log apart. I asked everyone to notice that the two pieces could *never* be put back together.

The impact of this rather dramatic demon- stration was better than I had hoped: the eyes, the faces, the silence. I managed to make a very critical point and have it com- pletely absorbed. For a few minutes longer we talked about the split log and how it was a very close comparison to what each of us does to other people when we constantly keep putting down with cuts and back stabs.

Things were a lot better after that session. It was one of those rare occasions where the group realized a problem and wanted to do something about it.

Mike Gillespie
Lexington, Kentucky

See also 16) BRICKS, 34) NEIGHBORS AND FRIENDS, 37) THE WALL, 38) GOSSIP BLOCKS, 39) SHORT PEOPLE, 44) FIRE, 76) TEA TIME, 215) THE UNFORGIVING BROTHER

37. THE WALL

Our high school youth group was working on the topic of handling emotions. We gathered together some large-sized children's building blocks to help us understand how our emotions affect our behavior. On the blocks we taped pieces of paper with labels identifying different things, such as anger, not talking, fear, selfishness, materialism, prejudice, etc. All of these problems had surfaced and been identified from an earlier discussion.

We built a wall out of these "emotional" blocks. Then we discussed how the wall not only kept others out of our life, but we also noted that the wall kept us locked in. The building of the wall and some of the realizations that came about as we worked on it provoked a deep, moving time of sharing.

Margaret Simpson, Bethel Park, Pennsylvania

See also 16) BRICKS, 36) PUTDOWN WEDGE, 38) GOSSIP BLOCKS, 76) TEA TIME, 82) LEMONS, 130) PRAYER CHAIR

38. GOSSIP BLOCKS

We were in the midst of a discussion about gossip. Our texts were James 3:5-8, 4:1-3, 4:11-12. I asked for two volunteers. These two sat back-to-back on the floor in the middle of a circle of youth. Each person was given an identical set of building blocks. With no chance for asking questions, one person was instructed to listen and obey as the other person gave the directions for the building of a structure (as the giver of instructions also built the same structure). It is best if the blocks are all one color. Or simply rule out the use of colors if your sets of blocks are multicolored. After the building is completed, have the two volunteers step aside and view the structures. It does not happen very often that the two structures will look exactly alike. This is an excellent exercise to point out how words can mean many things to many people.

Patricia Bronstad, Omaha, Nebraska

See also 36) PUTDOWN WEDGE, 37) THE WALL, 76) TEA TIME

39. SHORT PEOPLE

It was difficult for our junior high youth to accept those who for some reason "didn't fit in." A probe of Jesus' relation with Zacchaeus in Luke 9:1-10 helped our group to accept and respect each other.

HOW TO ACCEPT SHORT PEOPLE
(and everyone else, too)

Describe a time when you felt like Zacchaeus (shoved aside, not important). How were other people acting toward you that made you feel like Zacchaeus? Tell about a time when you felt like the crowd (pushy, arrogant, in control). How do you think others feel when you're being pushy or arrogant?

Who in your life has ever done for you the same thing Jesus did for Zacchaeus? Who are some people in your life who need to be accepted like Zacchaeus? What are some ways that you can be like Jesus for some of these people?

After all have answered, divide into small groups, sharing responses to the questions.

Our study made quite a change in the ways our youth felt toward themselves and others. There was a marked increase in acceptance.

Earl R. Eckhart
Belleville, Illinois

See also 9) BIBLE EXPLORATIONS, 34) NEIGHBORS AND FRIENDS, 76) TEA TIME

40. GOOD SAMARITAN MIME

We have developed a learning process for young people built around the story of the Good Samaritan (Luke 10:25-37). Volunteers acted out the parts of the traveler, robbers, innkeeper, donkey, Samaritan, rocks, priest, inn and Levite. Each actor got a name card. A roadway was marked on the floor with chalk, and the rocks and the inn were placed in position.

As someone read the Bible story aloud, actors mimed the story. Then the actors explained why they behaved as they did. Each actor received an "attitude" card:

1. "Whatever will be, will be" (traveler)
2. "What's yours is mine" (robbers)
3. "What's mine is my own" (priest, Levite)
4. "What's mine is yours" (Samaritan)
5. "What's mine is mine, and what's yours is yours" (innkeeper)

We took a break while everyone collected 17 pebbles from outside. Keeping in mind the five attitudes, each person divided the 17 pebbles into five piles. Each pile contained the number of stones that best represented each attitude in the young person's life.

Leigh Wilson
Shepparton, Australia

See also 9) BIBLE EXPLORATIONS, 34) NEIGHBORS AND FRIENDS, 42) CAMP PRODUCTIONS, 54) CHEAP ROLE PLAYS, 167) CLOWNING, 211) GOOD FRIDAY SACRED DANCE, 216) THE GOOD SAMARITAN

You can design simple, yet special, courses to help your seniors prepare for life after school.

41. SENIORITIS

There seems to be a disease prevalent among high school seniors in our church. It strikes every year during December and January. The symptoms of the disease are the failure to be a participating member of the Sunday morning church school class and a general lethargic attitude toward what's going on at church.

We treated the symptoms by designing an eight-session course. The sessions center on some of the areas of interest and growth that the seniors will be dealing with in the next several years: vocational concerns, family concerns, interpersonal issues.

We set up this series with a teacher who moderated each session and lead those we

since added a session on affirmative action for women, competition and equality. We have at various times had a senior breakfast to close out the session. The outline that follows will give you some idea of our structure.

Objectives:
- To combat senioritis
- To provide a forum for discussing vocations
- To provide a challenge to enter full-time Christian ministry in a paid position.

continued

SENIORITIS

Session 1:

A general look at vocations through a very old filmstrip, "The Meaning of Vocation," from the Vocational Guidance Series, available from Media Resource Center, 1211 North Park Street, P.O. Box 2050, Bloomington, IL 61701, and discussion of it using an accompanying guide. The first chapter of a now out-of-print resource that you may happen to have in your community, **You and Your Lifework: A Christian Choice for Youth**, is also most helpful. It deals with vocation as God's call and does a biblical study as well as considering the calls of Moses, Isaiah, Jeremiah and Peter. It also asks students to think of people they feel are called today.

Session 2:

"Understanding Your Interests and Abilities." We called on vocational guidance counselors from the public schools to lead this discussion. (They need to be reminded that these are seniors and have already been through a lot of testing.) If counselors are not available, **Where Do I Go From Here?**, available from Science Research Associates, Inc., 259 East Erie St., Chicago, IL 60611, pages 9-13, can be used. "Analyzing the Pluses" is particularly helpful.

Session 3:

"The World of Work and the Needs of the World: Career Decision-Making." We called on a State of Illinois Employment Counselor and a personnel director of a major employer in town to discuss how to apply for a job, how to write a resume and how to forecast the job market.

Session 4:

"Working for the Church." Chapter 8 of **You and Your Lifework** can be a beginning point for this discussion. Pamphlets from church vocations agencies can supplement this chapter. A graduate student who is still considering the possibilities for his own life has led this session.

Session 5:

"On Being a Freshman." Most of our seniors are college bound, so we asked three students, two recent graduates of our church's own senior high program, and one who is now attending our worship regularly, to talk about what it is like to register, make new friends, face new decisions, be a college freshman away from home.

Session 6:

(optional) "Living Responsibly as a Sexual Being." We borrowed a film from Planned Parenthood which dealt with decision-making. Saying no to sex (by both boys and girls) was one feature, but the emphasis was that one should make decisions about sex before one gets caught up in an emotional moment.

Session 7:

(optional) "It's My Choice. Where Do Parents Fit In?" Another filmstrip from the Vocational Guidance Series. Our seniors have not taken us up on this one. I want to have parents come, too, to see the filmstrip, and try to deal with who makes decisions about college (where to go), career, and what difference paying the bill makes.

Session 8:

(optional) "Parenting Adults." A mother and daughter who have gone through growing up, both away from each other and together, will be the guests. (This is our first time through this session.) They will discuss their feelings regarding separation and togetherness. We may or may not invite parents to this one.

Anne Eaton
Normal, Illinois

See also 27) OVER THE RAINBOW, 57) LET YOUTH TEACH, 60) SEX EDUCATION, 63) TEN CAREER CHOOSING TIPS, 64) CAREER CLARIFICATION, 65) WHAT'S IN THE FUTURE, 66) VOCATION, 105) SPIRITUAL PUZZLE, 128) "COMPUTER" DATING NIGHT, 204) SENIOR SHEET

Every year, a group of young people from Connecticut meet in a week-long camp to write and produce their own musical.

42. CAMP PRODUCTIONS

"Sing Praise" is a week-long camping program for junior highs (seventh and eighth graders) which features an original musical written and produced by the young people themselves. On Monday, we start with what's on the minds of the youth. These may be biblical themes, problems or dreams. We move through a process by which these probes become a refined theme. This is done by Monday night. On Tuesday, we expand the theme in all kinds of creative directions. Some of the young people work on lyrics, dances or music.

One year the campers chose Jesus' boyhood—from Jesus' perspective. They included his birth and childhood.

The staff helps as the lyrics are put to music. By Wednesday night, the campers have

the musical put together. They practice all day Thursday and present the musical on Friday for the parents. It is amazing how 50 young people can come together for a major show that makes a sound theological statement. They agreed to present it eight times during the year at different churches in our region. This enabled the young people to serve the church and promote the camping program.

Obid Hofland
New Haven, Connecticut

See also 15) WONDERS, 40) GOOD SAMARITAN MIME, 127) TALENT NIGHT, 164) WORSHIP ENVIRONMENT, 165) WORSHIP TASK FORCE, 188) JAZZ UP THE CHURCH, 189) SING OUT, 191) JEWISH/CHRISTIAN CELEBRATIONS, 207) PARTICIPATORY CHRISTMAS PAGEANT, 211) GOOD FRIDAY SACRED DANCE, 213) THE FIFTH GOSPEL

43. BLUE TASSELS

We were focusing attention on the Ten Commandments and some misconceptions of them during a senior high retreat. Using sheets of butcher paper and marker pens, we wrote down all the commandments they knew plus any other "thou shalt" and "thou shalt nots". Each person picked the one commandment which was the most difficult to follow. I then gave everyone a pea-sized pebble and had each person place it in the bottom of his/her shoe.

The group then embarked on a fairly long outdoor hike. At one point in the hike they stopped and read Numbers 15:37-40 which refers to blue tassels reminding the people of God's law. I gave them each a 30-inch piece of heavy blue yarn. They made bracelets and necklaces out of the yarn. I announced that we were now knights of the blue cord, and they read passages about forgiveness from the Bible (Luke 17:4, 15:11-32, John 8:1-11, Matthew 6:12, Mark 2:5-12 and Matthew 5:38-40). We then removed the pebbles from our shoes and returned to the retreat center.

Jake Jacobson, Clear Lake, Iowa

See also 9) BIBLE EXPLORATIONS, 15) WONDERS, 51) MOUNTAINTOP TO PLAIN, 52) RETREAT FEEDBACK, 193) ROOTED IN WORSHIP

44. FIRE

Fire can spark creativity. We used fire at camp to ignite the participants' imagination. The youth pointed out two symbolic values of fire. Half looked to the refining quality of fire. The other half saw fire as a means of destruction.

Everyone was to find a piece of wood. If they had looked at fire as a refining symbol, we asked them to write on it one or more gifts that they felt they had. Then they came together and built an altar. We fired up the altar, offering our gifts to God. We asked the youth to relate the fire to the way God refines their gifts.

If they chose the destroying quality of fire, we asked them to write ways they were prevented from using their gifts. Similarly, we constructed an altar fire to symbolically burn the obstacles.

The experience moved us to sing a hymn together. Someone offered a prayer.

On another occasion, a strange thing happened. The two fires were set together because the leaders were aware of two symbolic meanings of fire. The embers of the "refining" fire flared long after the other died out.

Trevor Smith
Townsville, Australia

See also 36) PUT DOWN WEDGE, 52) RETREAT FEEDBACK, 72) CREATIVE CONJURING, 164) WORSHIP ENVIRONMENT, 176) COMMON OBJECT MEDITATIONS, 178) SIN BURN-OFF, 180) OUT OF THE DARKNESS

45. TOUCH OUR MISSION

"Reach Out and Touch . . . Our Mission" was the theme we selected for our weekend retreat for high school youth. It combined the magic of fantasy (Star Wars, etc.) with the power of reality (human suffering). Each person received a diary. A sharing/reflection process was built into the weekend event. A T-shirt with the symbol of two hands reaching out toward each other was given to each person.

Jim Powell
Indianapolis, Indiana

See also 30) BEING HAN-DICAPPED, 31) HANDI-CAPPED RETREAT

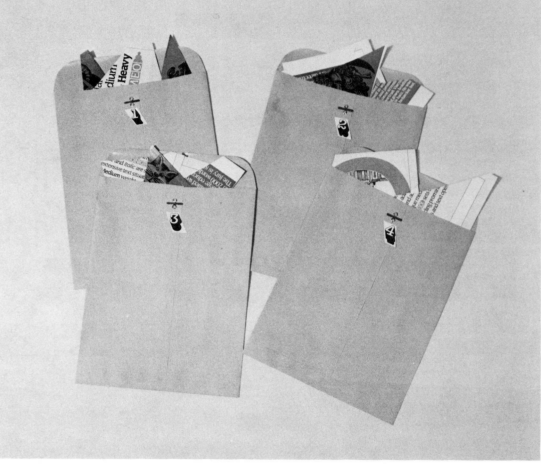

46. HAVES AND HAVE NOTS

I put together the following game as a workshop in a senior high weekend retreat. It was intended to increase awareness of the struggles between the "haves" and "have nots." The suggested questions are only starters. A leader can develop more probes from the dynamics of the game as it unfolds.

Take posters you no longer can use and cut them into pieces as though you were making a puzzle. Use your judgment as to size of pieces, depending on size of poster. Keep the cut-up posters separate, storing

each one in its own envelope. For socio-political awareness game, use four big envelopes. There is one envelope for each group in the game. Number envelopes like this:

#1—put one poster puzzle into the envelope (the rich).

#2—put one poster puzzle minus all the border pieces (middle class).

#3—put one poster puzzle minus some center pieces (middle class). (Note: It helps the game dynamic if #2 and #3 are exactly the same poster and cut exactly the same. Be sure to keep the extra pieces for these two puzzles in smaller envelopes that are out of sight during the game.)

#4—put very few, randomly selected pieces of a poster in this envelope ("have nots" or poor). Put several of the pieces from this poster into envelope #1 and distribute the rest between #2 and #3. (Note: You may want to number pieces on the back if you are going to use puzzles more than once so you can easily reassemble them.)

Newsprint and felt markers or a blackboard and chalk are needed. Other materials needed are four tables, chairs, and a timer or watch.

Instructions for game leader:

● Go over directions for game carefully before leading game.

● During the game, give directions, keep time and enable discussion. (Note: The game is somewhat abstract, but that's okay. Political-social issues often seem abstract until they touch our lives.)

Directions for the game:

1. Number off by fours (1-2-3-4) around the group.

2. Get into your group.

3. In your groups, discuss some questions:

   a. What does the word "awareness" mean to you as a Christian? You will have three minutes. At the end of that time, one person will report back to the total group. List responses so everyone can see them as reporters share. Give individuals and groups time to agree, disagree, respond, comment, but don't linger.

   b. Discuss in each group: "What does it mean to be political as a Christian?" Ask one person to report back to the group again. Allow five minutes. List responses, give individuals and groups a chance to respond.

   c. Now discuss in each group what social means to you as a Christian.

Allow three to five minutes. List responses, give time for comments on them.

4. Pass out envelopes containing puzzles. "When we get ready to start the game, it is important that all members work in groups to get the puzzles completed. No one is to start until all the puzzles are passed out." It is important that the leader does not answer any questions. Leave the room for a time if at all possible. Just disappear! If you are asked questions, try to ignore them or just shrug your shoulders. Try not to communicate verbally.

5. Call time. Be sensitive to what's happening. Don't stop too soon, as important dynamics develop in this part, but don't let it drag, either. Usually group #1 finishes the puzzle first and sits around awhile or wanders and watches others. #4 often gives up. Groups #2 and #3 usually get into it and often work together.

6. Discussion. This follows the attempts to put the puzzles together. Be sure that participants stay in their own groups for this.

7. Ask general questions for discussion openers: "What happened? How did you feel?"

8. Move into more specific questions: "What did you anticipate when I passed out the puzzles? What happened when I ignored your questions? Did you feel the instructions were inadequate? Why? How did you feel about my leaving the room? Why?" You can make comments on what you as leader observed.

9. Logistic questions: "Are all of your pieces there? Where are they?" (Take time to get the rest of the pieces from the other groups at this point.) "Why

continued

HAVES AND HAVE NOTS

did you think you needed pieces? Did your group (or individuals) decide to look for pieces? Why? How? Why not? Group #1, how did you feel about your extra pieces? Group #2 and #3, how do you feel about your puzzles? Group #4, how do you feel about group #1's puzzle? Would more instructions have been helpful? Why? What would they be?"

10. Move into relating this experience to everyday life. "Can you see parallels between this game and what happens in school, government, church, business, home, other places?" The leader will also want to draw a parallel to the fact that one group is poor, one rich, while two are middle class. "A partial poster is like life for those who get only part of what is really theirs. How can those without get what is needed?" The leader can ask group #1 why they had extra pieces in the puzzle. Groups #2, #3, and #4 can be probed about the fact that #1 was given pieces which were not wanted or needed. What did the groups do about it?

11. The leader and group can make final connections between this game and some possible experience as being a Christian. There is a saying: "Action comes from awareness." Action is another word for witness. Ask the participants if they have a new awareness from this game? What can they do about it?

12. A concluding thought might go something like this: "It is important as we go through life to be aware of what is happening socially and politically so we can witness to the Word."

Alice Ann Glenn
Paradise, California

See also 26) FLIGHT 108, 51) MOUNTAINTOP TO PLAIN, 52) RETREAT FEEDBACK, 61) DISCIPLESHIP, 139) HUNGER IDEAS, 140) BIG DOGS, ARMS SALES AND HUNGER, 174) YOUTH AND SOCIAL ISSUES

47. LIVING IN TANKS

We experienced an exciting weekend retreat with the senior highs. The theme of the retreat was "Living in Tanks." We also discussed how to get out and live outside a tank. Included in the material of the weekend was a simulated activity, a short film, "The Man Who Had to Sing," and another set of pictures. This is the design we used:

LIVING IN TANKS

SESSION 1: Spotting Your Tank

Reflections on a modern parable by James Baxter. (**Jerusalem Day Book**, James Baxter, pages 1-3, Price Milburn and Co., Ltd. Book House, Boulcott St., Wellington, New Zealand, 1971.)

We divided into groups of four or five. Each group built a tank—its own version of the military tank. On the basis of Baxter's parable, I tried to lead the group to see tanks as a form of escape from pressure in a negative and non-productive way and as legitimate and positive fencing-off of certain areas of life.

I have had groups "build" their tanks as a verbal or written exercise. I have also tried it in the form of having cardboard sheets cut in tank shape for the groups to give imaginative and creative form to their tanks. Surprising and delightful products have come out of both avenues.

SESSION 2: Volleys of Bullets

Reflections on the parable by Baxter and Romans 6:3-5. I emphasized the way in which Jesus can open and liberate lives. Such a liberating process involves a "dying and rising of Christ" and can often be a painful and hurting process.

The tanks are "shot full of holes." This is a group process in which each group exposes its tank and other groups take shots at it, verbally and with rubber bands. In the context of the parable, I encourage and aim for

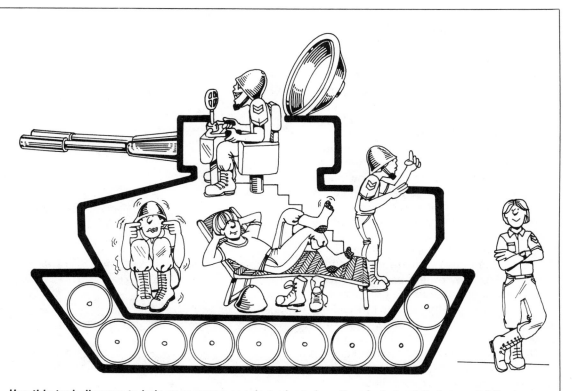

Use this tank diagram to help your young people evaluate how they feel about their own spiritual journey.

a positive, affirming volley of bullets. There should be no ridicule or self-destructive process. But at the same time, the tearing up of tanks can be a bit painful, especially in an intergenerational context.

Close with the film,"The Man Who Had To Sing" (Mass Media Associates, 1270 Chouteau Avenue, St. Louis, Missouri 63103).

SESSION 3: Learning to Live Outside Tanks?

Open with the showing of the film, "The Man Who Had To Sing." Reflect on how we open our lives to Jesus Christ. What happens to our relationships with other people in the process. How solitary and uncompromising can you be outside your tank?

Close with an exercise in which groups are again asked to sketch a picture of the

life they lead outside the tank. I used a simple sheet with a large tank outlined in broken lines. I also asked the group to give some shape to life and ended with an analysis of whether we wind up back in a new tank without realizing it.

Complete the lines, if you think you're moving into a new tank. Name the new tank. Evaluate it. (I got some very surprising results in this exercise.)

I had more fun and more response out of this design than any I have done in some time. I loved doing it.

Richard Teaford
Louisville, Kentucky

See also 23) DISCUSSION BASICS, 51) MOUNTAINTOP TO PLAIN, 52) RETREAT FEEDBACK

48. DEATH STUDIES

It was a most exciting experience. Originally scheduled for four weeks we wound up running for six sessions over an eight-week period.

I began by outlining the projected course of study. Next, I invited people to write down how old they thought they would be when they died and of what causes. They also drew a line graph of their life showing the ups and downs as it has been to date and project until their death age as just guessed. They also wrote their own obituary which reflected the graph of their life.

From this, we discussed feelings, emotions, joys, sorrows that are raised and experienced as they reflect upon their life and death. What patterns in the group's responses are apparent? Is any particular age or type of death predominant? What things may the group be avoiding or neglecting?

Our second session concerned matters of faith, an area of great misunderstanding. We discussed personal experiences of death and how we saw the community of faith responding to our needs: services, providing of meals, fellow parishioners responding with calls, letters, official acts of the church and clergy. How did the community of faith fail to respond? What do we understand the role of the community of faith to be? The participants seemed somewhat surprised at the questions, and it took awhile for everyone to get into the discussion. Soon, however, people began to understand the importance of the community of faith in dealing with death.

Our third session was to be a visit to a funeral home, but the class chose instead to concentrate on the faith elements again. So the third session also incorporated a study of the scriptures and the promises of faith.

Session four was a real "barn burner." Since the people in the seminar were familiar with the standard funeral practices, we

Death is one of the greatest fears young people face. Special learning experiences can help youth deal with those fears from a biblical perspective.

decided to discuss alternative methods of disposing of the deceased's body. In our case, we worked with the Pine Tree Memorial Society, which encourages its members to procure inexpensive funerals. The local funeral directors read about our program in the newspapers and without warning or seeking permission sent the secretary of their state organization to "sit in" on our meeting.

The director of the memorial society did a commendable job of explaining the laws pertaining to the disposal of the corpses, what a private individual could and could not do, permits that are required, etc. The funeral director representative did all he could to dispel these realities and to lift up "frightening consequences" of handling corpses. (All in all he did more to hurt his profession than to help it.)

The fifth session found us tying up the

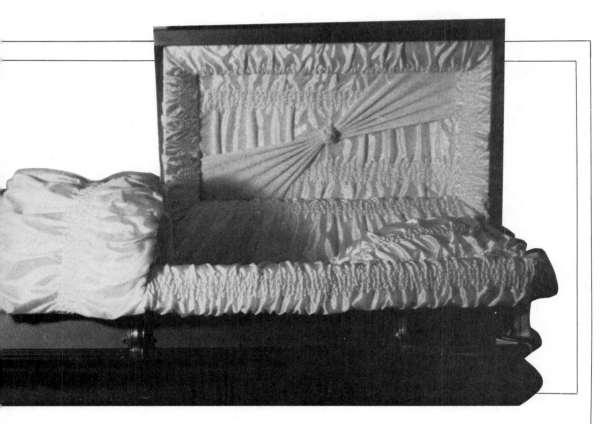

loose ends and unclear areas. Many were still having difficulty with the faith dimensions of death and dying. So my colleague and I set out one more time to help our people. This time we listed all the scriptures which we used in funeral services. Then we proceeded to discuss how these all dealt with death and the promises of faith.

Slowly but surely the young people began to understand. They understood the scriptures and could "intellectualize" them; however, they couldn't incorporate the promises into their own beings. All in all this session was rather enjoyable as it became more of a faith exploration in scriptures than anything else.

In the final session we discussed, reviewed, reacted on the entire seminar.

At all our sessions we provided a table of brochures and books. I got a lot of material from the local representative of the National Funeral Directors Association. Some of the material is extremely good; other is basic propaganda, so I just got what I thought was good and useful. I had material from the memorial society available. There were copies of the standard texts, Kubler-Ross's books and several by Edgar Jackson. I also contacted our denominational library and they sent me 15 books on death. These were an amalgam consisting of personal experiences or reflections, novels, short stories or spiritual reflections on death and dying. This proved to be invaluable as many of our people read several of the books. Most participants took some of the brochures.

Tim Morrison
Auburn, Maine

See also 23) DISCUSSION BASICS

49. ALL NIGHT TALK

We were used to staying up all night on overnight retreats and being wiped out for the next day's meeting. We changed this design for one all-night retreat.

It began with an all-church supper and program. After the adults went home, the kids stayed and we had a series of discussions on different topics all night. We told the kids not to bring sleeping bags. It was made clear that we would be staying up all night.

It was very exciting! We talked about things like, "What do you expect from your parents?" and "What do you expect from God?" We then turned the focus around and probed questions of what the young expected from themselves in terms of parents and God. Some of the youth fell asleep in the middle of the discussion. Most seemed to relax as they shared deep feelings. Perhaps the fatigue reduced the tension. I know that this was the best discussion we have had. Most of us slept all day Saturday!

Stephen Johnston
West Willington, Connecticut

See also 23) DISCUSSION BASICS, 26) FLIGHT 108, 33) OPINION LINE-UP, 70) LEARNING CENTERS, 75) A SPOONFUL OF HONEY, 98) PROBLEM SHARING, 173) YARN WEB

50. GUILTY

If approached in a new way, a rather ordinary experience can be extraordinary. That's what happened when about 400 high school youth from all over the country were gathered for a national convention. We wanted to hear the stories about what was happening in their part of the country. That, however, can sometimes be lengthy and dull.

Taking our clues from Micah 6:1-2, we reconstructed the courtroom symbolism in that chapter. We asked, "Your group is on trial for being Christian. Is there sufficient evidence to convict you?" The youth were then called upon for evidence to support their "guilt." They did this by telling of their local ministry to do justice, love tenderly and walk humbly. As the reports were made, the room was filled with exciting stories. The jury was reminded again and again that they were to judge on the basis of the evidence. Finally the whole body was encouraged to applaud the vital ministries being carried out by these young people as they gave their testimony of "guilt."

Terry Grove
Rocky Hill, New Jersey

See also 14) JURY BIBLE STUDY, 23) DISCUSSION BASICS, 51) MOUNTAINTOP TO PLAIN, 52) RETREAT FEEDBACK

51. MOUNTAINTOP TO PLAIN

I have spent years organizing exciting national youth events, including summer workcamps and the National Christian Youth Congress. These "mountaintop" experiences are fantastic. However, it is important to work on "coming down" as one leaves the conference and heads home. It seems that when we get into a peak experience of a retreat or conference, it is sometimes tough to reenter the home situation. This state can sometimes bring on depression or bad feelings. But this doesn't have to happen.

You and your group can take the experiences at the special event and blend them into your home situation. There are some steps to facilitate this process.

First, each person should gather with other members of the trip or retreat and spend some intentional time debriefing. Begin by focusing on a personal reflection of the warmest moment of the event. Ponder this question, for example: "What was the best thing about the National Christian Youth Congress?" It might help to write down that memory. After everyone has recorded or focused on that one aspect of the event, each person shares it with the group. If the memory is too personal, go on to the next person.

The next step toward reentry will be the group's brainstorming on how your group can use some of those retreat experiences in your youth program. This may be a small idea or memorable moment. A workshop or worship idea can suddenly have an application in your program. You might remember something that another young person shared about his or her youth group. You might begin this step as individual reflection and then move into a group sharing and discussion. During the youth session, be sure to write every idea on a piece of newsprint or blackboard. You will be amazed how the space will be filled with ideas. As one person remembers a useful idea, it will trigger a new idea in someone else.

The last step draws these highlights into your program. Have the group members develop the ideas for use in next week's meeting or in following weeks.

Mountaintop experiences need not stay on the mountain. This procedure I've described can make them beginning points in youth ministry long after returning from the mountain.

Thom Schultz
Loveland, Colorado

See also 52) RETREAT FEEDBACK, 115) RETREAT CHECKLIST, 173) YARN WEB

52. RETREAT FEEDBACK

We often spend a lot of time preparing for a youth retreat or conference and feel strangely depressed after it is over. What have we accomplished? Even a great event can be depressing when we hit the hard reality of our church basement. Reflection not only helps leaders to plan other experiences, it also helps participants to apply what they have learned.

We designed the following questionnaire for a large youth gathering. We deliberately waited six weeks before mailing it to the participants. The feedback was great. Many youth groups focused a whole program on discussion around the completion of these forms. It triggered a lot of creative energy. We suggested that the participants utilize the journal they kept during the event. The questionnaire was a perfect stimulus for discussion and reflection in the home church. Here's the questionnaire:

1. Since coming back home, I find:
   ____The music, ideas, images of what happened there are still with me.
   ____I remember what happened there, but it is hard to share with others because it was such a personal experience.
   ____I like me better and can better accept others.
   ____None of the above, but *this* happened:_____

2. Since coming back home, I have found:
   ____My youth group really grabbed hold of being a part of a greater Christian community.
   ____My youth group couldn't care less about me, and I have not picked up the program ideas I learned at the conference.
   ____I still feel good about the experience, but the program ideas presented there are too confusing for me to explain to others in my group.

3. As I look back on what happened at the conference, I wish I could have _____

4. I would recommend to the Planning Committee that the next event be different in the following ways: _____

5. I need help in the following areas: _____

Skip Herbert
Madison, Wisconsin

See also 4) WHAT'S A LEADER?, 31) HANDICAPPED RETREAT, 51) MOUNTAINTOP TO PLAIN, 115) RETREAT CHECKLIST, 156) REACH

53. RESOURCE CONSUMER TIPS

With the ever-increasing volume of media appearing on the market and considering the many types of media resources (from magazine articles to videotape equipment), it is becoming more important to develop some criteria for evaluating the usefulness and applicability of various media. It is no longer enough to make selections on personal preference alone. Many other aspects should go into a choice. Though not exhaustive, the following questions suggest important criteria for resource use.

Video, films, books, records—all are media at your disposal. You can determine which medium best fits your needs by asking yourself a few basic questions.

1. Does the resource open up a subject by presenting basic information clearly, objectively and creatively?

2. Does the resource focus on significant questions or issues which persons must consider seriously?

3. Is there a direct or indirect relationship between the resource and our biblical traditions?

4. Does the resource focus too much attention on itself or does it invite students to think, reflect, dream and respond with all the creativity and insight of which they are capable?

5. Are the students encouraged to discuss, explore, research or act further?

6. Is the resource flexible enough to be utilized more than once?

7. Are there accompanying guidelines to assist the teacher in using the resource effectively to the best advantage?

8. Is the resource appropriate for the age group for which it is intended?

9. If the resource is new, how much time should be allotted for familiarization?

10. Is the resource so familiar that it has become boring to the teacher and students?

11. Does the resource involve the student? (Avoid resources so novel or distracting that they call attention only to themselves.)

12. Will the resource provide the students with a sense of satisfaction and achievement?

By applying these questions to specific media or other resources used with youth and others, it should be possible to determine whether an item is worth your investment of time and money. Determine some guidelines for yourself with these questions. If a resource accumulates several "no" responses to the above questions, don't buy it.

Skip Herbert
Madison, Wisconsin

See also 3) TEN YOUTH MINISTRY CONCERNS, 4) WHAT'S A LEADER?, 22) FILM CRITICISM

54. CHEAP ROLE PLAYS

We noticed that several companies publish books and role play board games for youth discussions. We are limited in our funds. We had the advisors and the young people design their own situation cards. We used newspapers and all kinds of stories to make up these ethical situations.

The process of creating the cards was great. We divided the group into two units. We chose the subject of conflict and asked each person to draw a cartoon of an open-ended situation with a narrative underneath.

This cartoon approach was really neat. The youth then traded cards and each group role played the card they received. And, they went on to conclude the open-ended conflict.

I am glad that we don't have enough money to buy published role plays. The teens seem to get so much more out of the process by creating and resolving the situations.

Jim and Ervin Bullock
Decatur, Alabama

See also 23) DISCUSSION BASICS, 26) FLIGHT 108, 30) BEING HANDICAPPED, 32) CARING, 42) CAMP PRODUCTIONS, 59) WEEKEND PARTY, 68) SUPER SUNDAY, 74) PARENTING AN EGG, 129) COME AS YOU AREN'T LOCK-IN, 169) LOAVES AND FISHES

55. STUDENT/PARENT CONFIRMATION

Our confirmation class this year involved both the students and their parents. The parents met one hour for every three hours that the students met. We were pleased with the results of this combination.

The goal was to involve eighth graders and their parents in a confirmation class. After several sessions of study, the youth were invited to be received into the church.

The purpose was to provide a concentrated study for eighth graders and their parents. The assumption was that confirmation is not the goal. Confirmation was defined as only the beginning of a Christian faith.

We involved the parents, to see and know what their children were learning and to challenge them in their own faith. The leaders of the confirmation class were a pastor and two lay persons. The three of us met at least three hours each week to evaluate, plan and prepare each session.

The following issues were covered: Personhood (self-identify), relationships, God (Trinity), Jesus, church history, proclaiming the church, worship, prayer and faith. The youth went on field trips to witness church-related institutions. They visited a church-re-

lated hospital, a retirement home, a home for youth and a college. We also attended a service at a Jewish temple.

This is the outline of the class:

● **Youth and Parent Session:** Getting acquainted, orientation, definition of confirmation.

● **Youth Session:** Relationships and self-identity (Genesis 1:27). They wrote a story about relationships. ("If Jesus came back today who would he relate to?")

● **Parent Session:** Relationships. Their experience was the same as the youth session except they did not write the story.

● **Youth Session:** People-on-the-street interviews with tape recorders. The young people asked people about God and then listened to the various statements. Creeds about God were read. They then wrote statements about how they saw God in the creed. They collected advertisements about statements that describe God and made posters or collages.

● **Parent Session:** They interviewed each other about God and listened to the youth tapes.

● **Youth Session:** We asked for words de-

Confirmation isn't the end result of a life of faith. Rather, it's the beginning. Parents can play an important role in this development process.

scribing Jesus. We looked at characteristics of Jesus in the scriptures, showed paintings of Jesus (how differently artists see him), talked about the resurrection, and studied creeds and wrote statements about Jesus.

● **Youth Session:** We drew a time-line from Abraham to the present, made slides of the Ten Commandments, and studied symbols of Jewish community in preparation of attending a Jewish service.

● **Youth Session:** Each young person wrote a newspaper account of the field trip to the temple. We compared and contrasted the functions of the New Testament church to the present-day church. We studied creeds and wrote statements about the church.

● **Parent Session:** Jesus, history and proclaiming. They experienced the same things as youth except they did not go on a field trip.

● **Youth Session:** Worship, prayer and faith. We designed the worship service for Confirmation Sunday. The students wrote statements on: "What it means to me to be a member of a church" and "Why I wish to be confirmed or why I do not wish to be confirmed."

● **Youth and Parent Session:** Evaluation. This was a summary of the entire course. The parents and youth together made symbols of what confirmation meant to them.

The pastor held a 15-minute personal interview with each young person during the week prior to Confirmation Sunday. The Confirmation Sunday service was designed and led by the youth. The parents as well as the pastor laid their hands on the young person's head for the confirmation.

Ron Rich
Winfield, Kansas

See also 13) HOW-WE-GOT-OUR-BIBLE GAME, 56) CONFIRMATION RING, 58) PARENT/YOUTH ENCOUNTER, 61) DISCIPLESHIP, 78) LORD'S PRAYER DANDELIONS, 81) REDACTION IN ACTION

56. CONFIRMATION RING

Confirmation marks a certain point in maturity and understanding. It is an opportunity for the church to create a memorable experience for the youth.

Many churches give a cross as a symbol of this important passage rite. I am wondering if a "confirmation ring" might hold a strong appeal to new members. It's an idea worth some exploration.

Doug Whiting
Lancaster, Pennsylvania

See also 55) STUDENT/PARENT CONFIRMATION, 199) I WILL SERVE THE CHURCH

57. LET YOUTH TEACH

In our small congregation, senior highs don't feel comfortable in a church school class with their parents, aunts, etc. So they teach in the classes for younger children. Working and planning with adult teachers, they often conduct entire class sessions on their own. Children appreciate them, and the senior highs have a sense of accomplishment.

Roger Kemp
Crittenden, New York

See also 41) SENIORITIS, 70) LEARNING CENTERS, 124) YOUNG PEOPLE AS LEADERS, 125) LET THEM LEAD

58. PARENT/YOUTH ENCOUNTER

During a three-part series for junior highs we focused on that very relevant but often hard-to-talk-about subject—parents. Both the junior highs and their parents were involved in this series although in different groups and sometimes during different sessions.

Session one opened with the junior highs writing questions about their parents (and parents about junior highs) on slips of paper. These were unsigned. Groups of parents of these young people gathered together and responded in writing to the questions that had been raised. Similar groups of young people answered parents' questions. The answers were read to the whole group.

During the second session each person assumed the role of a family member (father, mother, siblings, grandparents). These roles were not according to age. All members

were from different family units. Time was given for each person to communicate with each member of the "family." Changes were made several times so that there was a variety of encounters.

Session three focused on making decisions about drinking. A very helpful (and free) resource is the annual report of **Alcohol and Health** (National Institute on Alcohol Abuse and Alcoholism, 5600 Fishers Lane, Rockville, MD 20857). There are, however, many other excellent books and films you might use.

Adolph Quast
Waukesha, Wisconsin

See also 17) ENCOUNTER BIBLE CHARACTERS, 18) PRODIGAL DAUGHTER/SON, 55) STUDENT/ PARENT CONFIRMATION, 59) THE WEEKEND PARTY, 74) PARENTING AN EGG, 214) THE LOST SON

59. THE WEEKEND PARTY

Our youth love parties. Our area is known for its wild and undisciplined events. I put together a role play game that centers on a party that got out of control.

Setting

John's parents are going away for the weekend. They do not trust John (who is 16) to stay alone. However, they could be convinced to allow John to stay at the house if his friend George (who can do no wrong) would stay with him.

Playing the game

Two people will be picked to be the parents. They will leave the room after they have been convinced to let John and George stay at the house for the weekend. After they leave the room, they will be given the instructions on how to react after the weekend.

Each person will be given one role only. A moderator will set the stage and bring in initial characters. After that, it should flow without the moderator. The moderator will decide when to ask John for his decision. Mary will then respond according to instructions. The parents will be brought back into the room, having been told the outcome of

the weekend. The moderator will decide when to break off the game and move to discussion of what had happened.

Roles of each character. (Make up ahead of time on 4 x 6 cards)

John: He really is upset that his parents do not trust him. All the other parents trust their kids to stay alone.

Before your parents leave

Convince your parents they can let you stay home alone.

You really do not want George to stay with you as a babysitter (he is also 16), but will accept that if it is the only way to get your parents to let you stay home.

After your parents leave

Your friends may try to convince you to have a party at your house. The decision is yours.

continued

THE WEEKEND PARTY

You have been trying to get a date with Mary Cheerleader for over a year. This could be your chance.

George: John's parents think you are the perfect teenager. Convince them to let John stay home and offer to stay with him. Assure them that you will keep John straight.

As soon as John's parents leave

Try to convince John to have a party. You really think John's parents are square and you know you have really got them snowed.

Call some friends and get them to come over and help convince John to have a party. You know a guy who can get beer. Call Ann (the captain of the cheerleaders). She could talk Mary into coming. John really wants a date with Mary. You are really to play the bad guy.

When John's parents come home

You take all their praise or credit. If John does have the party, tell them you tried to talk him out of it.

Ann: (captain of the cheerleaders) You try to convince John that you can get Mary to come to the party. All the cheerleaders will come if you tell them to. You really have to make John want to have this party.

Mary: You really do not want to go out with John. Ann pressures you into saying you will go to the party. Go along with the gang.

After John makes his decision

If he has the party, tell him you are not coming; you just said that to make him have the party.

If he does not have the party, tell him you are proud of him and will be glad to go out with him anytime.

John's parents

Before the weekend

Try to convince John to go to his grandmother's house while you are away. You do not trust him to stay home alone. The only way you will let him stay home is if George stays with him. Give all the instructions and rules for the weekend and tell John to do whatever George says.

After the weekend

If John has the party, blame everything on John and ask him why he didn't listen to George. Ask George what happened, but assure him you know it wasn't his fault. Really blow your stack at John.

If John doesn't have the party, give all the credit to George for keeping him straight. Really lay it on heavy.

After John's parents have reacted to the weekend, let the dialogue between John and his parents go on as long as it is productive.

Discussion questions

Appropriate questions will vary greatly, based on the outcome of the game and amount of peer pressure actually applied. The following questions are possibilities:

1. Did John's parents treat him like an adult?

2. Why did they think George was so great?

3. Did John react in a responsible manner?

4. What type of person was George?

5. If you were a social worker or pastor, how would you resolve this family's problem?

6. Have you ever felt like John? Have your parents ever wanted you to be like someone else?

7. Have you ever been in a position like George? Have parents of your friends ever thought you were better in some way than their own children?

Ken Scarborough
Ithaca, New York

See also 54) CHEAP ROLE PLAYS, 58) PARENT/YOUTH ENCOUNTER, 74) PARENTING AN EGG, 214) THE LOST SON

60. SEX EDUCATION

The area of sex education and discussion is one that is so often overlooked. Church people have a variety of viewpoints regarding the propriety of sex education within the school, the church, and the family. Often, youth move through their early adolescence with very little opportunity to be involved in a serious discussion with adults other than one of their parents.

We designed a seven-week course. It began with an orientation session for the parents of the youth. This was an important part of the planning of the course since it enabled us to go over the material that would be covered during the course of the next six weeks. The parents felt much more relaxed when they knew the content of the course.

When the high school youth gathered together for the first time, they were given several pieces of paper and asked to write questions regarding sex that had always bothered them. No names were to be signed. After collecting the questions, the gathering was divided into smaller groups, each of which had a physician and an adult leader. During that session (and future sessions), discussion centered on the questions that the students had written down. The medical folks were quite surprised by the questions. There are many areas of ignorance among our young people. The course also brought in a young married couple who were happy to share with the group the journey of their love. And, the whole course was undergirded by the Christian understanding of agape love.

Bill Wolfe
Nashville, Tennessee

See also 1) TRY TO REMEMBER, 23) DISCUSSION BASICS, 25) THE HOT SEAT, 41) SENIORITIS, 128) "COMPUTER" DATING NIGHT

61. DISCIPLESHIP

A core of youth in our group enjoyed the Sunday evening fellowship group, yet felt the need for in-depth study and outreach. We came up with an intense program for these youth, combining serious Bible study, prayer and outreach. This group met early on weekday mornings in homes. It was not to substitute for the Sunday evening group.

The first element was Bible study. Adults helped them to decide what they wanted to study. Then, each week teams of two came prepared with some kind of dialogue about the scripture passage. They were to apply the lesson to their school and home life. They then came back the following week and reported on their application. Meanwhile, a different team prepared the next lesson and the group repeated the process.

The second element was prayer. Prayers were given for each other, for their friends (and enemies) and for their schools and homes. They were to pray for each other's

continued

DISCIPLESHIP

needs throughout the week. They committed themselves to help bring inactives and non-Christians to youth activities and Sunday morning services.

The final element was outreach. The group gave volunteer time to organizations that needed help. For example, the group volunteered eight hours to a hospital per week. Each of the four young people gave two hours a week. This was a big commitment, since all of them were already involved in 20 or so different things.

The youth discovered a lot about themselves, about their faith and developed a close fellowship. It was never intended to be, nor did it become, a clique.

This approach gave bone and flesh to our beliefs. It helped the group discover and probe the promises of discipleship. It was an experiment in faith. We believe it was successful.

Gary Weaver
New Mexico

See also 12) DISCOVERY BIBLE STUDY, 46) HAVES AND HAVE NOTS, 55) STUDENT/PARENT CONFIRMATION, 62) THE "AVERAGE" KID, 78) LORD'S PRAYER DANDELIONS, 93) SMALL GROUPS, 146) DOWN-AND-OUTS

62. THE "AVERAGE" KID

I believe that the "average" kid needs to be a star. The local church can do so much to develop the talents of young people. If we have a good idea for a song, we like to give it to music-loving young people and ask them to sing it. If we find other young people with an interest in photography, we ask them to go out and take pictures or slides to fit the theme of a song. If there are producer-types, we ask them to mix the song and slides into a presentation. These kids might never have worked together before. They might never have used their cameras other than for taking pretty scenes on trips. They may have written songs for only themselves. I look around and try to see kids who have a little inkling of talent that can be spotlighted and polished. I would like to make professionals of many of them in their own fields. It gives them self-confidence. More than that, they perform a creative ministry.

Young people want to contribute their talents. I don't care if they haven't been trained in singing, dancing or acting. If they want a chance, I'll give it to them. Often they say, "I can't do that," but I stay with them until I know that they can. Even if they make a mistake, they still appreciate the opportunity to share talents.

Pauline Hubner, Brisbane, Australia

See also 4) WHAT'S A LEADER?, 127) TALENT NIGHT, 183) MULTIMEDIA WORSHIP, 185) SLIDES AND PRAYERS, 187) POP MUSIC POSSIBILITIES

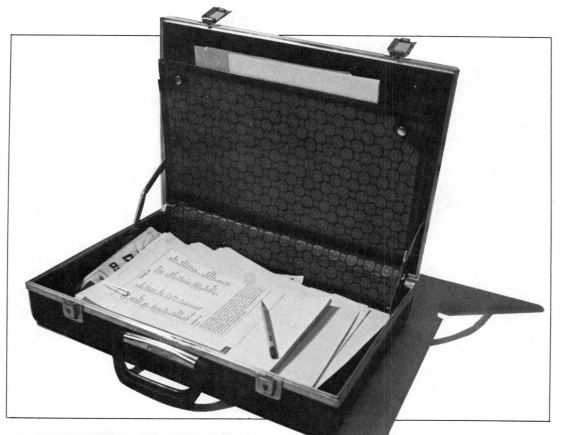

63. TEN CAREER-CHOOSING TIPS

1. Don't make your final occupational decision until you have studied it from every possible angle. Learn about the field you are considering by reading everything you can find on the occupation that interests you. Do this exploratory work before you start training for your chosen career.

2. Based on what you personally need— intellectually, socially, psychologically, financially—the best thing to do is make your own checklist when you are investigating occupations. Decide if a particular occupation measures up to your personal needs in all areas. How close does it come? Which of several choices comes closest?

3. Consult a qualified career guidance counselor for objective advice on your career plans. Make sure, however, the counselor spends enough time with you to gain a good insight into your particular situation and personal needs.

4. Remember, one of the most important factors in choosing an occupation is to pick something you are psychologically suited to handle. Take advantage of any psychological aptitude tests that are available. They may show you the type of work for which you are best suited.

5. Because everyone can do some things better than others, choose a field suited to your own particular abilities. Find out if there are any special mental qualities, such as the capacity for learning quickly and easily, imagination, originality, or good memory that are essential in the vocation in which you are interested.

6. Discuss your career plans with several

continued

TEN CAREER-CHOOSING TIPS

people already established in the fields you are considering. You'll get a clearer picture of both favorable and unfavorable sides of the job, and a better understanding of the type of work involved.

7. Find out in detail about the actual work done in the vocation you are considering. Try to learn precisely what is done during a typical day or week on the job. Are the same tasks done again and again, or are they varied? What are those duties you would be called on to perform only once in a while? Be sure you are aware of all the occupation's duties. It's the job's day-to-day experiences that make it agreeable or disagreeable.

8. If you can, work summers or part-time in offices, laboratories, or plants and talk to other workers about their jobs.

9. Don't allow your parents, teachers or counselors to decide on an occupation for you.

10. Don't attach too much importance to what others may think of your vocational choice. Take into account the effect of your work's prestige, but don't overestimate it. There are types of work that are less crowded, more highly paid, and provide a higher standard of living than some of the white-collar jobs we generally think are so prestigious.

To summarize, the things that should influence you most in your choice of careers are high school courses in which you did well, reading about careers, talking with friends and teachers in the field that interests you and summer or part-time work experiences.

John H. Boller, Jr.
San Diego, California

Title: "A Career List"

Objective: The students make a list of 10 careers which interest them and identify some of the factors which influenced their choice.

Activities:

1. Ask the students to list 10 careers or jobs which interest them. If the students have trouble thinking about possible careers for their list, hand out a copy of career lists from sources such as the **Dictionary of Occupational Titles** (available from high school counselors).

2. After the students have compiled their lists, ask them to do the following:
   a. Put a "$" next to the careers in which you could make a lot of money.
   b. Put an "O" next to the careers which involve working with or helping other people.
   c. You are at a party where the only thing you know about the people is their job. Put an * next to those careers which signify the person you would be most interested in talking to.
   d. Put a "P" next to those careers your

parents would approve of.
   e. Put an "F" next to those your friends consider to be good jobs.
   f. Put an "M" next to those you want to find out more about.

3. Discuss the following questions:
   a. Are the careers that have the most marks next to them the careers that you have spent some time thinking about?
   b. How much have your parents influenced your choice? How much have your friends?
   c. Why did you want to talk to certain people on your list and not others?
   d. Is money an important consideration?
   e. What can you do to find out more about the careers on your list?

John H. Boller, Jr.
San Diego, California

WHAT DO YOU WANT OUT OF A CAREER?

Which of the following are *most* important to you (indicate at least four but not more than six with a +).

Which are of *least* importance to you (indicate at least four but not more than six with a −).

Most	Least	
___	___	An opportunity to be original and creative.
___	___	An opportunity which has the potential for rapid and great success as well as the possibility of immediate and much failure.
___	___	An opportunity which offers much contact with people but little involvement.
___	___	A pressure job where you have to put a lot into it and the pace is very fast.
___	___	An opportunity where one lives and works in the world of ideas.
___	___	An opportunity which permits the use of leadership and power.
___	___	An opportunity which permits a great deal of independence.
___	___	An opportunity where one becomes much involved in management and assumes responsibilities.
___	___	A job which has a wide variety of tasks.
___	___	A job where long-term goals

Most	Least	
		are involved rather than the emphasis on immediate results.
___	___	A chance to earn a good deal of money.
___	___	An opportunity where the emphasis is on ethical behavior.
___	___	An opportunity where I can choose my own geographical location.
___	___	An opportunity to use my abilities.
___	___	An opportunity to serve and work with humanity.
___	___	A job where I can see immediate results.
___	___	An opportunity to work with things (objects).
___	___	An opportunity which gives me status, prestige and recognition.
___	___	An opportunity for moderate but steady progress.
___	___	A chance to earn a comfortable income and dependable employment.

John H. Boller, Jr.

See also 41) SENIORITIS, 64) CAREER CLARIFICATION, 66) VOCATION

64. CAREER CLARIFICATION

I put together five practical exercises that can be used by those interested in Christian career development. I found them very helpful to youth groups. Following are instructions I used in these exercises:

As you get involved with these exercises, you may notice that it's difficult to focus only on your vocation, occupation, career or whatever you call it. You will find some dreams of places you want to visit creeping in, some things you want to experience and other non-job goals. Don't omit these.

Practical exercise #1: Analyze your hobbies. List all the hobbies you have done over the years. Then rank them in order of greatest enjoyment. What skills were you using? What were the results of these hobbies? Hobbies reveal skills you may find useful in making career decisions.

Practical exercise #2: What makes you happy? This exercise consists of a very simple question: If you could have any kind of job, what would it be? Sometimes the question is put like this: Where do you want to be a year from now? 10 years from now? 20 years from now? Try them all. This exercise presumes you know what makes you happy. Maybe, however, you have a much clearer idea of what makes you unhappy. The next exercise thrives on that.

Practical exercise #3: What makes you unhappy? Compile a list of what things make you unhappy? Then, separate what you have listed into two categories:

1. Things that lie within my control.
2. Things that lie outside my control.
When you are done with that, review the second list to be sure these things are really beyond your control or power to alter.

Now go over the first list and separate those things into two categories:

1. Things which I could change through a change of environment (e.g., my job, or the place where I live, etc.).
2. Things which I could change through

working on my interior life (e.g., working on personal hang-ups, emotions, growing spiritually).

Finally, write out realistic resolutions, setting time goals beside them.

Practical exercise #4: Who am I?
1. Take 10 sheets of paper. Write on the top of each one the words: "Who am I?"
2. Then write, on each sheet, one answer to that question. Each sheet will have the same question, but you'll have 10 different answers.
3. Now go back over the 10 again, looking at each answer. Then write below how you feel about that particular answer.
4. Now go back over the 10 sheets and arrange them in order of importance. The most important identity goes on top, the least on the bottom.
5. Finally, go back over the 10 sheets, looking particularly at the answers you wrote about how you felt about each answer. See if there are some common denominators. The answers you felt good about may be some things that your career (calling, vocation, job or whatever) can use to help you be truly happy, fulfilled and effective.

Practical exercise #5: Look to the future. Spend as much time as necessary writing an article entitled, "Before I die, I want to . . ." (things you would like to do before you die). Or, you may prefer to write the article on a similar topic: "On the last day of my life, what must I have done or been so that my life will have been satisfying to me?" When it is finished, go back over it and make two lists: "Things Already Accomplished," "Things Yet to Be Accomplished." Next to the "Things Yet to Be Accomplished" list, write some particular steps that you will have to take to accomplish these things.

John H. Boller, Jr.
San Diego, California

See also 41) SENIORITIS, 63) TEN CAREER-CHOOSING TIPS, 65) WHAT'S IN THE FUTURE, 66) VOCATION

65. WHAT'S IN THE FUTURE?

Planning for the future, both individually and as a community, is an important part of maturing. Our youth group spent some very special time focusing on making plans for the future.

The following letter will give you a quick overview of the Career Education Program we offered in our church. The program was successful in focusing and inspiring youth (even more so for their parents) to consider the kind and quality of future they hope for themselves.

Dear Parent:

You are invited to invest six hours in your child's future.

Starting on January 21, the First Congregational Church is offering for all junior highs and their parents three two-hour sessions on "Career Education." "Career Education" is one of the most neglected areas in the upbringing and schooling of our youth. You are especially encouraged to attend and participate, because no other person can influence as directly and as profoundly the career choices of your son or daughter. Through these sessions you will gain a better understanding of your child's career aspirations and how you might help him or her in the pursuit of a career and other life choices. God calls each of us to contribute the best of our gifts, to the best of our abilities, for the best of our world.

continued

WHAT'S IN THE FUTURE

When I Grow Up?

SESSION 1:
Crystal Ball Gazing

Goals: 1. To open up before participants the variety of work opportunities and the reasons for work.
2. To think about short- and long-range goals.

Theses: 1. Our limited knowledge and work experience doesn't allow us to know of the variety of job opportunities available to all of us.
2. Dreaming about our future can make our present clearer.

Each session began with a get acquainted or ice breaker activity. Only those materials that were to be used in the particular session were distributed.

Introduction:

Have you ever thought about what you want to be when you grow up? I think we all have.

Over the next three weeks we're going to take the time to allow each of us (both you and parents) to make some definite plans for your future. I can't convince you of the need to make those plans. (Right now is not too early to begin making them.) But I do ask you to be open to all the things we've planned for you to do. I know it will be helpful to you. I guarantee you that you'll learn a lot about yourself.

Since only you can convince yourself of the importance of career education, setting goals and making plans, I want to share with you a few statements which I think make a great deal of sense and which I think point to the reasons why we're going to be doing the things we've got planned for the next three weeks.

1. This first statement is from a poster. "Plan ahead. It wasn't raining when Noah built the Ark." In order to accomplish anything, you have to plan to make it happen. Examples: being an athlete, getting good grades, getting a date, saving money.

2. "Aim at nothing and you'll reach your goal." Wishes, hopes and dreams don't happen if there's no action.

3. "It takes 40 minutes to boil an ostrich egg!" Taking a look at your future is a lot bigger concern than merely making plans for tomorrow (although that is important). It only makes sense that you'll have to do a lot of hard thinking now in order to make those plans. And that's what I'm asking you all to do. Be open now and give the best of yourself, to the best of your ability, for the best of your world. That's what God asks of each of us.

4. "I don't know where I'm going, but I'm on my way." Today we'll be dreaming about our futures. Since the meaning of most dreams isn't immediately obvious or clear, we don't expect a lot of answers today or next week. We also realize that our vocational dreams begin to happen through what we do together in Session 3. But don't expect all the answers then either. They will take a lifetime.

Today we'll dream about your whole life: what you want to do, what you want to learn, where you want to go, what you want to do for others, what you want to do for yourself, where you want to do it.

Next week we're going to look at specific jobs, careers, and occupations you might want.

In the last session, we will put it all together and find ways we can begin to make our plans happen!

In all these activities, remember three things:

1. **Be honest.** Write down only what you want for your life. Don't put down what you think I, your parents, friends or teachers want. These programs won't mean a thing unless they are your answers.

2. **The only right answers are your answers.** This time together and these exercises we'll do are not a test. No one has to see what you write unless you want to share it. So put down whatever you really feel about your hopes and dreams and goals.

3. **Use your imagination.** Dream (Astronauts, Hula-Hoops, and Frisbees weren't known 30 years ago.)

"The trouble is not in achieving goals but in imagining them." We first have to imagine what we want before we can then do it. Let's begin right there and start dreaming (with our eyes open) about our futures. Let's imagine, not just a future, but many futures for ourselves.

Since most of us will probably spend almost 40 if not 50 or 60 years working, it is exciting to think we might be able to have two or three completely different careers in our lifetime.

After the introduction, we began with a filmstrip and cassette presentation produced by Newsweek Magazine called, "Working Americans." (Most cities and colleges have the filmstrip. Another good free resource is the film "What Will I Do With My Time?" Order from Association Films, Inc., New York Life Insurance Company, 866 Third Ave., N. Y., NY 10022.) After the filmstrip was

shown, we discussed the following questions: Why do people work? Do people's jobs provide satisfaction and fulfillment? What do you expect from a job? from your life?

Exercise 1: Use the "I Want To" sheets to dream about *all* the things participants think they might like to do at some point in their lives. This includes anything whatsoever. An "I Want To" sheet might look something like this:

I Want To (some examples)

- Have a job that I love
- Have a good marriage
- Spend time with interesting friends
- Have a comfortable home in the suburbs
- Live overseas in a beautiful village by the sea
- Have enough free time and money to travel
- Be in good physical condition
- Run my own company, laboratory, ranch or office
- Live in a modern apartment resort in the heart of an exciting city
- Produce a great work of art, make an important scientific discovery, devise a better master plan for a city, make a run-down farm profitable
- Have people come to me because I am an expert
- Make enough money to travel, educate my children, and buy good art
- Work in an important government post, influencing what is happening in our country.
- Learn to cook Chinese
- Learn to cook French
- Learn to cook Norwegian

---

continued

WHAT'S IN THE FUTURE

Exercise 2: We used the "In Service" sheet in the same way. On each of these first two exercises, participants were asked to put a check beside their top 10, to put dollar signs beside all those that cost money, and to put the date beside those checked as to when they wanted to accomplish those dreams and goals. An "In Service" sheet might look something like this:

In Service (some examples)

- Defeat cancer
- Lick inflation
- Equal opportunities for all
- Get rid of sexual and racial stereotyping and discrimination
- Eliminate hunger
- Stop constant warring
- Clean air and water
- Provide equal justice
- Promote understanding of conflicting, opposing or differing viewpoints
- Jobs for all
- Eliminate crime
- Break down barriers between people
- Eliminate America's "consumerism-itis"
- Encourage and support individuals' natural creativity
- Develop the human mind to the fullest potential
- Preservation of natural wildlife
- Natural healthcare programs
- End physical abuse of children
- Humanizing death and dying programs
- A cure for baldness

- Sharing of money, skills, time
- Assist people in getting a better handle on their identity
- Increase awareness of spiritual identity
- Conserving energy resources
- End the drug problem
- More family cohesiveness
- Loving care of the dying
- Family education
- End conflict between religious groups
- Humane correction systems for all offenders
- Five-cent phone calls
- Meaningful retirement
- Eliminate or alleviate tedium at work
- Creative leisure programs
- People taking responsibility for themselves
- Six-hour work day
- Humanistic working conditions and environment
- Elimination of violence through a nurturing environment, starting with . . .

Exercise 3: "In Service" was followed with one of the "Interview Sheets." Youth were to interview an adult. (The youth enjoyed this exercise. They took their role as interviewer seriously. Some were, however, reluctant to speak with an adult and role playing one interview might have helped them get started. This exercise helped people experience how to get needed information by interviewing.) An "Interview Sheet" might look something like this:

Interview Sheet

1. Of all the jobs you've had, which one have you enjoyed most?
2. What one thing do/did you like best about the job?
3. What did/didn't you like about the job?
4. How did you come to choose this job?
5. What is the average salary for that type of job?
6. List three benefits of the job.
7. List three drawbacks of the job.
8. Would there be a future in this job for me in five years?

Session 1 ended with people evaluating the class session as well as completing their own individual evaluation. I commented on the next session and encouraged everyone not to be concerned with what all these exercises might mean until the third week. (We kept the folders at the church between sessions so people would make sure to have them for the next session.)

SESSION 2:
At the Library

Our second session met at the local public library. I began by interviewing three adults who worked in different career areas. I also encouraged the young people to ask any questions they wished.

We also introduced and studied the different resources we had made available that could help young people make life choices.

continued

WHAT'S IN THE FUTURE

Exercise 1: We reviewed the career/occupation information sheet and people filled in the parts of it they could. The adults gave youth help at this point. (Youth were not expected to fill out this sheet but to use it as a beginning for their own exploration in interviewing out in the "real" world.) The sheet looked like this:

Exercise 2: We then spent a considerable amount of time going over the wealth of resources in the community that could help the youth plan their futures and fill in other parts of the information sheet.

Community Resources:
- Local libraries
- Adults doing what you think you want to do some day
- Agencies which will employ youth or take them on as volunteers in fields of the youth's interests
- School guidance departments
- Local college career guidance and placement services
- College financial aid offices

Exercise 3: We asked the kids to write a letter to themselves about some of the things they were going to do as a result of the class. We mailed the letters to the kids five months after the sessions, hoping they would continue work on some of their future dreams and goals.

Larry Gaffin
Walla Walla, Washington

SESSION 3:
Now What Do I Do?

Goal: To help participants see how to begin working toward some of their short- and long-range goals.

Thesis: Clarifying and taking charge of our dreams and goals is a step toward living out more fully God's calling for each of us.

The introduction reviewed the first two sessions and moved into discussion about how to begin to bring all the work of the last two weeks together.

See also 41) SENIORITIS, 63) TEN CAREER-CHOOSING TIPS, 64) CAREER CLARIFICATION, 66) VOCATION

Career/Occupation Information Outline	Choice 1 Type of Job:	Choice 2 Type of Job:	Choice 3 Type of Job:
1. **Nature of Work**—What daily tasks are performed?			
2. **Interests Required**—What things should you like to do?			
3. **Abilities Required**—What things should you be able to do well?			
4. **Personality Traits Required**—What attitudes, values do you need?			
5. **Preparation Required**—High school subjects? Technical training? Apprenticeship? College degree? Graduate work? How many years of schooling?			
6. **Other Requirements**—Union membership? State license? Approval by professional organization?			
7. **Working Conditions**—Regular hours? Shift work? On call at all times? Pleasant surroundings? Adequate equipment? Opportunities for improving skills?			
8. **Location**—Where would you have to go to do this work? What are living conditions there?			
9. **Employment Outlook**—How many workers are employed in this work nationally and locally? Is there a demand for these workers now? Is the demand increasing or decreasing?			
10. **Salary and Benefits**—What is the starting wage? Will it probably increase? Are there paid vacations, compensation plans for illness and accidents, retirement program?			
11. **Personal Satisfaction**—Does this work enable you to realize some of your real values? Are those values worthy of a person on the way toward spiritual maturity? How many years would you like to work in this job?			
12. **Social Importance**—How does this work meet human needs?			
13. **Vocational Potential**—How can this work possibly become God's call to you? Can God speak to you through its demands, and can you respond to God by faithfully performing it?			

66. VOCATION

Vocational choice is a trouble facing every age group. However, our young people really feel the pressure. We designed an exciting event to confront this challenge.

A Retreat Design: A Place for You

The following material is part of a design that evolved out of several discussions of our Youth Activities Committee regarding vocational choice. We wanted a solid theological base for helping youth with the frustrating task of choosing a career or job situation. We also wanted kids to see how people integrate their faith into their vocation, especially folk who have non-ministerial roles. Remembering that our Lord occupied four or five vocational roles (prophet, priest, king, shepherd, carpenter), we began asking each other where we saw people being pastoral toward each other, or priestly, or kingly, etc. We discovered we needed definitions that young people could understand, so we listed some of the concepts you see on the "Debriefing 'Kotch' " sheet (see right).

We live in a media-saturated world. How could we unsaturate it by draining meaning from the media? We hunted through catalogs, looking for a flick that would involve contemporary issues. "Kotch" is a film about a pregnant runaway youth and a rejected senior citizen who get involved in a non-sexual relationship which ministers to both of them. ("Kotch" is available from Films, Inc., 5625 Hollywood Blvd., Hollywood, CA 90028.)

We then assembled some objective and theological questions to use in small groups.

Asking questions is another technique we all like to use, but who will do the asking, and why are we asking, and what would be the nature of the questions? We felt that kids need to know real Christians who carry their faith into their vocation, and vice versa.

We're all more comfortable on our own turf, so we decided to send our kids out with cassette recorders to interview people in the churches in our city—people who were deeply involved in their faith and vocation. The interview questions were put together by the kids and small group leaders. "Playback" was a time set aside to discover processes of vocational choice and to see how Christ could intertwine the lives of people, vocations, and church.

The other items on the schedule were natural spin-offs (posters, banners, graffiti board, poems, worship). We had people in the churches cook meals for us while we were responsible for cleanup.

There was quite a sense of community from having worked with each other on such a crucial issue. Our kids now have an understanding of God's will for their lives, which involves more than "Where shall I go to college?" or "Who shall I marry?."

Debriefing "Kotch"

Objective questions
1. Which scene sticks in your mind? Why?
2. What major character impressed you most?
3. What problems were evident in the characters' lives?

Subjective questions
1. How would you describe your mood during the film?
2. Did you get angry or upset with any of the characters? At what point?
3. Were you appalled at any scenes or characters?

Theological questions
1. Where did you see "sin" in the film?
2. Where did you see "grace" in the film?
3. What pictures of God or Christ did you see in the film?
4. Was there any sense of death and resurrection—leaving an old life and gaining a new one—in the film?
5. How was the brokenness of the characters changed to wholeness in the film?

Role models
1. Where did you see someone acting pastorally toward another person? That is, where was someone showing love and counseling with concern for the well-be-

ing of another?

2. Who acted in the role of a priest, giving faith or hope to someone, forgiving or giving another an opportunity to confess? Also, where did someone intercede (plead their cause) on behalf of another? How did they share the gospel with the other person?

3. Where did you see someone being prophetic with another person? That is, raising specific questions about what others are doing with their energies or resources. How were they correcting injustice in life situations?

4. Was there anyone who was involved in governance of another? This means someone who guided another in making decisions for the good of humanity as well as themselves. How was this done?

Randall R. Scheer
Sterling, Kansas

See also 41) SENIORITIS, 63) TEN CAREER-CHOOSING TIPS, 64) CAREER CLARIFICATION

67. AROMA

We once had a most exotic evening at youth fellowship. We invited everyone to bring a favorite fragrance (perfume, aftershave, etc.). We talked about how each person had received that particular perfume or fragrance and why it was especially liked. Then we discussed Luke 7:36-50, where the sinful woman anoints Jesus. The discussion focused on the analogy of Christian living and fine fragrances: our Christian witness attracts people to Christ. We then anointed each other with the fragrances.

Bobbie and John Rankin, California, Pennsylvania

See also 72) CREATIVE CONJURING, 75) A SPOONFUL OF HONEY, 76) TEA TIME, 82) LEMONS, 118) STOP AND SMELL THE ROSES, 176) COMMON OBJECT MEDITATIONS

68. SUPER SUNDAY

A couple of years ago we evaluated our Sunday school for junior highs and came up with a pretty sad picture: the hour-on-Sunday-morning wasn't working! The usual problems: lousy attendance, poor continuity, not enough time each session and not enough continuity in the class to have a sense of building from one week to the next, poor morale, boredom, frustration among both students and teachers. Teacher recruitment was a crisis each year.

So, SuperSunday was hatched! We meet monthly for four hours on a Sunday afternoon instead of weekly for an hour. (By the way, people who initially object to "such a long time in class" seem to have a terribly restricted idea of a church school class—they assume we sit around tables reading and discussing the Bible the whole time!) Young people are encouraged to worship with their families on Sunday morning, and their parents are urged to mark the SuperSunday dates on the calendar well in advance. We make no apology for our insistence to parents that this important experience should have a high priority for the young people and their families.

SuperSunday begins with lunch, about one-half hour after the close of worship. At lunch, we informally begin to focus in on the topic for the day. There is no standard process for SuperSunday. We simply make sure that it is fun and active. A particularly successful SuperSunday was "Hershey Bars," which grappled with The Fall in Genesis.

On the "Hershey Bars" occasion we all brought sack lunches. A huge bowl of Hershey bars was placed prominently in the room. When we finished lunch, the teachers asked the students to clean up while the teachers made final preparations in another room. We made a point of telling the kids not to touch the Hershey bars!

All the teachers left the room, leaving the students with Steve, our high-school-age assistant. All the kids liked and admired Steve. Since he had been in on our little scheme, he knew he was to play the role of the "Serpent." He easily persuaded the class that it wouldn't hurt to take the Hershey bars, that the teachers were probably only saving them for a treat for the class later on anyhow. The kids responded to Steve's enticements readily—some of them even got sneaky and reassembled the wrappers so they would look unopened. Then—caught in the act! The teachers returned, feigning shock and anger that we had been disobeyed. Of course, the kids were quick to blame Steve—and each other! The whole thing—from the end of lunch to the time the fingers of blame got pointed—took about 10 minutes. It was intended to provide experiential "common ground" before the class looked at Genesis 3.

But we also wanted the kids to see the connection with their own individual experience. Immediately after the above episode, and still before we had opened a Bible, we passed out 3 x 5 cards and asked students to write about a time when they got into trouble for disobeying. We decided that one of the teachers should read these aloud, to preserve the anonymity of students. We discussed feelings as the cards were read. We talked about disobedience, punishment, forgiveness, reconciliation.

This conversation was interrupted suddenly when one of the teachers burst into the room and read the following news "hot off the wire": *"Flash! Adam and Even have just been expelled from the Garden of Eden! God is said to be furious! The Serpent is in big trouble! Adam and Eve, often celebrated as the world's most original couple, were thought to have "had it made" in their garden paradise. Early reports from the scene indicate that the couple disobeyed a direct command from God, and that their removal from the Garden of Eden is permanent. It has not yet been disclosed exactly what the crime was, nor the full extent of the punishment."*

Now the class took on the role of a newsroom crew. They divided into groups to go out and get the full story: each group had a teacher-helper. Four crews were assigned to interview the main characters: Adam, Eve, God, the Serpent. These groups had to come up with appropriate interview questions and get the details of the story from that character's point of view. They were to choose one of their number to portray the character being interviewed, and one to do the interviewing. They had materials to make costumes and simple props.

A fifth crew was assigned to provide a summary version of the story. They were also to prepare a background description of the Garden of Eden and its blessings, and a commentary on what life will be like now that Adam and Eve have been expelled.

The groups had 40 minutes to do research and preparation. They read and discussed Genesis 3. Then they prepared their portion of the news broadcast. From hindsight, we should have borrowed videotape equipment and taped this whole news broadcast. But we didn't think of it in time, so we presented it "as if" it were on television.

After a 15-minute recreation break for the whole class, each group was permitted another few minutes to make final preparations, and to coordinate its part of the presentation with the others. They presented the broadcast itself—it took about 20 minutes.

Now the class was well-acquainted with Genesis 3, and in the debriefing they soon made the connection between the Adam and Eve story and their own experiences with the Hershey Bars. But we needed some more intentional discussion of sin and reconciliation. So . . .

We showed the old Laurel and Hardy movie "Two Tars". (Some public libraries have it; or you can buy a super 8mm print for about $20 from Blackhawk Films, Box 3990, Davenport, Iowa 52808.) This is a silent movie, though some prints have musical soundtracks. We used a record of ragtime music; it always seems better when there is music in the background. This is a very funny movie—remember? It's the one where Laurel and Hardy get into a traffic jam, and every car on the road gets systematically demolished. It's really a great film about sin (yes!), and also about scapegoating, disobedience, authority, retaliation, relationships. The class was quite eager to discuss it afterwards. We took pains to keep the discussion light-hearted, in the mood of the movie itself.

Our kids love to make collages of magazine clippings, so we did one on sin. We tried to emphasize the kinds of sin that have to do with relationships, rather than the individual varieties. We made our collage on a long piece of butcher paper. Then we put it up and talked about our feelings, and how God must feel about sin.

That talk led right into our closing worship, during which (about 20 minutes) we debriefed the whole afternoon's experience. We believe "Hershey Bars" SuperSunday did far more than traditional Sunday school to help junior highs understand themselves in sin, grace and reconciliation.

Dick Craft
Elmwood Park, Illinois

See also 54) CHEAP ROLE PLAYS, 69) SUNDAY SCHOOL PUBLICITY BLITZ, 70) LEARNING CENTERS, 79) HAPPINESS IS . . ., 109) ROOM DYNAMICS

69. SUNDAY SCHOOL PUBLICITY BLITZ

We decided to give our church school a real boost in publicity. We created a large brochure featuring a complete preview of the coming weeks in Sunday school. Attractive art helped draw attention to the content. Much of the artwork, type, and numbers were drawn from catalogs, magazines and books.

Rob Gregg
Medfield, Massachusetts

See also 68) SUPER SUNDAY, 87) STICKY FLAPS, 88) YOUTH DIRECTORY, 89) PHONE-A-THON, 156) REACH, 166) GETTING THE WORD OUT

70. LEARNING CENTERS

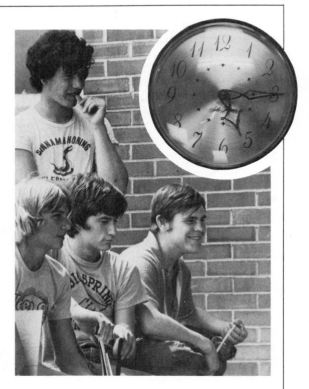

Instead of the standard 60- to 90-minute meeting on a single theme or issue, why not break the time into several shorter units? I call these shorter units learning centers. A learning center should concentrate on a topic for three to 15 minutes. Just keep rolling along on several themes. And, vary the kind of activity for a learning center. You may use role plays, another discussion, another game, or some other kind of media. This barrage of experiences should appeal to short attention spans.

Steve Sonnenberg
Topeka, Kansas

See also 23) DISCUSSION BASICS, 49) ALL-NIGHT TALK, 57) LET YOUTH TEACH, 68) SUPER SUNDAY

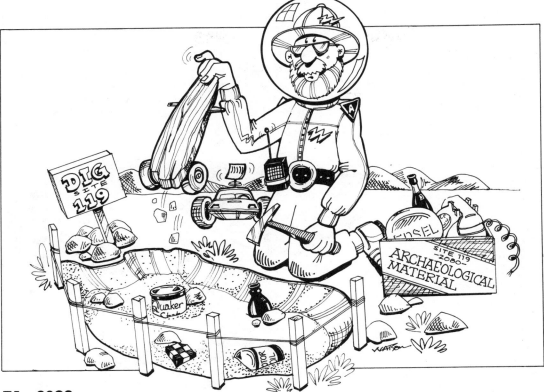

71. 2083

What facts will the people of 2083 gather about us from the items we discard along our rivers and streams? This was the question put to our youth group.

We set our clocks ahead 100 years. The group was divided into three research teams. Each team gathered items along the shore of the Chester River in Maryland. All of these items had been discarded approximately 100 years prior, around the year 1983. The items were presented to the group after each team had determined what they were. A spokesperson for each team described the item and its use.

The following is a partial list of items:

Dark brown bottle—had been used for alcoholic beverage which many consumed for relaxation.

Bottle marked "illegal to refill"—this was when a law actually forced the public to use a bottle or can once and throw it away to clutter the earth.

Quart can marked "oil"—this was a petroleum product people had discovered under the earth which had provided fuel and lubrication; however, every known oil well has since been pumped dry.

Many other items which had been used for packaging, construction, transportation, and pleasure were found and discussed.

The discussion that followed each team's presentation touched on many areas of ecology and ethics. The people of 1983 appear to have had little regard for the natural resources or the litter that they left behind for future generations.

We ended our project with a prayer that we, the inhabitants of the year 2083, would make better use of our resources than our forebearers.

Ken Scarborough
Townsend, Delaware

See also 2) THE FUTURE GAME, 15) WONDERS, 142) CAN-A-THON

72. CREATIVE CONJURING

I introduced experiential learning to my class of junior highs in various ways. One Sunday, I asked them to come up with some experiential ideas. I suggested the topic of kinship. They responded: "Put different colored M&M's on cookies. We could then talk about how they are the same cookies, but the M&M's make them different. However, they only appear to be different."

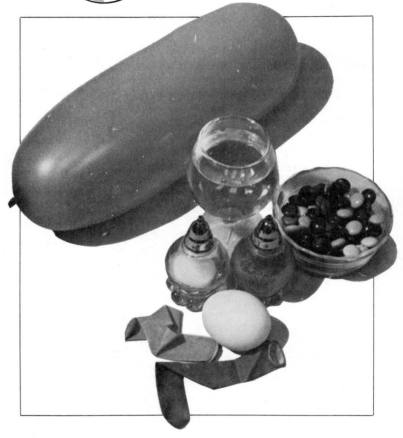

We then used salt as a clue. They suggested that we shake some salt into a glass of water. Then add some pepper and a drop of soap. This could mean that some elements will mix, some will separate and stay apart. Their point was that all elements do react to each other.

I gave them the theme of creation and a balloon. The students inflated it and let the air out. For them, this relates to our responsibility to replenish the earth. If we aren't good stewards of God's gifts and responsibilities, we will overpopulate the earth (the balloon pops).

I also gave them objects and let them set the themes. For instance, I handed them an egg. They said that it was like the Trinity. Three in one: shell, white, yolk. We need all three and each is beneficial and complementary.

Another time I used water. They said that plain water represents people. Fire represents hell. If the water is heated long enough it evaporates. They also noted that by adding salt to boiling water, the water will evaporate but not the salt. Jesus is like that salt.

It is amazing what these imaginative young people can discover. The group did not begin this way. When they first came to me, they expected the usual "dumping" process of teaching. However, after several weeks of experience, they began to bloom with creativity.

E. Jane Mall
Westmont, Illinois

See also 4) WHAT'S A LEADER?, 9) BIBLE EX-PLORATIONS, 12) DISCOVERY BIBLE STUDY, 15) WONDERS, 44) FIRE, 67) AROMA, 74) PARENTING AN EGG, 77) SPONGE BITS, 82) LEMONS, 92) AIR BANDS, 104) SHOPPING BAG VALUES, 176) COMMON OBJECTS MEDITATIONS

73. MEDIA PROBING

I am one of those teachers who feels that good teaching involves a learning experience for the teacher as well as the students. I frequently ask my high school students to bring into class media forms which mean something to them. It can be a recording, a poem, or anything important. The beginning of the class is devoted to the sharing of these media items. The response is fantastic! A person does not have to explain why he or she finds meaning in that which is shared. However, students soon begin to make such statements. I have found a whole new understanding of pop art forms through my students.

Michael E. Moynahan, S.J.
Berkeley, California

See also 22) FILM CRITICISM, 49) ALL-NIGHT TALK, 80) TV WISDOM, 81) REDACTION IN ACTION, 163) EXTRA! JESUS LIVES, 172) BURLAP, 176) COMMON OBJECT MEDITATIONS, 183) MULTIMEDIA WORSHIP, 187) POP MUSIC POSSIBILITIES

74. PARENTING AN EGG

A friend gave me this idea. I was working with our youth on the demands and joys of parenting. I wanted a project which would help our youth understand what it means to be a parent.

I gave each member of the youth group a raw egg. They were to care for it during the next 48 hours. Each young person kept a journal of the experience. The instruction sheet was entitled, "My Egg—An Experiment in Sharing, Caring and Parenting." I in-

cluded the following explanation: "What is it like to be a parent? One way to discover some of the feelings is to be completely responsible for something which is vulnerable. This egg is in your care. For a period of 48 consecutive hours you are parent and guardian for this egg. It is breakable, it can be injured, and there are known cases in which eggs have been eggnapped and even held for ransom. One unfortunate egg was stolen on a school bus and dropped from the window. You must keep a journal and record events during your 48 hours including signed statements from baby sitters which include the time and fees paid." We also noted the condition of the egg upon its return.

The response to this experience was fantastic! We created more conversation with families from this project than any other church event in years. One fellow confessed that he would never be much of a father. "I was a terrible guardian of my egg," he said.

We shared our stories at the Sunday worship service. Some of the youth made houses for their eggs. Others colored them and put faces on them. One girl went to the store and got her egg a friend. I know that many folks have tried this experiment. However, this is a great idea. Imagine what a fine Lenten experience this would be!

Gabe Campbell
Akron, Ohio

See also 54) CHEAP ROLE PLAYS, 58) PARENT YOUTH ENCOUNTER, 59) THE WEEKEND PARTY, 72) CREATIVE CONJURING

75. A SPOONFUL OF HONEY

At one point in our youth group meeting when the energy seemed to be at a particularly low ebb, I passed around some tablespoons to the youth. I asked each person to look into the spoon and to share some of the pain or disappointment he or she had experienced recently. After an open reflection among the group, I passed around a jar of honey. Each person took some honey from the jar with the spoon. As they spooned the honey into their mouths, I talked about how God gave goodness even in the midst of stark pain.

Dr. Paul Perry
San Antonio, Texas

See also 24) SPINNING TOP, 49) ALL-NIGHT TALK, 67) AROMA, 76) TEA TIME, 176) COMMON OBJECT MEDITATIONS

76. TEA TIME

Tea bags were an important part of my first class session with the new eighth grade Sunday school class. I found a variety of tea bags at the local supermarket—strawberry leaves, peppermint, and ginger. I passed these around to the students and asked them to guess what the three ingredients were. They could identify the peppermint, but not the other two kinds. There were sounds of disdain about the unknown ingredients in the other two tea bags.

On the blackboard I wrote: "You don't know anything about this tea except that you don't like it." Then I gave everyone a cup of hot water. Everyone brewed a cup of tea. They tasted their tea and said it was a little better. On the board I wrote: "Adding hot water makes it better." Then I gave each

person a cookie, and they agreed that helped the tea taste better. I wrote on the chalkboard: "Adding a cookie to go with the tea helps even more." Then we discussed things and people in our lives that were as ugly as those tea bags, such as arguments

77. SPONGE BITS

I carried an empty drinking glass into my high school class with me. As we got into our lesson/discussion for the day, I told the class that their lives were like this glass. Describing the bits and pieces of their lives, I began dropping small pieces of a sponge into the glass. It seemed to become filled with the sponge, just as the lives of high school youth are so quickly filled up with school activities, friends, social events, etc. Then I poured water into the glass and the seemingly full glass was able to hold a considerable amount of water. It filled in the spaces and was absorbed by the sponge. In much the same way we talked about how Christ fills up our lives, moving in and through the various pieces and activities.

Mike Shaughnessy, Avon, Minnesota

See also 72) CREATIVE CONJURING, 176) COMMON OBJECT MEDITATIONS

with friends, teachers or parents.

I changed the first statement on the board to read: "You don't know anything about this person except that you don't like him." We talked about how adding the water and making a cup of tea made the unliked tea bag better; and how adding Jesus and his love to any situation makes it better.

Then I changed the second statement on the board: "Adding Jesus and his love makes it better." We talked about the love we are to have for others. We received the love of Jesus as a gift and we must do something also—because of his love, we love.

I changed the third statement by writing: "Adding our love helps even more." I passed out pieces of paper and envelopes and asked them to write the date, the person or situation that was troubling them, the ways in which they could add "water" (prayers, etc.), how they would add a "cookie" (their

love and understanding) and what they hoped would happen.

The young people sealed and addressed the envelopes to themselves. On the back of the envelopes they put an American Bible Society stamp which read, "There is a miracle inside you." (I collected the envelopes and mailed them to the students three months later.)

We moved on to a discussion on Paul's epistle. I wanted them to see that Paul saw situations that needed correction, so he wrote letters telling the people that Jesus would make a difference. He reminded them that their own actions, through Jesus' love, would change things.

E. Jane Mall
Westmont, Illinois

See also 36) PUT DOWN WEDGE, 38) GOSSIP BLOCKS, 39) SHORT PEOPLE, 67) AROMA, 75) A SPOONFUL OF HONEY, 82) LEMONS, 118) STOP AND SMELL THE ROSES, 176) COMMON OBJECT MEDITATIONS

78. LORD'S PRAYER DANDELIONS

One idea sparks another. It is neat to transform ordinary objects into teaching tools.

Our high school class was studying the Lord's Prayer, especially the phrase, "Thy kingdom come." The catechism (Reformed Church) explains "Thy kingdom come" as: "Rule us by your Word and Spirit in such a way that more and more we submit to you. Keep your church strong, and add to it. Destroy the devil's work; destroy every force which revolts against you and every conspiracy against your Word. Do this until your Kingdom is so complete and perfect that in it you are all in all." The answer is in the form of a prayer to Almighty God.

I wanted an unusual way to discuss the Lord's Prayer. I decided to recycle some of the dandelion plants I had in my yard. I pulled (root and all flower parts) enough weeds for my class and placed them in a shoe box.

At the class session I made a big deal about the surprise in the box. We first read and discussed the Lord's Prayer. Then I handed a weed to each student. (I provided paper towels with the plants.)

I asked the class to look at the world with "dandelion" eyes. What is your goal? (Spread over all.) What do you plan to do about grass that gets in your way? (Destroy it.) How do you plan to survive the summer? (Send roots down for strength.) How do you plan to cover the lawn? (Grow more plants from roots.) What is your hope? (All grasses and other weeds will submit to dandelion rule.) What will be your success? (When dandelions are all in all.)

The negative character of the dandelion (at least here in Iowa) was changed to the positive character of the spread of God's Kingdom.

Both the students and I found this a helpful way to see in a new way the commonly uttered prayer of our Lord.

Tom Hydren
Pella, Iowa

See also 9) BIBLE EXPLORATIONS, 15) WONDERS, 55) STUDENT/PARENT CONFIRMATION, 61) DISCIPLESHIP, 72) CREATIVE CONJURING, 82) LEMONS, 172) BURLAP, 176) COMMON OBJECT MEDITATIONS

79. HAPPINESS IS . . .

I'd like to pass on the highlights of one of our happiest Sunday mornings with our junior high Sunday school class. We began with some old, hardbound copies of "Happiness Is a Warm Puppy," and "Security Is a Thumb and a Blanket." Most folks will recall these "Happiness Is . . ." or "Security Is . . ." illustrated books.

Our class looked over the books for a few moments, and then I turned and wrote on the chalkboard, "Being a Christian is . . ." and left the rest up to their active imaginations.

Using brightly colored construction paper, crayons, and marking pens, the class worked together to make a single book, whose colorful pages were fastened together at the end through a hole in the side. I was very proud of some of the pages, such as "Being a Christian is taking time to enjoy beauty" (a hand-sketched illustration of Snoopy lying on his back on top of his house with a vase of flowers on his tummy). Others included, "Being a Christian is making friends with a lonely person," "Being a Christian is making others feel happy," and "Being a Christian is loving your neighbor."

Ken and Cathy Yost, St. Louis, Missouri

See also 11) COMIC STRIPS AND THE BIBLE, 68) SUPER SUNDAY, 154) RECIPE CARDS AND KIDS, 175) PNEUMA TIME

80. TV WISDOM

We have stimulated several discussion groups with the use of audio input. I have used audio tapes of the epilogue usually given at the close of the "Mork and Mindy" show. The youth in our group respond well to this kind of audio stimulation when it is well-focused on the topic that we are discussing. I have also used these audio pieces as a part of a slide presentation.

Beverly W. Rice
New Baltimore, Michigan

See also 183) MULTIMEDIA WORSHIP, 185) SLIDES AND PRAYERS, 186) DEAD FILMSTRIPS

81. REDACTION IN ACTION

I was working with the senior high Sunday school class on the redaction theory of scripture. The redaction theory maintains that several sources were edited into a single book in the Bible. The Book of Job is an example of the result of redaction.

I gave each class member a copy of Edward Arlington Robinson's poem "Richard Cory" (the Simon and Garfunkel version could also be used). They also received a copy of a recent newspaper article about a local suicide. They were given pencils, paper, paste and scissors. Each was to cut, paste and write transitions to combine the two original sources into a single continuous narrative.

After reading the results and looking at their appearance, we looked at modern translations of Job (which showed the difference between the prose and poetry). After noting the differences in prose and poetry content (e.g., the prose has Job a nomad with livestock, and the poetry has him a farmer), we talked about redaction theory and God's message of hope and comfort even in pain and suffering.

John Rawlinson, Oakland, California

See also 9) BIBLE EXPLORATIONS, 11) COMIC STRIPS AND THE BIBLE, 13) HOW-WE-GOT-OUR-BIBLE GAME

82. LEMONS

I am a lemon freak. I love lemons. It was a particular pleasure to travel in Australia. I could actually see lemons growing on trees in the backyards of my hosts! One Sunday morning, I was invited to lead the youth class of a large church. As we were leaving the house, I noticed the lemon tree. It was winter and the pieces of fruit were spotted, bruised and wrinkled. I filled a shopping bag with these discarded lemons.

The church school leader introduced me to the class. The 120 young people were not impressed when I was presented as an American who was going to show them how they should do Sunday school. These young people were raised on a school system which focused on hard, cold knowledge rather than on experiencing life as they learn.

I formed the group into clusters of six or eight teens. I read Isaiah 53 and gave a lemon to each group. "How does your lemon represent the idea of the Messiah or the suffering servant as presented by Isaiah? Pass the lemon around and share the first thoughts which come to your mind." There was a wall of silence. I started thinking about getting the car ready for a fast escape. Slowly the level of conversation began to increase. Soon the room was buzzing with discussion. After 10 minutes, I brought the group to order. I asked each cluster to share some of the comments. The insights were striking! The bruised and discarded fruit was related to the servant who was uncomely and disfigured.

The group really came alive when a 13-year-old boy said that he felt like a lemon. "If I accept Christ publicly, I will lose my mates," he said. The culture in Australia doesn't even pretend to be Christian. Most young people, in fact, have few friends who are Christians. Immediately another young person who was a bit older responded. "Hang in there, mate. You may lose some friends at first, but be faithful to Christ. You will gain real friends after a while." Others joined in to support this young person.

One classmate said, "Smell the room. Christians have a special smell!" The lemon odor filled the class. The handling of the fruit had released the rich lemon fragrance. After a parting prayer, the young people crowded around and thanked me for the morning. One young person stopped and asked if she could take the lemon home. It had special meaning to her now.

Dennis C. Benson
Pittsburgh, Pennsylvania

See also 12) DISCOVERY BIBLE STUDY, 15) WONDERS, 37) THE WALL, 67) AROMA, 72) CREATIVE CONJURING, 76) TEA TIME, 78) LORD'S PRAYER DANDELIONS, 176) COMMON OBJECT MEDITATIONS

FELLOWSHIP

COMMUNITY

Fellowship is a favorite youth group word. Some experts will claim that the strongest attribute of youth ministry is the sense of community that the young people and adults enjoy among one another. In fact, most parachurch youth programs are built around the fellowship aspect of the program. If youth are enjoying themselves, they will follow any creed and any leader. Unfortunately, many leaders abuse young persons' need for fellowship.

The community of saints is the foundation for the faith. It is the context in which the Holy Spirit is active. The communion of brothers and sisters in the faith is the birth of all worship, outreach, learning and sharing. It is this theology-reality which you are celebrating as you approach the fellowship dimension to your group.

We hope that you will not view this section as a collection of tricks to create community. The Holy Spirit has already created the community of faith. We are simply called to draw from this source.

In Christ there is no "Greek or Jew." Fellowship activities should be planned regarding young people as our equals in Christ. We should help them in their quest for maturity and all the uncertainty such a journey reveals. We are called to be aware of the school systems, economic status and other secular divisions among our youth. Fellowship helps to heal these divisions.

The items in this section will provide some exciting ways to battle those walls between people. They will help you restore the basic covenant relationship which God has maintained with his people. These contributions from our friends will provide many clues to good fellowship experiences.

It's often frightening and painful to give a great deal of yourself to another person. Yet, this giving is what faith is all about.

83. BEING THERE

Our church became interested in the relational model of youth ministry, and I developed for them a study based on perceptions, experiences, and observing others. The suggestion of this study is that youth ministry at its best involves "availability" to the youth on the part of many different people.

Youth ministry is the response by the entire Christian community to the needs and desires of youth as real people as they encounter God and others in the relationships of daily life. The response calls together the entire Christian community to minister to each other in openness, reconciliation and trust. A key to this process is "availability."

Availability for the pastor means:

- being responsive to the needs of youth.
- being able to listen with sensitivity and understanding.
- keeping your office door open—both physically and emotionally.
- being exposed to the things youth are exposed to.
- reinforcing positive values and openly forgiving negative incidents.
- asking youth questions and listening sincerely for their answers.
- letting young people see and share your humanity.
- supporting those who work with youth.
- being a part of the crucial decisions which young people must make.
- being where young people congregate, relating to them on a one-to-one basis, i.e., school and its activities.

Availability for the professional youth worker/youth pastor means:

- relating to all ages of youth in the church.
- being sensitive to the individual youth within the larger group.
- seeing each youth as a unique individual.
- being around and familiar with those places where youth "hang out."
- relating to all youth of the church and community, not just the "straight" or active youth.

- being excited about being a Christian.
- achieving a personal identity with the congregation's youth.
- being present at major youth activities.
- being free enough to sit down and relate personally with youth as their needs arise.
- being able to totally share your faith, values and goals with youth.
- encouraging youth to become responsible for ministering to others.
- trusting young people and their ability to be responsible.
- helping young people discover their talents.

Availability for the church member/volunteer youth worker means:

- assisting pastor/professional youth worker in any way possible.
- taking time to develop relationships with youth based on open and honest communication.
- listening to the feelings and frustrations of youth.
- supporting and encouraging youth activities.
- being open to the new ideas of youth even though they may conflict with "tradition".
- being contagiously excited about the things youth are doing and feeling.
- encouraging people who work with youth.

continued

BEING THERE

- being open to sharing authority in the church's decisions with youth.
- taking risks that allow youth to feel significant parts of God's kingdom.
- being more concerned about people than things.
- opening the church up to the community.
- actively seeking out ways to become involved with youth.

Availability for the church council means:

- keeping an open mind while supporting youth.
- seeing that young people are also given positions of responsibility.
- providing an open atmosphere in church, seeing that the church building is made available to youth at non-conventional times.
- sharing with the youth the goals and objectives of the church and its ministry.

Availability for the parent means:

- being interested and supportive in the youth program.
- talking with those working with youth, volunteering help whenever possible.
- sharing your time and resources.
- participating with youth as enablers and not disciplinarians.
- identifying with youth, their goals, dreams and ambitions.
- sharing openly in the ministry of the church as co-workers and co-searchers.

Availability for the district churches/clusters means:

- being open to share ideas, successes and frustrations.
- providing a larger group for fellowship and support.
- scheduling "big events" which single churches could not, such as retreats and special outreach ministries.
- providing opportunities for the cross-pollination and sharing of ideas, resources, and programs.
- forming cooperative task forces to meet the needs of the larger community.
- being the "yeast" which allows others to grow and develop.
- sharing facilities.

Availability for youth means:

- assuming responsibility for ministering to other youth.
- being yourself and accepting other youth as equals.
- being alert and sensitive to the lonely and alienated youth of today.
- befriending the newcomer.
- supporting each other in taking a stand for Christ.
- being understanding and accepting of the feelings of adult members of the congregation.
- developing patience.
- being willing to set priorities in favor of people rather than "fun" and excitement.
- being willing to ask what you can do rather than having to be told or asked to do something.
- being willing to be open and committed to the study of God's Word, the spirit of his love and the power of prayer.

Availability in youth ministry is a *people* ministry built on a person-based support system, sharing the community of Christ's love at all levels, allowing the Spirit to work and shape and guide that ministry. This system allows growth and development in the community of youth ministry in direct relationship to the people and resources available to the ministry of Christ to his disciples, the church, and the community.

Paul Krupinski
Minneapolis, Minnesota

See also 4) WHAT'S A LEADER?, 5) BIBLICAL LEADERSHIP, 32) CARING, 35) STAY FRESH . . ., 94) YOUTH LEADERS AND RELATIONSHIPS, 95) LEADER SUPPORT

84. JOGGING FELLOWSHIP

Our youth group didn't really have a good group identity. There were a number of kids attending but they weren't really working as a group. I knew that a number of the guys were active and liked to get rid of energy. Since I often get rid of extra energy by running, I dreamed up an idea. I started out by running to another boy's house and having him run with me. We ran to each other's houses until we had picked up the whole group. There were five to eight of us. The idea was that we would be running together. We had some great conversations along the way.

We then gradually ran each other home. The first we dropped off was the first who had been picked up. The last one was the boy who had joined us last. It wasn't an intellectual thing. We just enjoyed each other. I felt that those who ran together got along a lot better at our meetings.

Marc Gibson, Auckland, New Zealand

See also 85) STRETCH, 86) KARATE CHOP, 120) PIZZA FRISBEE, 121) PHYSICAL RISK, 141) WALK FOR HUNGER

85. STRETCH

Since being in good physical shape is an important part of our summer adventure camp for high school youth, we used to begin each day with calisthenics. But this year I tried something different. Instead of the routine exercises, we now do stretching exercises.

Several weeks before the camp began, I purchased a book of stretching exercises, read it carefully, and did daily stretching exercises myself. During camp the kids really enjoyed this new form of exercise. It provided a great deal of variety and actually prepared the young people for the climbing, canoeing and caving they did each day. Stretching exercises could become an interesting part of Sunday youth group activities, too.

Charles Martin, Pittsburgh, Pennsylvania

See also 84) JOGGING FELLOWSHIP, 86) KARATE CHOP, 121) PHYSICAL RISK

86. KARATE CHOP

Rev. Robert Connolly is a priest in our town who has found a wonderful way of reaching both youth and adults. As an assistant pastor at a local church, he draws upon a hobby of his own youth. He is highly skilled in the art of karate. He has been able to combine this ancient art with his Christian faith. In fact, he has found that the discipline is an excellent foundation for modern Christians.

Rev. Connolly runs weekly classes in the sport. Both men and women attend. He's seen a remarkable change in the lives of many of the youth. A sense of physical confidence frees many young people from the violence which fear breeds. Some of his young people have progressed far enough to teach others.

The demand for practice produces a sense of patience, missing from many of the experiences of contemporary culture. Youth learn karate in a gradual, disciplined style. I'm certain other youth could benefit from karate lessons from committed Christians.

Dan Reed, Natrona Heights, Pennsylvania

See also 35) STAY FRESH . . ., 84) JOGGING FELLOWSHIP, 85) STRETCH, 121) PHYSICAL RISK

87. STICKY FLAPS

I ordered a set of envelopes to go with a special letterhead. The package containing the envelopes somehow got soaked. They arrived with all the flaps glued securely to the envelopes. So I was stuck with a large pile of empty sealed envelopes.

Just before trashing the envelopes I got an idea. I compiled a list of all the youth who were absent the last few weeks from church school, youth fellowship, and confirmation class. I addressed an envelope to each young person and had a note typed on the back: "You will discover that this envelope is empty. There is nothing in it, only a wide and deep void. That is how we feel when you are absent from us. We feel empty. We miss your presence." It was signed, "The Youth Fellowship Cabinet and Randy Griffith."

Randy Griffith, Fort Lauderdale, Florida

See also 28) DEAR ME, 69) SUNDAY SCHOOL PUBLICITY BLITZ, 88) YOUTH DIRECTORY, 89) PHONE-A-THON, 156) REACH

88. YOUTH DIRECTORY

We consider our youth program at our church to be one of the vital ministries of the congregation. Knowing that the youth come from various schools and parts of the community, we have found it essential to publish an annual youth directory.

Each student's name, address, telephone number, school, and birthday (month and day) and grade in school is given. A school-by-school listing of our youth is also included. We made the directory as attractive as possible by adding artwork on the cover and throughout.

The directory has been helpful for our active youth to keep aware of the youth who were not quite as active in all the programs. As their leader, I use it nearly every day.

David Shaheen
Silver Spring, Maryland

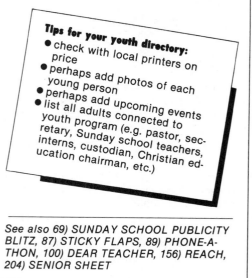

Tips for your youth directory:
- check with local printers on price
- perhaps add photos of each young person
- perhaps add upcoming events
- list all adults connected to youth program (e.g. pastor, secretary, Sunday school teachers, interns, custodian, Christian education chairman, etc.)

See also 69) SUNDAY SCHOOL PUBLICITY BLITZ, 87) STICKY FLAPS, 89) PHONE-A-THON, 100) DEAR TEACHER, 156) REACH, 204) SENIOR SHEET

89. PHONE-A-THON

A "phone-a-thon" is a way to make a young person feel very special. We organized them for birthdays, when someone is ill, when a person hasn't been around for several meetings, or for whatever other reason.

We organized a phone-a-thon to wish Jim a happy birthday. We sent a card to all the other youth saying, "May 5th is Jim's birthday. In order to make this a special day for a special person, we're planning a surprise phone-a-thon during which Jim's special friends will be calling to offer him happy birthday greetings. So that you don't get a busy signal, we have reserved a time slot for you at 7:30 a.m. The number is 222-1111. We hope that you will plan on being a part of this celebration."

We organized phone-a-thons for each person's birthday. When someone was ill, a phone-a-thon really perked up the sick person's spirits. Regardless of the reason for calling, young people sure enjoy talking on the phone.

Oscar E. Twedt
Valders, Wisconsin

See also 32) CARING, 69) SUNDAY SCHOOL PUBLICITY BLITZ, 87) STICKY FLAPS, 88) YOUTH DIRECTORY, 113) "I CARE" VALENTINES, 156) REACH

90. FALL DOWN HELLO

Our youth group has a special greeting. Whenever anyone in the club sees another member, he or she says "hi" and falls down. If we are walking down the street in the middle of a busy shopping center and see another member of the group, we have to say "hi," and fall over. The other person has to do the same thing or get the penalty. So far no one knows what the penalty is because nobody has ever failed to fall over.

Grant Nichol
Melbourne, Australia

See also 91) DEAD ANTS!, 119) BALL OF ENERGY

91. DEAD ANTS!

"Dead Ants" evolved from the soldiers in bars during World War II. To decide who paid for drinks, someone would yell out "Dead Ants!" The last person on his back with his hands and legs in the air had to pay for the drinks. The idea took off in our youth group. If we have dishes to wash, someone yells "Dead Ants!" The whole youth group in half a second is flat on the floor, hands and legs in the air. The last two or three on the floor must do the dishes. We ran a camp in the same way and the kids loved it. Every meal they would be waiting for a leader to yell "Dead Ants!" Sometimes we would yell it out and sometimes we wouldn't. At one of the country railroad stations someone yelled out, "Dead Ants!" The people in the station gazed in amazement at those kids lying on the floor with their hands and legs in the air. It is a zany thing that kids really like.

Grant Nichol
Melbourne, Australia

See also 90) FALL DOWN HELLO, 119) BALL OF ENERGY

92. AIR BANDS

We have utilized the "air band" concept. This design is quite simple and the kids love it. Choose a popular record and ask for "band" volunteers. Ask them to choose an instrument or vocal part in the record. The music is then played and the people on the stage mime singing, guitar pickin' and frantic drumming. It is amazing how they really get into the act. The participants and the audience love it. This is especially effective for large group activities.

Marcy Posner and Terry Caywood
Pittsburgh, Pennsylvania

See also 72) CREATIVE CONJURING, 119) BALL OF ENERGY, 127) TALENT NIGHT

93. SMALL GROUPS

I would like to share with you a model that we have used successfully with our junior highs. The emphasis is on small groups.

WHAT?

Situations in which smaller numbers of youth are brought together in terms of interest, community or tasks.

WHY?

To develop growing relationships with a few "significant others" and thereby develop leadership through shared cooperative work.

WHEN? WHERE?

Youth in their homes, church or special situations, such as retreats.

HOW?

1. Secure dedicated leaders from the congregation.

2. Set up workshops for these leaders to develop insights into the youth culture, techniques of building open relationships and confidence in themselves as youth workers.

3. Put these leaders into teams of four or more so that no one will feel totally alone or

94. YOUTH LEADERS AND RELATIONSHIPS

I made a radical career change. I was a civil engineer. Now I am a full-time youth ministry worker. It was a long agonizing process deciding whether I wanted to change occupations and get into youth ministry. The biggest factor in the decision was my observation that many youth workers I knew had poor relationships with their families. I had seen a youth worker's marriage fall apart.

I thought hard about going into youth ministry because my relationships with people are very important. I was not prepared to sacrifice them to youth work. I prayed a bit and talked about the career change with my girlfriend. She was supportive and encouraging. We openly shared the potential problems, not the least of which is sexual temptation.

I think if you are not careful, you can get into big trouble. I realize that in youth work there are young people who look at me and love me. It's a sort of hero worship. I look at them and try to give some love back. I put an arm around their shoulders or squeeze their hands from time to time. It is only a supportive thing. There are many different kinds of love and I think it is very important that the youth minister keep the love on a friendship level.

Stay away from heavy relationships in which people are always touching each other. It's easy to fall into temptation in touchy-feely situations.

Perhaps the best way to stay out of trouble is to be a professional. Professionals strive to keep the relationship with clients cordial, caring and helping. Professionals do not manipulate. Be careful to maintain an "intimate" distance between yourself and your group. That distance will keep you away from relationship-destroying temptations.

Grant Nichol
Melbourne, Australia

See also 1) TRY TO REMEMBER, 4) WHAT'S A LEADER?, 8) RECRUITING TEACHERS, 83) BEING THERE, 95) LEADER SUPPORT, 97) TRANSPARENCY, 99) SELF AWARENESS, 107) DIVERSIFY YOURSELF, 126) YOUTH MEMBERS FIRST

unable to schedule time for relating to youth.

4. Emphasize that the purpose of groups is to develop meaningful relationships among the youth and lay leaders. Openness, trust, forgiveness and freedom to be oneself are goals to work toward.

5. Provide resource ideas and materials to small group leaders.

6. Divide the youth into small groups to meet leaders and share some fun experiences together.

7. Develop a schedule of outreach tasks along evangelistic or social ministry lines for each group to do on a weekly or monthly basis.

8. Schedule periodic all-group activities.

Paul Krupinski
Minneapolis, Minnesota

See also 3) TEN YOUTH MINISTRY CONCERNS, 4) WHAT'S A LEADER?, 7) PLANNING STRATEGY, 14) JURY BIBLE STUDY, 23) DISCUSSION BASICS, 61) DISCIPLESHIP, 97) TRANSPARENCY, 99) SELF AWARENESS, 109) ROOM DYNAMICS, 161) YOUTH EVANGELISM

95. LEADER SUPPORT

Another youth leader can be a youth leader's life-support system. That's why our church's state office formed S.O.Y. (Sponsors of Youth). Youth group sponsors meet with each other to exchange ideas, share problems, and compare notes. **Soy Sauce** is the name of our newsletter.

We've held retreats which really fired up our youth sponsors. This first retreat focused on thinking about programs, service projects, fund raising and general policies. A large part of the retreat was designed to "hear" individual needs and suggestions. So, S.O.Y. asked each person to come prepared to share responses to four items:

1. Discuss your most miserable problem.
2. Share your most triumphant success.
3. Bring three resources you really find useful in working with your group.
4. Take a long look at the goals, needs,

etc., on the enclosed sheet. How would you add to or change it to meet your needs?

The sheet mentioned in number four is as follows:

The Problem

Our discussions with several sponsors and other youth leaders around the state reveal a common list of difficulties:

1. A need for support in efforts with youth. Typically this was couched in phrases like "Am I doing okay?"
2. A shortage of ideas for programs and service projects.
3. A separation from and a lack of communication with other youth groups and sponsors in the state. This has resulted in considerable duplication of efforts.
4. An unclear theology of youth ministry.
5. A feeling of isolation, resulting in depressed attitude about possibilities.

An Approach to the Problem

The best approach seems to be to form a support group for those involved in youth work. Since the problems affect both junior and senior high youth group leaders, all youth ministers and volunteer leaders should benefit from the state-wide support group.

Goals

Short Term:
1. Acquaint sponsors with one another.
2. Establish lines of communication between sponsors of youth.
3. Lay the foundation for a support group made up of all sponsors of youth in the state.
4. Compile a manual containing basic information and resources to all sponsors of youth in the state.

Long Term:
1. A "unified" approach to youth programming for state-wide events.
2. A broader base of youth program support.
3. Involvement of youth ministry in other forms of ministry.
4. Greater involvement of youth in life of the state and national levels of the church.
5. A strategy for recruiting sponsors.

Our first S.O.Y. retreat was a success (and a relief) for the participants. A common statement was "You, too? I thought I was the only one who had this problem?" Informal conversations seemed to help us "sharpen" each other. I think the support group model is an exciting idea for local churches. Youth leaders from several churches in a community should take time to join and share in a support group. The group may time and again act as a life preserver.

Quentin B. Jones
Shreveport, Lousiana

See also 1) TRY TO REMEMBER, 4) WHAT'S A LEADER?, 6) PLANNING SKILLS, 94) YOUTH LEADERS AND RELATIONSHIPS, 101) GROWTH THROUGH LOSS, 107) DIVERSIFY YOURSELF

96. BIG QUESTIONS

I work with a lot of youth leaders. I try to help them look at what youth ministry is all about. Does a church's youth ministry make a difference? Or is it simply something that we do because some adults in the church think that the kids in the church should have something planned for them? Does it make a difference in the kinds of things we feel, think, yearn and dream about?

During a training event for youth ministers and advisors, I ask them to examine a number of questions. What difference does your work back in your congregation make? Does the group really get after those questions that you really get excited about? Do you go below surface feelings? Where are the connection points between the group and how you feel about yourself? Does the local group deal with how youth relate to parents, friends or the other sex? Does the local group deal with life issues?

One way of looking at the validity of the youth group is to cast yourself into a situation in which a reporter is interviewing you on the street. He asks: "Who are you?" The reporter wants more than just the surface labels. "Give me a list of five or six of those characteristics which really tells me who you are," he demands. Does the local program touch these facets of our lives? This is the real test of a church's youth ministry.

Roland Martinson
St. Paul, Minnesota

See also 1) TRY TO REMEMBER, 3) TEN YOUTH MINISTRY CONCERNS, 4) WHAT'S A LEADER?, 5) BIBLICAL LEADERSHIP, 6) PLANNING SKILLS, 100) DEAR TEACHER, 107) DIVERSIFY YOURSELF

YOUTH MINISTRY PHILOSOPHY

97. TRANSPARENCY

Someone who is just starting out in youth ministry must be transparent. The people who stimulate the most positive comments from the kids are those who open up themselves. Leaders must reveal who they are inside. The adults who get no response from the youth are those who put a barrier between themselves and the young people. They want the youth to cross the barrier in discussions and then continue to hide behind it. One of our more popular youth advisors we have is a man in his late 50s who is willing to risk sharing his true self. The kids wanted him to continue as their teacher because he is not afraid to share personal reactions to whatever the class studies.

Stephen Johnston
West Willington, Connecticut

See also 1) TRY TO REMEMBER, 4) WHAT'S A LEADER?, 5) BIBLICAL LEADERSHIP, 16) BRICKS, 23) DISCUSSION BASICS, 35) STAY FRESH, 93) SMALL GROUPS, 172) BURLAP

98. PROBLEM SHARING

We have often found that there are many resources to be shared in a youth group. Sometimes one youth can provide fresh insight on another youth's problems.

A particular exercise that we have used to enable this kind of sharing is easy to do. Divide the group into pairs. One person shares a need or want, while the other listens carefully. The need or want may be better grades in school, direction for a career, new clothes, a better relationship with parents or brothers and sisters or whatever. Having listened to the other person's need, the listening partner has five minutes to quietly search the room for an object that would symbolize the fulfillment of that need or want. The person presents the object to his or her partner, explaining the object's symbolism.

Repeat the exercise, switching roles. After this, ask volunteers to share any new light shed on problems, needs or wants.

Donald W. Davidson
Kansas City, Missouri

See also 16) BRICKS, 23) DISCUSSION BASICS, 32) CARING, 34) NEIGHBORS AND FRIENDS, 49) ALL NIGHT TALK, 61) DISCIPLESHIP, 104) SHOPPING BAG VALUES, 138) OBJECT-IVE REFLECTIONS, 176) COMMON OBJECT MEDITATIONS

99. SELF AWARENESS

I've found it helpful to be aware of my feelings in the dynamics of youth ministry situations. I guess you might call this "situation dynamics."

Before I get to a youth group meeting, I take an informal inventory of the feelings churning inside me. Am I nervous because I'm not really prepared? Am I tired or ill? How will that affect me at the meeting?

If you recognize your own feelings, then you'll be able to take inventory of the situation at the meeting. If you are not aware of your feelings, you may be out of control and won't pick up the needs of the youth.

Yohann Anderson
San Anselmo, California

See also 1) TRY TO REMEMBER, 23) DISCUSSION BASICS, 93) SMALL GROUPS, 94) YOUTH LEADERS AND RELATIONSHIPS, 107) DIVERSIFY YOURSELF, 109) ROOM DYNAMICS

100. DEAR TEACHER,

Junior high and early teen years are times of great sensitivity and uncertainty about one's own self and qualities.

I had been working with a church school class of junior highs for almost a year and had really grown to love their many different strengths. I asked each student to write (privately) on a piece of paper what he or she thought that I (as the teacher) felt and thought about him or her. They were really quite shy about doing this task, but then proceeded with great sensitivity.

My response to each student was to write a personal letter, listing all the positive attributes that I appreciated and saw in that person. It is my hunch that lifting up those positive qualities may strengthen their development in the coming years.

Joan Eastley
Verona, Pennsylvania

See also 4) WHAT'S A LEADER?, 16) BRICKS, 27) OVER THE RAINBOW, 28) DEAR ME, 33) OPINION LINE-UP, 88) YOUTH DIRECTORY, 156) REACH

101. GROWTH THROUGH LOSS

The marriage and subsequent departure of our youth director was a painful time for the group. But it also gave us an opportunity to use that time to do some evaluation of the group. We talked a great deal about where the group had been and where we wanted to go. The next step was to outline goals for the future. We included these goals in the job description for the next youth director. The youth then became involved in the search for a person to fill the newly-defined youth director's position.

Carol Seibert
Barrington, Illinois

See also 4) WHAT'S A LEADER?, 95) LEADER SUPPORT

102. CHRISTMAS NOSTALGIA

For some unknown reason we had an unusual youth group meeting on a Sunday before Christmas. In a relaxed, cozy atmosphere, sparked by appropriate Christmas decorations and goodies, I asked the group to share some of their Christmas memories. What did they remember best? What was their first memory of Christmas? What was the happiest moment? What was the neatest gift they ever gave/received? What do they treasure about Christmas? The nostalgic feelings began to roll, and the youth really opened themselves up.

Timothy A. Morrison
Auburn, Maine

See also 153) CHRISTMAS OUTREACH, 154) RECIPE CARDS AND KIDS, 164) WORSHIP ENVIRONMENT, 207) PARTICIPATORY CHRISTMAS PAGEANT, 208) CHRISTMAS STORIES, 209) THE MESSAGE OF THE CAROLS

103. GRADUATION DINNER

I was not very happy with the traditional ways our church honored graduating seniors. On the Sunday morning service prior to graduation, few seniors would show up for the presentation of a gift book.

One year, an interested member of the congregation handed me $60 and told me to spend the money for the graduates. In addition to this gift he also offered to let us use his membership in a local business and professional club (which serves great meals).

I made reservations at the club for lunch following the Sunday morning worship service. All the invited seniors came. We used our time together to talk about the people who had been most inspiring to them in the past year. They also shared their plans for the coming year. Each graduating senior also received a gift book. It was a good time of fellowship, celebration and looking to the future.

Phineas A. Washer
Beaumont, Texas

See also 114) WELCOME BACK PLANTS, 203) PEANUTS AND BACCALAUREATE, 204) SENIOR SHEET, 205) BACCALAUREATE

104. SHOPPING BAG VALUES

We did an interesting exercise that helped all of us share with the group some of our feelings on values. Each person was given a shopping bag. During the next 20 minutes each person was to find an object of value. Each person looked for the object alone, placed it in the bag, and did not tell anyone what had been chosen.

As each youth returned, a number was marked on the shopping bag. After all had returned, I told the others what it was that I had chosen as an object of value. I shared with them "why" I chose this particular object. Then each person, in the order of the number marked on the bag, shared in a similar fashion with the group.

Ken Scarborough
Townsend, Delaware

See also 72) CREATIVE CONJURING, 73) MEDIA PROBING, 98) PROBLEM SHARING, 138) OBJECT-IVE REFLECTIONS, 171) PAPERBAG CONFESSIONS, 176) COMMON OBJECT MEDITATIONS, 210) SNOW WORSHIP

105. SPIRITUAL PUZZLE

I bought a United States map puzzle (the pieces were cut along state lines). I passed out pieces of the puzzle to the youth and asked them to work together to complete the puzzle. I gave some one piece, others several pieces, some large states and others small states. I purposely left out two or three states. As the puzzle was assembled, it became obvious that it couldn't be finished if some of the pieces were not there.

This led excellently into a discussion of the variety of spiritual gifts. Some may receive more spiritual gifts, but all have some spiritual gifts. This important point was made: The body of Christ cannot function as it should if everyone isn't participating or if someone is missing.

Charles Goza
Andrews, Texas

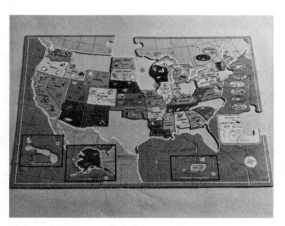

Idea on how to use this idea:
● Use with study on 1 Corinthians 12

See also 41) SENIORITIS, 46) HAVES AND HAVE NOTS, 87) STICKY FLAPS, 106) PICTURE PUZZLE CROWDBREAKER, 173) YARN WEB, 179) BIS-QUICK COMMUNION

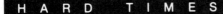

106. PICTURE PUZZLE CROWDBREAKER

I found a way to do a crowdbreaker with puzzles my children outgrew. These 10-12 piece puzzles are made for three- or four-year-olds. I jumbled two or three puzzles in a box and passed them out to a large group. Each person took a piece. Everyone had to find the other members of the group who had pieces of the same puzzle. When the puzzles were assembled, we had a number of small groups.

Another way of using this idea is to take a 4 feet by 5 feet card and cut it into puzzle-like pieces. You can also use a poster or some other big picture for this puzzle. I have also pasted large-print material on cardboard, such as Jesus' parables. The cardboard was then cut into pieces. When the group members assembled the pieces, they discussed the parable. This process provides an excellent discussion spark.

Obid Hofland
New Haven, Connecticut

See also 68) SUPER SUNDAY, 105) SPIRITUAL PUZZLE

107. DIVERSIFY YOURSELF

While you work with young people, be sure to find someone else your own age to relate to. Better still, organize a support group to help you clarify and grow in your ministry. And, be a part of a Wednesday morning Bible study, choir or other group that you enjoy as a member. In short, balance your roles in the church. As you freely give, make sure your own spiritual needs are satisfied in the church.

Susan Hay, Nashville, Tennessee

See also 1) TRY TO REMEMBER, 4) WHAT'S A LEADER?, 94) YOUTH LEADERS AND RELATIONSHIPS, 95) LEADER SUPPORT

108. FIVE-PART MEETING DESIGN

After much trial and error, we found a design/format for our Sunday evening youth fellowship that seemed to provide a good variety of experiences for our high school youth. The evening usually contained several segments out of the following group: team games, humorous skits, biblical message and brief worship, and a short media show.

The youth produced a new media piece almost every week. These presentations were the favorites of the high school youth. Usually two slide projectors or two movie projectors were used. The show was never over three to five minutes in length. Discussion always followed.

We encouraged the members of the group to bring their friends to these evenings of enjoyment, and the group is still growing.

Steve Knox
Alhambra, California

See also 3) TEN YOUTH MINISTRY CONCERNS, 68) SUPER SUNDAY, 183) MULTIMEDIA WORSHIP, 186) DEAD FILMSTRIPS

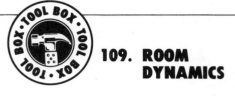

109. ROOM DYNAMICS

Instead of the ordinary ways of sitting on the floor in a circle or in chairs around tables, why not try a different room dynamic? Instead of setting up as always, divide the group into two subgroups. The leader sets up in the middle, between these subgroups. It's a nice change of atmosphere.

Yohann Anderson
San Anselmo, California

See also 23) DISCUSSION BASICS, 68) SUPER SUNDAY, 93) SMALL GROUPS, 99) SELF AWARENESS, 110) BILLBOARD WALLPAPER

110. BILLBOARD WALLPAPER

Creating an exciting learning environment is a challenge—especially when that environment is a sterile church basement. We found billboard ads a terrific way to create a warm atmosphere. Billboard art comes in large sections of heavy paper. It is applied like wallpaper. Contact your local outdoor billboard advertising company. They often have extra sections of ads. You will be surprised how these sections really add color and action to a sterile basement.

Dale Duncan-Smith
Chicago, Illinois

See also 109) ROOM DYNAMICS, 116) GROUP BANNER

111. MELT THE DEVIL

Those of us who live in the northern United States sometimes feel confined by the drastic weather changes. Our group found an interesting use of the environment during a winter retreat. Our theme for this retreat was an exploration into evil. As a part of this event, we built a huge "devil" out of snow. Red vegetable dye converted the snowman into a real "devil." After discussing the theme, we gathered around the sculpture and began pouring pails of water on it. As the devil melted, we talked about the power of water as used in baptism.

Gary Logan
Fremont, Ohio

See also 138) OBJECT-IVE REFLECTIONS, 177) LIVING WATER, 194) ON THIS ROCK, 210) SNOW WORSHIP

112. KITE DAY

We made good use of March winds by having the high school youth make kites. They discussed the relationship between kites and the Christian life. On the day we had set aside as "Kite Day," the youth came with their homemade kites. It was a striking sight to see the dozens of floating creations. Each kite had a prayer concern painted on it. A young person observed that when we floated the kites our prayers were lifted up.

Keith Curran
Amsterdam, New York

See also 176) COMMON OBJECT MEDITATIONS, 192) IDEAS FROM OTHER CULTURES

113. "I CARE" VALENTINES

As Valentine's Day approached, our Sunday school class decided to undertake a project which would benefit both the members of the congregation and the class. We decided to solicit, create and deliver "I CARE" Valentine greetings in our church.

Three weeks before Valentine's Day, we signed people up for "I CARE" valentines during a coffee fellowship. We wrote down the valentine's recipient and its message. The cost was 10 cents per "I CARE" greeting. The class made the greetings the next two Sundays during the church school session and handed them out to the congregation the Sunday just before Valentine's Day. The folks savored their Valentine messages. Also, we earned enough money to buy a table for the classroom.

Donna Ackerman and Donna Richards
Covina, California

Ideas on how to use this idea:
● can create and simply give away—fund raising not essential
● good meeting idea
● perhaps add scripture

See also 89) PHONE-A-THON, 114) "WELCOME BACK" PLANTS, 154) RECIPE CARDS AND KIDS, 155) PALM SUNDAY FAIR

114. "WELCOME BACK" PLANTS

The folks at our church have an interesting way of saying, "Welcome back" to the college students when they return each September to this college town. During the year the congregation is encouraged to root cuttings of coleus, impatiens, geraniums, Swedish ivy, and other suitable plants. These are potted and attractively prepared by the middle of August. We give these small plant offerings to the students at enrollment time as a symbol of the church's care for them.

Stephen Fletcher
Lawrence, Kansas

See also 103) GRADUATION DINNER, 113) "I CARE" VALENTINES

Retreats are one of the most unforgettable youth ministry programs your group will ever experience.

115. RETREAT CHECKLIST

Retreats bring some of the best growth moments for youth. However, details in planning are very important for the success of these special times. Here is my checklist for a youth outing:

RETREAT CHECKLIST

- [ ] when are we going?
- [ ] where are we going?
  - do we need reservations?
  - how much for lodging?
- [ ] food
  - how much?
  - menu?
  - who will buy?
  - how much cost?
  - who will clean up?
- [ ] who is going?
  - who needs a special invitation?
  - counselors?
    - who and how many?
- [ ] transportation
  - when will we leave?
  - when will we return?
- [ ] what needs to be done when we first arrive?
- [ ] theme of retreat
  - resources
  - films, projectors, etc.
- [ ] worship
  - when?
  - who will lead?
  - where?
  - special resources?

- [ ] singing?
- [ ] recreation?
- [ ] other events or programs?
- [ ] other resources?
- [ ] goal or hope for retreat
  - (list two or three)
- [ ] lights out time
- [ ] sleeping arrangements
- [ ] free time
- [ ] any special rules?
- [ ] publicity for retreat
  - who will do it?
  - how long before?
- [ ] weather problems
  - what if it rains, snows, etc.?
- [ ] what needs to be done to make whole group welcome?
- [ ] in case of emergency or accident, where is the nearest clinic or hospital?
- [ ] other
- [ ] now, why is it we are going?
- [ ] *LET'S GO!!!*

Wesley D. Taylor
Oregon City, Oregon

See also 6) PLANNING SKILLS, 51) MOUNTAINTOP TO PLAIN, 52) RETREAT FEEDBACK

116. GROUP BANNER

In an attempt to build the idea of a community at an area-wide event for junior high school students, I came up with the idea of making a community banner. Each young person received a small felt square as he or she registered for the event. The youth were then directed to a table where there was a variety of materials available for them to create their mini-banners. Each person was instructed to put his or her name on the front side of the banner. While the group was involved in the first session of the retreat, I went to work with my portable sewing machine and stitched all of the pieces together. When the young people returned to the main meeting room for the evening meal, they found their banner covering one wall. They were all symbolically joined together.

Katherine Ingleheart, Kansas City, Missouri

See also 27) OVER THE RAINBOW, 110) BILLBOARD WALLPAPER, 172) BURLAP

117. FREE TIME RETREAT

Kids seem to love free time at retreats. We decided to give the young people a full free day. Everyone was told the day before that the next day would be completely free. They could do exactly as they liked.

When everybody got up in the morning, they discovered that the cooks were free also and there was no breakfast. This, of course, brought all kinds of gasps about what was going to be done. Interestingly, the kids formed groups to get work done. Some even elected to cook the cook's breakfast. They had a time to do their own thing. Everything was a group decision. We believe the youth learned that discipline is essential, especially in youth groups. It was a great exercise for teaching that freedom involves great organization and hard work.

Diane Hoag
Townsville, Queensland

See also 52) RETREAT FEEDBACK, 115) RETREAT CHECKLIST

118. STOP AND SMELL THE ROSES

I once read that our sense of smell is directly rooted in the brain's memory system. Certain odors evoke years-old memories. We tested this theory in our group.

We used the fragrance of the rose at a junior high camp to help young people associate the scent with the camp experience. We made mealtime table centerpieces with roses the cook brought from her garden. I purchased rose scented solid air fresheners for each cabin. Prior to some of our gatherings during the week, I sprayed the meeting area with rose scented aerosol air freshener.

One evening we had a foot washing service at the swimming pool. I washed and dried the counselors' feet; they did the same for their youth. I squirted a dab of Rose Milk cream on each person's hand. I then asked everyone to turn to a person sitting next to them and rub the lotion into the backs of that person's hands. This was a very tender, "touching" experience that created greater community among youth and leaders.

The scent of the rose became special with our group. Several campers said they remembered the week every time they smelled a rose.

Lynn Potter
Mount Ayr, Iowa

See also 52) RETREAT FEEDBACK, 67) AROMA, 72) CREATIVE CONJURING, 76) TEA TIME, 82) LEMONS, 138) OBJECT-IVE REFLECTIONS, 172) BURLAP, 179) BISQUICK COMMUNION

119. BALL OF ENERGY

Young people (like the rest of us) love to laugh. No kidding. We designed a weekend retreat which used what came to be known as a "ball of energy." We first got the kids to laugh and immediately directed that energy into messages of Jesus Christ. Here are a few examples.

We opened an evening with the "movie" skit. Four chairs were placed in the front of the room. I played the straight man. I was the square pastor. We introduced the experience by stating that this man is coming into the movie theatre. I sat down with a bag of popcorn. Next, a messy person came into the scene. He then mixed the popcorn with bubblegum and finally spat it on my coat. A man dressed in women's clothes sat down next to the messy man. They started necking. Then a woman dressed as a man came into the scene. She played the husband of the woman. A fight broke out and everything ended up on me. I continued to ignore what was going on. The husband and wife finally left. The messy person was all beaten up. He sat down next to me and asked, "Don't you care about anything?" I then stood and sprayed whipped cream all over his head. I

put a cherry on his head and walked out.

By this time, the whole place was rolling with laughter. We quickly organized into small groups. We got them very close and had them discuss how people are treated. What is our responsibility to others as Christians?

As the weekend unfolded, we would interrupt an event with brief commercials. For instance, a person appeared before the group while an off-stage announcer proclaimed that M&M candies do not melt in your hand. The performer showed M&M's in his hand. The voice then informed us that "they do melt in your mouth." At this the person opened his mouth and chocolate streamed out of it. He had poured half a can of chocolate into his mouth before coming before the group.

At the dinner times, an empty pill bottle was placed at each person's place. Each contained directions to do something crazy to another eater. One, for example, was to eat off a neighbor's plate.

After each "ball of energy," we gathered as a staff and evaluated the flow of the event. We knew what we had planned, but we checked on what adjustments should be made in light of the group's reaction.

We had one girl at the retreat who risked coming. She had a lot of emotional problems and had just joined the youth group. She was sitting off by herself at the beginning. We asked another youth to be her Christian friend for the weekend. They became very good friends. The humor helped ease tension. When the humor was related to Christ, I believe the kids were reached with his message.

James Boos
Saxonburg, Pennsylvania

See also 32) CARING, 52) RETREAT FEEDBACK, 90) FALL DOWN HELLO, 91) DEAD ANTS!, 92) AIR BANDS, 115) RETREAT CHECKLIST, 129) COME AS YOU AREN'T LOCK-IN

120. PIZZA FRISBEE

We had a group of junior high youth who had not yet truly become a group. Some of the kids were rather withdrawn, others a bit stuffy, and some aloof. I hit upon an idea as I purchased some frozen pizzas for the youth group's snack (the kind that are sealed in plastic with a cardboard backing).

As group meeting began that afternoon, I tossed one of the frozen pizzas, like a Frisbee, to one of the youth in the group. It caught on very quickly, and soon we were into a pizza version of Frisbee. Everyone was drawn into the action. By the end of the meeting there was much more unity in the group.

By the way, call a halt to the Frisbee game before the pizza becomes too tattered to eat.

Randy Scheer
Sterling, Kansas

See also 84) JOGGING FELLOWSHIP, 93) SMALL GROUPS

Support, trust, caring become more than words when a group shares risky experiences together.

121. PHYSICAL RISK

Several years ago I rafted down the Rio Grande with several other adults. We had to work together or end up taking a splash in the river. Rock climbing and hiking also were part of the week. This one-week barrage of experiences helped me put some things back together in my life that had sort of been loosened up and scattered around.

The elements of physical challenge and risk helped me see the possibilities of adventure experiences with Christian youth. I like to take them out of the comfort of the church walls and challenge them to stretch their limits. They learn how to trust, how to be responsible, how to care, how to cooperate and how to be a friend.

Even if you can't take your group hiking, or rafting or whatever, you can do some risking adventures on the church grounds. (Read the next page for specific activities.) It's amazing to see people come alive in these risking situations. The support from others and sense of accomplishment are rewards for taking risks. The youth readily connect these risks and rewards to those in the Christian life.

Earl Sires
Cleveland, Ohio

See also 35) STAY FRESH . . ., 84) JOGGING FELLOWSHIP, 85) STRETCH, 86) KARATE CHOP, 157) SKATEBOARD OPEN, 189) SING OUT

ADVENTURE CAMPING

Try a weekend version of adventure camping. Set up the following simple obstacles. Then divide into teams of five or six and turn the teams loose on the following course. Debrief afterward. Get some construction trade guys in your church to help you set up the course.

1. **The wall:** Make an imaginary wall by stretching a rope between two trees about five feet above the ground. The objective is to get the entire team over the rope without touching it or any other part of the wall.

2. **The platform:** Suspend a three-foot square piece of plywood about five feet off the ground. (Use heavy plywood, chains and heavy eyebolts.) The object is to get the entire team onto the platform.

3. **Rope bridge:** Check the **Boy Scout Handbook** for directions on constructing a rope bridge. Get the ropes and have the teams construct the bridge. Then have fun crossing it.

4. **The gorge:** Place two platforms about 12 feet apart. (Plywood placed solidly on two sawhorses for each platform works well. Give each team two 2-inch × 6-inch boards, each eight feet long. The object is to get the group from one platform to the other using only two boards and the team's ingenuity.

"The Wall," a 14-foot obstacle, is just one challenge you can use in a homemade version of adventure camping.

122. MID-WINTER SUMMER CAMP

It is often difficult to stir up enthusiasm about summer camps during the frigid winter months. However, that is when planning must be done.

We decided to go all out in our promotion of the summer camping program. We picked a Sunday in March and called it "Camping Sunday." Youth and their parents were invited. They arrived to find the fellowship hall filled with pitched tents, a canoe (complete with paddles and life-jackets), a fire area with real rocks and wood and many other camping items. Posters and pictures relating to the natural world covered the walls. The group sang camp songs and read Psalm 33:1-9, which tells the beauty of God's creation. Slides from previous camps were shown while campers talked about their experiences. It was a fine evening of enthusiasm for the coming summer camping program.

Michael F. Miller
St. Paul, Minnesota

See also 123) CAMP TAPES, 136) THE WOOD CARVER'S GIFT, 137) WORKCAMPING

123. CAMP TAPES

Leading an adventure camp for high school youth has been an activity I have enjoyed being involved in for the past several summers. This kind of experience enables the young person to face the challenge of mountains, caves, streams and weather in the context of Christian fellowship.

In preparation for the summer event, I had interviewed the camp leaders. After editing their comments into a 60-minute cassette, I sent a copy of these edited comments to each registrant prior to the camp. Many questions that would be asked were quickly answered on the tape. In addition, the new registrants were much better able to pick up

124. YOUNG PEOPLE AS LEADERS

the "flavor" of this camping experience than they would be able to do from print alone.

During the adventure camp, I interviewed the youth about what they were experiencing physically and about their feelings in regard to these experiences with nature. Their responses were amazing, and I am now using this material to build the tape that will be sent out prior to next year's camp. I feel very good about the fact that we have now gathered many of the stories of these youth which would be quickly forgotten or very hard to retrieve at another time. We also have an audio history of our adventure camp.

Charles Martin
Pittsburgh, Pennsylvania

See also 122) MID-WINTER SUMMER CAMP, 138) OBJECT-IVE REFLECTIONS, 206) WEDDING CASSETTE

Kids are responsible for most of what happens in our group. We have some real problems, some real weaknesses. But it is amazing how people pull together and pull us through. We have had our share of flops. I am surprised the church would hire me if they knew my record of flops from the last church where I was. But in our flopping and fooling around, and in making our mistakes, I think the kids learn some tremendous valuable lessons about the way life really is. It also gives them a lot of confidence.

We probably had the only church spaghetti dinner in the country that didn't have any spaghetti! They put it in the pan before the water was boiling, and it all sunk to the bottom. It took us about three hours to feed 125 people because we had to run out to the store and buy more spaghetti. The kids had worked so hard. The salad was ready, the dessert was ready, the sauce was ready, but not the spaghetti. The one fellow who led this event had a tough time. Mark had to

deal with running the kitchen, getting things organized, etc.

Later we went to Maine with a group of kids during the summer, and he was the leader. When the group had some real hassles, it was Mark who calmed everyone and said, "Now, what can we do to pull together?" Here again was that theme of something out of nothing. Here was a fellow, an average sort of guy, who became the leader. He had emerged.

Adults need to guide things along, but not control with an iron fist. If something doesn't go quite right, sit everyone down and debrief the problem. Once it is worked out, return responsibility and control to the group.

Tiff Bates
Elgin, Illinois

See also 4) WHAT'S A LEADER?, 7) PLANNING STRATEGY, 57) LET YOUTH TEACH, 125) LET THEM LEAD. 126) YOUTH MEMBERS FIRST, 198) THE "CALL"

125. LET THEM LEAD

We give young people jobs which they are capable of doing. Our clerk (who is also an elder) began her job at age 19. We appointed two young men, ages 17 and 15, "associate trustees," and put them in charge of some work projects at the church. They took on their calling quite well and performed several essential jobs around the church.

Roger Kemp
Crittenden, New York

See also 4) WHAT'S A LEADER?, 7) PLANNING STRATEGY, 57) LET YOUTH TEACH, 124) YOUNG PEOPLE AS LEADERS, 199) "I WILL SERVE THE CHURCH"

126. YOUTH MEMBERS FIRST

We owe a great deal of respect to the youth member. He or she deserves integrity in the planning, developing, membership development and personal relationships of Christian youth groups. The whole power of the youth group, we feel, lies in the members and their communion with God, rather than the spotlight always on the youth director as "star."

The personal needs of young people are the needs that have been around forever. Self-image is important. A youth group can do so much to build self-image and relationships with peers. A youth group can do it like no other group can. Some groups are successful at it and some are not. Again, that all goes back to our philosophy of putting the power in the hands of the members. They have a great deal of power to fulfill their own needs within the group if they can develop that kind of community and communion among themselves as members.

A youth worker, either lay or professional, really needs to fulfill the role of a servant. A youth leader does not need to have a sparkling personality or bundles of original ideas. A youth leader needs the ability to love. It is the hard kind of love that lasts month after month, year after year. Kids need adults who love them, who will listen to them and be there week after week, month after month, and year after year.

Thom Schultz
GROUP Magazine
Loveland, Colorado

See also 1) TRY TO REMEMBER, 4) WHAT'S A LEADER?, 7) PLANNING STRATEGY, 94) YOUTH LEADERS AND RELATIONSHIPS, 124) YOUNG PEOPLE AS LEADERS

127. TALENT NIGHT

Our group wanted to recapture the enchantment of "homemade" entertainment with maximum participation. So, we sponsored a "talent night" at our church which involved minimal work and reaped lots of fun.

We recruited 17 acts, varying from a beautiful piano/flute duet by a father and daughter to someone retelling camp-like yarns. A mock hillbilly band was great fun. A sing-along was a fantastic climax to the talent night.

Make sure you secure a good emcee, someone who will be familiar with the acts and has a crazy sense of humor.

David F. Keller
Pittsburgh, Pennsylvania

See also 42) CAMP PRODUCTIONS, 92) AIR BANDS, 128) "COMPUTER" DATING NIGHT, 129) COME AS YOU AREN'T LOCK-IN

128. "COMPUTER" DATING NIGHT

"Computer Dating Night" was an experience we used to enable youth to enjoy a "computer" date for one or two hours. This experience was then used as the common ground for a discussion on loneliness and desperation.

As the youth arrived, they were given a form and a pencil. (The form asked for name, interests, etc.) They deposited the form in a large box which was decorated—lights and all—to resemble a computer. We gathered the group to explain the evening's program. We then saw "Comput-her-Baby," a four-minute film available from various film distributors. After the film, couples were matched by the "computer." Each couple met and left the room before the next couple was called. (If the number of boys and girls is not equal, the ones not getting assigned dates joined another couple.)

Various dating sites were set up on the church property, each one with adult supervision. For an hour, couples, double dates or group dates enjoyed a snack place, table game room, miniature golf, roller skating on parking lot, bowling (plastic kind in a room or hallway) and movie (a classic, short, silent comedy, such as "Two Tars" by Laurel and Hardy, available at your local library).

All couples reassembled at an appointed time and discussed (as couples) the items on response sheet #1 for 10 minutes. They then joined another couple and listened to Janis Ian sing "Seventeen." Then they discussed response sheet #2 for 15 minutes. After some group discussion, we closed in prayer.

D. Ray Wiggins
Brentwood, Tennessee

See also 18) THE PRODIGAL DAUGHTER/SON, 41) SENIORITIS

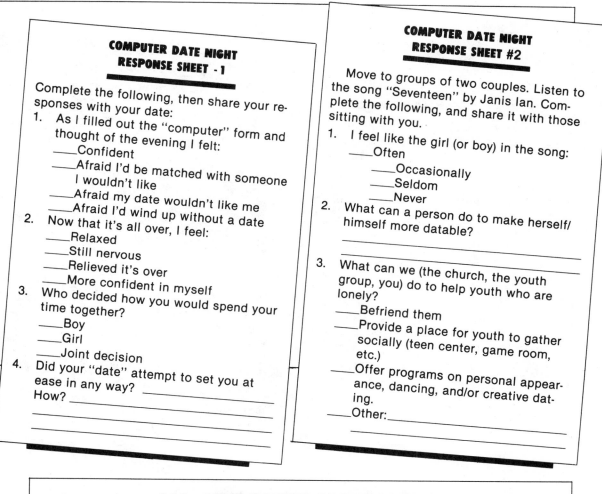

COMPUTER DATE NIGHT RESPONSE SHEET - 1

Complete the following, then share your responses with your date:

1. As I filled out the "computer" form and thought of the evening I felt:
   ——Confident
   ——Afraid I'd be matched with someone I wouldn't like
   ——Afraid my date wouldn't like me
   ——Afraid I'd wind up without a date

2. Now that it's all over, I feel:
   ——Relaxed
   ——Still nervous
   ——Relieved it's over
   ——More confident in myself

3. Who decided how you would spend your time together?
   ——Boy
   ——Girl
   ——Joint decision

4. Did your "date" attempt to set you at ease in any way? How? _____
   _____
   _____

COMPUTER DATE NIGHT RESPONSE SHEET #2

Move to groups of two couples. Listen to the song "Seventeen" by Janis Ian. Complete the following, and share it with those sitting with you.

1. I feel like the girl (or boy) in the song:
   ——Often
   ——Occasionally
   ——Seldom
   ——Never

2. What can a person do to make herself/himself more datable?
   _____
   _____

3. What can we (the church, the youth group, you) do to help youth who are lonely?
   ——Befriend them
   ——Provide a place for youth to gather socially (teen center, game room, etc.)
   ——Offer programs on personal appearance, dancing, and/or creative dating.
   ——Other:_____
   _____

129. COME AS YOU AREN'T LOCK-IN

Our youth fellowship has had very good experiences with lock-ins. We usually hold them for 12-hour periods (7 p.m. to 7 a.m.) at the church, with continuous activities: games, movies, skits, food, etc. People are encouraged to stay up all night, but they do bring sleeping bags and can collapse in the sanctuary when it becomes necessary.

"Come As You Aren't" is a fun variation that we have tried. Each person comes as someone else. The person decides who she/he wants to be and then dresses, talks, and acts like that person. Darth Vader, St. Paul, Robin Hood, Red Riding Hood, O.J. Simpson, etc., have come to our lock-ins. It's a lot of fun, but very hard to stay in character.

Roger Kemp, Crittenden, New York

See also 54) CHEAP ROLE PLAYS, 119) BALL OF ENERGY, 127) TALENT NIGHT, 158) CLOWNING OUTREACH

130. PRAYER CHAIR

Our youth group has developed an interesting tradition. We have often made use of what we call a "prayer chair." During retreats, or at times of close fellowship, a member of the group may choose to sit in this prayer chair. The others gather around. It is a time of prayer both for the person's concern and a time when the person in the chair may offer prayers. This is an intense time. We have had many amazing moments using the prayer chair.

Jack Kelly
Bethel Park, Pennsylvania

See also 126) YOUTH MEMBERS FIRST, 164) WORSHIP ENVIRONMENT, 173) YARN WEB, 181) LIGHT AND DARKNESS, 185) SLIDES AND PRAYERS, 196) STEP INTO THE OFFERING

131. CAR POOLS

When gasoline prices exploded, car pools became essential to our youth ministry. Our youth group members did not know where each other lived. So we printed up a map of the area with the exact location of each of our members, including the inactives. We gave the list to each youth and parent along with the regular list of members' addresses and phone numbers. Many inactives became active because rides and friendship were offered.

Jan Otto
Gig Harbor, Washington

See also 135) MAGIC BUS

154

132. THE GREAT PUMPKIN (OR WHATEVER) HUNT

Each year we sponsor a Halloween "Great Pumpkin Hunt" which has become very popular. The hunt is always fun and requires a little detective work.

Here are the instructions we pass out and read before the hunt:

1. You will receive one clue here (at the beginning point). Figure out what it means; go to that place to receive your next clue.

2. When you arrive at the next place, if you see anyone who looks like he or she may be a part of the hunt, go to that person and say, "Do you know where the Great Pumpkin is?"

3. If you ask the right person, he or she will respond with a clue to the next place to look by saying, "No, but I know where to look." Then you'll receive the next clue.

4. If you cannot figure out the next clue at any point within a reasonable amount of time, go by Charlie's house and get help on it.

Here are the clues we used:

1. Love 'em in the morning, when you see the dough a risin',
Go there in the evening, 'cause you'll get the clue today. (donut shop)

2. Don't bust your belt looking for this dude,
You'll probably find this clue at a place you eat food. (Dairy Queen)

3. We had lots of fun this summer each week,
As we got our exercise, now you know where to seek. (volleyball court)

4. You'll be all wet and you'll most likely fret,

If you can't guess the place where on July Fourth the town met. (city lake)

5. The father is a deacon, his wife is a teacher,
The youth are both active, by knocking you'll reach her. (A youth's home)

6. If you can't find this you'll really be sick,
So go there to wait, you'll get the clue quick. (hospital waiting room)

7. And now to this place you'll sure want to hurry,
And there we will meet you. Their last name is Furry.

These clues, of course, are simply a model. Other groups will need to create their own clues.

Other seasonal hunts might be fun: Great Snowman Hunt, Great Suntan Queen Hunt or Great April Fool's Hunt.

Charles Goza
Andrews, Texas

See also 131) CAR POOLS, 135) MAGIC BUS, 151) THANKSGIVING SCAVENGER HUNT, 190) A.D. 81

Variations of the well-known progressive dinner can spice up your youth meetings.

133. PROGRESSIVE DINNERS

Probably every youth group has had a "progressive supper," a supper served in three or four courses, each at a different location (usually in homes). The group "progresses" from appetizer to salad to main course to dessert. Here are some different ways to do a progressive supper:

1. Travel by bicycle, roller skates, skateboards, or any other kind of wheels (except cars).

2. Serve courses outdoors, picnic style.

3. Eat each course in a different restaurant, such as

- Appetizer at a health food store (juices, nuts, etc.)
- Salad at a pizza place
- Main course at a hamburger place
- Dessert at an ice cream place

4. Use four rooms in the church. Decorate them to represent four different foreign mission areas of your church. Serve the native foods of those areas. Briefly present each mission through slide shows, panel discussions or talks.

5. American ethnic meals can help youth become aware of other people's life settings. They can also deal with prejudice. Serve soul food and present information on black Americans; Polish food with a look at Polish jokes; Indian food; etc. In each case the group can deal with misinformation and generalizations regarding each ethnic group. This can really be a lot of fun and a great learning experience!

6. "Serve a scripture progressive supper" in which a passage of scripture and a group experience are set up at each course. Any kind of food can be used at each location.

● **Appetizer:** The group forms a circle on the lawn of the host's home. Read John 13:1-16. The leader explains why foot washing was a custom in a time of sandals and dirt roads and how Jesus used this task to teach his disciples about servanthood. A comparable custom in our time is the washing of hands before a meal, usually done alone, but this time the group members will wash one another's hands and all that is needed is a basin of water, a wet towel, and a dry towel. This can be done in silence, or the scripture read again or songs sung.

● **Salad:** The group forms a circle on the lawn of the host's home. Read Luke 14:16-24 regarding the parable of The Great Banquet. The leader points out that Jesus has invited all to believe yet many still give excuses for not giving ourselves to him.

● **Main Course:** The group circles up as before. Read Matthew 25:31-46; then present information on world hunger. Then read Luke 12:42-48. Encourage all to do what they can for the poor, hungry and oppressed.

● **Dessert:** Group circles up as before. Read John 21:4-17 where Jesus tells Peter, "If you love me, feed my sheep." Follow this with a modern day parable about the man who was given a glimpse of hell and heaven. Taken to hell, he saw people sitting at a lavish banquet, but all were in great grief due to the fact that long utensils had been strapped to their arms so that their elbows could not bend; therefore, they could not feed themselves. Then he was taken to heaven where he saw the same lavish banquet and the same utensils strapped to the people. Only these people were happy, full, singing, and joyous, for they were feeding the persons seated across from them. Then the leader asks group members to pair off and to feed each other dessert. A prayer ends the progressive supper.

D. Ray Wiggins
Brentwood, Tennessee

See also 9) BIBLE EXPLORATIONS, 139) HUNGER IDEAS, 150) BICYCLE SERVICE PROJECT, 182) FORTUNE COOKIES

134. OLDER FOLKS IN YOUTH MINISTRY

I am totally committed to kids. I have seven grandchildren. Perhaps that's how I know that older people have a tremendous amount to give. They have experiences they would love to share.

Most old people love young people. Don't make any mistake about that. Once basic relationships are built, young people realize that old people understand them, love them and will listen to them. Older people have a fantastic story to tell, an exciting story to tell, a meaningful story to tell. So often we don't give older people chances to relate. Let's give young people opportunities to hear stories older people tell out of the experiences of their lives.

Older folks can help out with youth activities. I love

to help our youth when I can. For example, our group decided to hike up a mountain. I did not go up the mountain. But I was at the base. When the group came down, I was ready to give them a cool drink of water and tasty snacks.

Young people can really help older people, especially the lonely ones of us. The trouble is to stop us oldies. We won't want to stop once we get started.

Bob Alley, Auckland, New Zealand

See also 8) RECRUITING TEACHERS, 136) THE WOOD CARVER'S GIFT, 153) CHRISTMAS OUTREACH, 162) YOUTH REACH ADULTS

Buying and fixing up an old bus can open up a new world of adventure to your group.

135. MAGIC BUS

We needed a bus, so I did all my homework and took the idea to the parish council. We had a big hassle session. Eventually the vote went in favor of the bus. We went to the next Brisbane city council auction of buses. The parish council had given me $3,000 to spend. How was I going to buy a bus for $3,000? We went to the auction and got one for $2,300. When we paid the registration and third party insurance, it came in at $4 under the $3,000. I felt that God was telling me, "Full steam ahead!"

A lot of amazing things happened. Angels appeared out of the woodwork. Spray painters painted the bus and mechanics fixed up the engine. We needed a particular piece of equipment for the bus. We bought it for $300. We got an anonymous donation for $300. We had a Christian friend who had a lot of friends that weren't Christians. He persuaded all of these non-Christian mechanics

continued

MAGIC BUS

to come over one night and work until 11 p.m. repairing the bus. Tremendous things have happened.

This bus has served the parish in a wonderful way. The people have fallen in love with it. They identify with it; they refer to it as "our bus." Every group in the parish has used it. It has proved its worth over and over again. In seven months we drove 8,000 miles and spent $700 in fuel. We have $1,000 in the bus account now, more than any other church account.

There are many answers to prayer that have come as a result of this bus. We had hard, bench-type seats in the bus. After an all-night trip one Easter with a family camp, we knew we would have to do something about the seats. I was doing a favor for a friend in Brisbane, and I happened to talk to someone about buses. He had a set of coach seats for sale. I asked how much he wanted for them. He replied that he would let me have them for $30 each for a double seat. I needed 20 ($600 worth) and we didn't have that amount of money. I told the parish treasurer that I wanted to buy these seats and get them into the bus. He said they would underwrite it, but I'd have to see if I could get the money. We ordered the seats and had them installed. I went to work on a publicity campaign to ask people if they would like to buy a bus seat. Within four days we had come up with the $600 to buy the bus seats.

We didn't even have to pay for installation because the fellow who installed them said that he'd take the other bus seats in trade to cover the installation costs.

There have been many other stories like that. It is great to have our bus. It is a great witness. We often drive it up and down the main street just to let people know that our church is on the move.

Glen Brown
Brisbane, Australia

See also 131) CAR POOLS, 146) DOWN-AND-OUTS

136. THE WOOD CARVER'S GIFT

I was standing in the vestry of a church where I had come to give the sermon. I bustled to get my thoughts together. An old man came up and befriended me. He was in his early 70s. He was a quiet, humble man and quite shy. But he went to great trouble to make me feel very much at home.

I went to a place for lunch after the service (with members of the congregation) and asked them about the old man. They told me an interesting story. The old man had never been a part of the church until just about a year ago. His wife died just about then. She had been a lovely person who really had helped out in the church. The man, however, had always stayed away from church. They all knew, though, that he was a great wood carver.

Shortly after the wife's funeral, the church planned a family camp. The people liked to do various crafts at camp. Wood carving was to be one of those crafts. They asked the old man if he would like to lead the wood carving. He was a bit nervous and didn't think he had anything to offer and that nobody would want to come to a wood carving class. He agreed, nonetheless, to come.

At the camp, many teenagers came to his wood carving class as well as people of other ages. He was teaching them how to make little wooden trains, trucks, etc. They weren't polished or anything, but they looked real. As he worked with the kids, they gained a real love for him, and in a matter of a weekend he acquired a whole new family. They weren't just feeling sorry for him; he felt he was contributing to the weekend. His group made some offering bowls for the communion service at which people shared something created in the crafts classes.

Several weeks later, I ventured to the old man's house and found myself starting to make something as he was talking with me.

He had such a love and a genuine interest in people, and he wanted to help so much. While I was there, some teenagers called in just to say hi. He had special little cups for them. His whole wood shop and shed were just for people. He was a young man of 73, not old at all. His spirit was really having an effect on the congregation. The church, especially the youth, had opened up for him a new life.

As I listened to this fascinating story, it occurred to me how God can work. He uses our special talents, whatever they are, for the benefit of both the church and ourselves. It seems to me that youth groups can learn so much from people who share their talents, whether it be wood carving or any other gift. And the person who shares with a group often receives young persons' love and respect.

Pauline Hubner
Sidney, Australia

See also 35) STAY FRESH . . ., 122) MID-WINTER SUMMER CAMP, 134) OLDER FOLKS IN YOUTH MINISTRY, 153) CHRISTMAS OUTREACH, 162) YOUTH REACH ADULTS

OUTREACH
MISSION

You may realize that this section is smaller than the others. Youth ministry generally focuses on the inner-directed part of the Christian life. It is our hunch that many youth have trouble going out to others because of the poor examples they have received from the adult church. They simply don't see the elders of the tribe reaching out to others.

One of the great benefits for youth in the mission or outreach aspect of the faith is that they will receive great gifts as they touch the lives of others. The answers to their own quest for the meaning of life can be found as they serve others.

It will be helpful to let your young people discover what they can do for others. For example, it is more authentic to train youth to interview people in a retirement home than to bring them cake. Telling their stories to someone is a far greater need than digesting something sweet.

Clowning, puppetry and other special skills can help youth focus on giving something important to others. We pray that you will develop this section of youth ministry. Work to make service a genuine part of your youth program. The 80s cry out for the gospel while Christians play with the temptation to focus their faith on themselves. We must again and again remember the message to our brothers and sisters in the early church: "What does it profit, my brethren, if a man says he has faith but has not works? . . . If a brother or sister is ill-clad and in lack of daily food, and one of you says to them, 'Go in peace, be warmed and filled,' what does it profit? So faith by itself, if it has no works, is dead " (James 2:14-17). Perhaps youth ministry can wake the church from its deadening sleep. Young people will discover a living faith as they work to give it away.

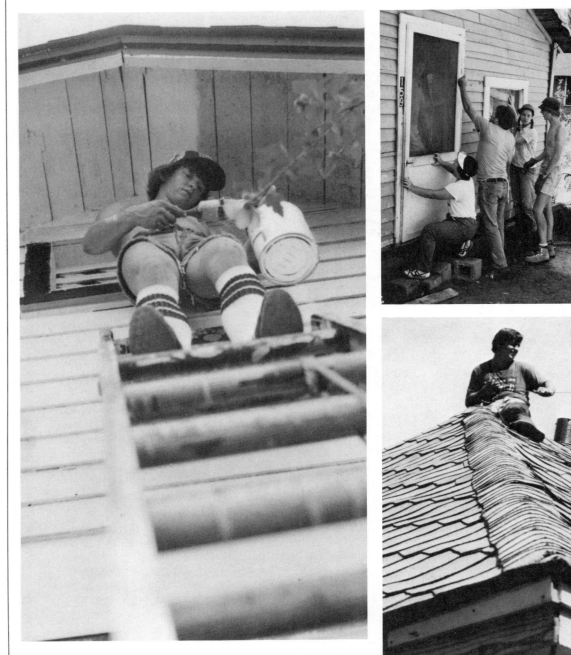

The effect of workcamping is greater on those doing the work than it is on those who receive the help.

137. WORKCAMPING

Last summer we took a group of senior highs and adults to work on a church in Kentucky. We spent a week living in their parish house and working with them. We moved out an old furnace, dug a hole for an outhouse and laid down linoleum. We worshiped with the host congregation on Sunday, worked Monday through Friday, returned to Pittsburgh Saturday and reported our work to our home church on Sunday.

In order to put together a work-camp trip, it is important to determine needs. Your denomination can provide a list of mission points in every part of the country. By writing to particular places, they will tell their needs. Some places need a group of visitors to teach vacation Bible school or some other ministry work. Some need rebuilding of facilities. But, my hunch is that if you look around in your community, you will find many ways you can begin serving human needs. No service is too small. And, the young people grow in Christian compassion as they discover the joys of giving themselves away.

Jack Bowers
Pittsburgh, Pennsylvania

See also 122) MID-WINTER SUMMER CAMP, 138) OBJECT-IVE REFLEC-TIONS

138. OBJECT-IVE REFLECTIONS

I took a work team of 18 young people to the Sierra Service Project for a week. We lived in a church and worked on Native Americans' homes. Most of the work involved weatherization.

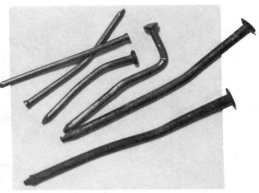

The work team was responsible for the worship service back home the day after we returned. One part of the service was called "Object-ive Reflections." I had asked four people to bring back objects we used or worked with and to say how the object symbolized something about our experience.

One girl brought back a bent nail. "For every nail we got into the boards, there were four like this," she said. The bent nail reminded her of the patience we needed.

Another person brought back her shoe coated with roof "goop," saying the goop was like the love she experienced in the group. It smoothed out disputes, helped to accomplish tasks and patched up mistakes.

"Object-ive Reflections" helped the youth find and articulate meaning in their experience. It also showed the congregation what the youth had accomplished and experienced.

Chris Shiber
Walnut Creek, California

See also 9) BIBLE EXPLORATIONS, 72) CREATIVE CONJURING, 98) PROBLEM SHARING, 104) SHOPPING BAG VALUES, 111) MELT THE DEVIL, 123) CAMP TAPES, 137) WORKCAMPING, 176) COMMON OBJECT MEDITATIONS

139. HUNGER IDEAS

Our youth held a "Lord, When Did We See You Hungry?" program that was a big success. Here are some of its elements other groups might use in their own hunger programs.

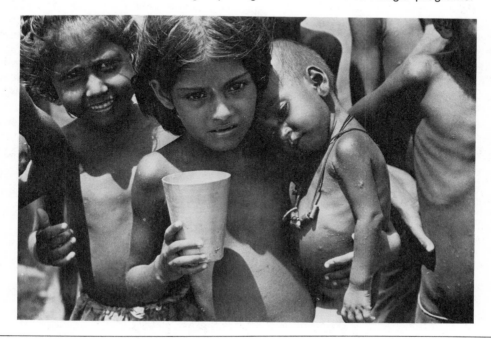

A Litany for a Hungry World

Leader: I was hungry . . .
Audience: And we circled the moon.
L: I was hungry . . .
A: And we told you to wait.
L: I was hungry . . .
A: And we set up a commission.
L: I was hungry . . .
A: And we talked about bootstraps.
L: I was hungry . . .
A: And we told you that you shouldn't be.
L: I was hungry . . .
A: And we had napalm bills to pay.
L: I was hungry . . .
A: And we said "Machines do that kind of work now."
L: I was hungry . . .
A: And we said, "The poor are always with us."

L: I was hungry . . .
A: And we said, "Law and order come first."
L: I was hungry . . .
A: And we blamed it on the communists.
L: I was hungry . . .
A: And we said, "So were my ancestors."
L: I was hungry . . .
A: And we said, "We don't hire over age 35."
L: I was hungry . . .
A: And we said, "God help those who are . . ."
L: I was hungry . . .
A: And we said, "Sorry, try again tomorrow."

continued

HUNGER IDEAS

A "Hunger Crisis" Myth.

We assume that our country has been generous in giving to the poor and hungry of the world. Some people even talk, somewhat resentfully, about how we are feeding the world.

Evidence indicates that such is simply not the case.

1. In the 1970s we Americans spent more than $375 per person on military services and articles, but . . .

2. We spent only $6 per person on eco-nomic assistance to poor countries.

3. Our food aid to poor countries amounts to one-quarter of one percent of our gross national product.

4. One-half of our aid is directly tied to political considerations rather than to greatest need.

5. Only Spain, Portugal and Italy of all the Western European nations give a smaller percentage of their national income than we do to overseas relief.

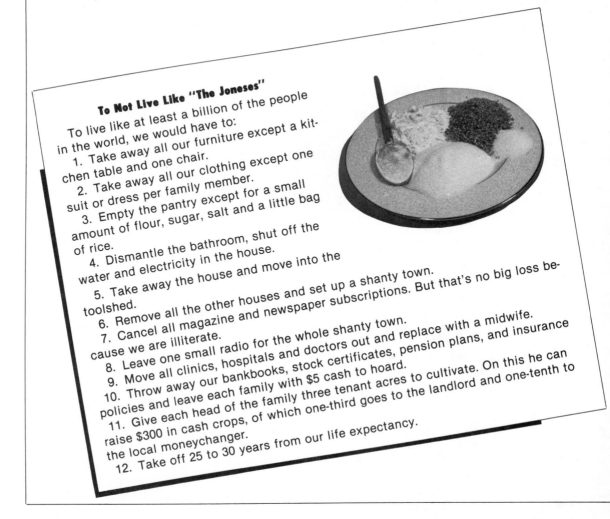

To Not Live Like "The Joneses"

To live like at least a billion of the people in the world, we would have to:

1. Take away all our furniture except a kitchen table and one chair.

2. Take away all our clothing except one suit or dress per family member.

3. Empty the pantry except for a small amount of flour, sugar, salt and a little bag of rice.

4. Dismantle the bathroom, shut off the water and electricity in the house.

5. Take away the house and move into the toolshed.

6. Remove all the other houses and set up a shanty town.

7. Cancel all magazine and newspaper subscriptions. But that's no big loss because we are illiterate.

8. Leave one small radio for the whole shanty town.

9. Move all clinics, hospitals and doctors out and replace with a midwife.

10. Throw away our bankbooks, stock certificates, pension plans, and insurance policies and leave each family with $5 cash to hoard.

11. Give each head of the family three tenant acres to cultivate. On this he can raise $300 in cash crops, of which one-third goes to the landlord and one-tenth to the local moneychanger.

12. Take off 25 to 30 years from our life expectancy.

A World Banquet

We adjourned to the basement of the church for our meal. (Please take a seat at one of the tables.)

Did you know? Did you know that there are just three kinds of meals in the world? That's right! And they are . . .

1. 29 percent of the world eats full scale meals, with large portions, plenty of meat, and lots of vegetables.

2. 33 percent of the world eats sufficient meals, which are made up of mostly rice or wheat, no meat, and few vegetables.

3. 38 percent of the world eats inadequate meals, which are made up of a cup of watery soup or a small portion of rice and no meat or vegetables.

Focusing our action on our personal consumption patterns

1. Have a family fast one or two major meals per week. Send the money saved to your church's hunger fund.

2. Question the values of an economic system which urges you to consume and waste rather than share food resources.

3. Channel savings achieved by moderation in your family to effective voluntary hunger agencies.

4. Believe that individual responses do indeed make a difference.

5. Assert the goodness of God's providence and his concern for all his children.

6. Uphold the dignity of sisters and brothers whose hunger brings shame not to them, but to us.

continued

HUNGER IDEAS

A Thanksgiving Hunger Litany

Liturgist A: Lord, we thank you that our Thanksgiving is increasingly a sharing of food with the hungry.

All: We are grateful that you have given us communication and transportation and resources so that the thrust of famine may be lessened.

Liturgist B: Yet, our hearts are troubled.

All: We know by this Thanksgiving that the problems of hungry people will press in on us the rest of our days.

Liturgist C: The world cries out despite our offerings.

All: Some even say hunger is not the issue. Help us to understand.

Liturgist A: Of course hunger is the issue. You can see it in the famine-stricken . . . the children with swollen stomachs, the listless eyes, the despairing silence in the face of starvation. What they need is food, good food.

Liturgist B: There's truth to what you say, but there's more to be said. The real need is for development. Hungry people must be enabled to develop their own resources, especially food production.

Liturgist C: The issue goes far beyond what either of you is saying. The problem is exploitation. We must rearrange world economics so that resources are distributed with more equity. Then all would be able to have the food they need. Those who can buy never go hungry.

All: Lord, the times are bewildering. We'd rather turn our faces away and pretend no problem exists. Nevertheless, give us translating hearts so that we may see the shapes of the question in many languages.

Liturgist A: You've seen the massive food airlifts. It's a great story in the Christian tradition of charity.

Liturgist B: But they'll starve anew if they aren't taught to help themselves. Not food but technical aid and example must be our assistance.

Liturgist C: We still buy their raw materials cheap and sell finished products back at high price. And two billion must live on $200 a year. Justice is required.

Liturgist A: If a man is dying of hunger you give him a fish.

Liturgist B: If a man is to live tomorrow you help him learn to fish.

Liturgist C: I say make room at the stream so that everyone *can* fish . . . and make a market where the fisherman can sell his surplus catch.

All: Lord, give us a new sense of community and a sense of being neighbors to people all over the world. We are proud to be Americans. Let not our pride prevent us from caring for others of the human family.

Liturgist A: It is the story of being a Good Samaritan.

Liturgist B: Even more it is the story of the talents and giving poor nations the chance to develop two talents into 10.

Liturgist C: Mary sang it in the Magnificat: "He has put down the mighty from their seats and exalted them of low degree. He has filled the hungry with good things and the rich are sent empty away."

All: Lord, is it possible we are to receive as well as to give? Can the world's poor give us new vi-

sions of how humanity should live? Do they have a mission to us as well?

Liturgist A: We can give of our surplus money, food, clothing.

Liturgist B: We can give of our know-how, our technology, our organizing ability.

Liturgist C: But the poor claim the right to have enough for life. We can let the system be changed so that all get a share of the earth— which God owns.

Liturgist A: We regret the dependency, but a dying man is willing to be dependent.

Liturgist B: Self-reliance is the word.

Liturgist C: We need a shift of power and wealth in an unbalanced world.

All: Lord, help us to learn the languages and to know the directions. Which side must we take? Where do you stand, Lord?

Liturgist A: Immediate relief aid for the starving.

Liturgist B: Assistance for self-help.

Liturgist C: Internal reform, international economic change, or in desperation, overthrow.

All: Lord, what shall we do?

Liturgist C: We haven't begun to give what is needed.

Liturgist B: We must support agriculturists, technicians, rural development projects.

Liturgist C: We need to lobby in Congress to change our policies of aid and trade.

All: Lord, this Thanksgiving as we renew our pledge of identification with the poor and the hungry by our gifts, deepen our lives in every way in order that we may have a world less hungry, more just, and more rooted in your peace. Amen.

continued

HUNGER IDEAS

"Four Possibilities"
—a hunger skit

Possibility 1:

A: Boy, have we had a good day.

B: Yeah, the fish were almost standing in line to jump on our hooks.

A: I have more than I need.

B: Me too. I don't know what to do with them.

A: Ah, let's just leave them on the bank.

B: Yeah, and maybe I will take a few home and feed them to my cat.

Possibility 2:

A: Boy, have we had a good day. The fish are really biting.

B: Yeah, I'm getting tired pulling all of them in. Let's quit for today.

A: Okay, I've got more than I need.

B: Me, too and I don't know what to do with the extra.

A: Well, maybe we could give them to ol' Silas, he likes fish but doesn't have any.

B: Sounds good, let's do it.

Possibility 3:

A: You know, we always seem to catch too many fish.

B: Yeah, we always seem to have more than we can use.

A: And then we always end up giving the extra to ol' Silas, since he likes fish, but doesn't have any.

B: Sure, it seems like the thing to do.

A: Well, I was thinking that maybe we could do a little more for ol' Silas. We could give him a fishing pole and some fishing tackle and then he could go fishing when he wanted.

B: That's a good idea. He wouldn't be so dependent upon us. And we could still give him today's extra fish to tide him over until he can catch his own.

Possibility 4:

A: Boy, this is great!

B: Can't beat it.

C: Yes, this sure works better, guys.

A: You sure caught on fast, Silas. You are really turning out to be quite a fisherman.

C: Well, you two are the reason. You not only gave me the equipment, but you made it possible for me to get a license, and then you shared your know-how with me. That made all the difference in the world.

B: I've been thinking. Bill doesn't know how to fish either. Maybe we could take him along with the three of us next time.

Oscar Twedt
Sharon, North Dakota

See also 46) HAVES AND HAVE NOTS, 140) BIG DOGS, ARMS SALES AND HUNGER, 141) WALK FOR HUNGER, 143) MONOPOLY MARATHON, 144) LIFE-SIZE MONOPOLY, 145) ROCK AROUND THE CLOCK, 152) BREAD, 169) LOAVES AND FISHES, 174) YOUTH AND SOCIAL ISSUES, 200) AMEN!

140. BIG DOGS, ARMS SALES AND HUNGER

To bolster our church's world hunger special offering, we tried a different kind of message. "Witnesses" were called to testify about the issue, an American arms salesperson and a dog.

Here is the reading for the American dog: "Woof, woof, woof! I am a dog, the pet in a well-to-do home in the U.S.A. I am either a boxer or a Saint Bernard or a Doberman pinscher, I haven't decided which. I'm a big dog, and I have a big appetite. Woof, woof!

"Of course, I am a rich dog, and I can afford to eat whatever I want. I get chunks of meat to eat from the cans of dogfood they feed me—meat that people in India or Somalia can't afford to eat. Gravy Train, Alpo, whatever I want I can have. My master says

when he was a kid, his dog ate just table scraps. But he buys me what I like. We have a cat in our house and he eats well, too. But let's not talk about cats. Woof, woof!

"You see, it's all like an auction. Food is being auctioned off in the "global supermarket." Those who have the money can buy what they want. But poor people can't buy much of anything. I'm glad I belong to an American family. Woof!"

"Here is the arms salesperson's reading: "I am a salesperson for a huge corporation. You'd be surprised at what I sell. It's not breakfast food or insurance or cars. I sell weapons. No, not just guns to individuals, so they can protect themselves against bur-

continued

BIG DOGS, ARMS SALES AND HUNGER

glars. I sell sophisticated weapons to military people, both in our country and in other countries. We have the latest and the best in electronic equipment: guided missiles, nuclear warheads, etc. If you want a real deterrent that will keep any enemy from thinking twice about attacking you, then you want to keep my corporation in mind when you go buying your weaponry. Well, of course, you wouldn't be buying what I have to sell, but your armed forces buy our products.

"My company is very strong. We make a lot of money on juicy, cost-plus defense contracts. And lots of money means lots of power. If we need to, we can afford to do a lot of lobbying to get Congress to approve some weapons we think our country needs.

"We have an arms bazaar about every year. It's a kind of sales convention for the defense industry. Once we had one in Chicago, and here came around those pinkos and pacifists and so-called Christians, telling us, 'We shouldn't make so many weapons. Our country should use the money to help poor, starving people, instead.'

"How stupid can you get? They don't understand the facts of life, the facts of survival in modern life. We need to be able to defend ourselves against the godless communists and their schemes for world domination. Besides, weaponry is good business, big business. Yes, and plenty of profits are to be made!"

We had other "witnesses" testify, such as a Meals on Wheels volunteer, the mother of a starving child and the prophet Amos. We invited the congregation to respond to these witnesses by giving generously to the special offering. The offering was great! We were able to see our folks responding to the needs of the world's hungry.

Milan Lambertson
Larkin, Kansas

See also 26) FLIGHT 108, 46) HAVES AND HAVE NOTS, 139) HUNGER IDEAS, 141) WALK FOR HUNGER, 152) BREAD, 166) GETTING THE WORD OUT, 169) LOAVES AND FISHES, 174) YOUTH AND SOCIAL ISSUES, 213) THE FIFTH GOSPEL

There is no question whether or not youth groups should help feed the world's hungry people. The question is to decide the best way to become involved.

141. WALK FOR HUNGER

There are several ways to raise money for the hungry. The most common is the walk for hunger. The walk has significance because we are walking symbolically with people who walk every day of their lives to survive: for water, for firewood, medication, food, and other kinds of things. Walkers solicit pledges per each mile.

Many of the walkers are youth. In New Jersey, where we have our program, we have something over 14,000 walkers each year. My hunch is that probably 75 percent of those are aged 12 to 18.

When we talk to the kids about why they walk, we get all kinds of interesting answers. Most answer that they want to be part of something. They are concerned. It gives them a visible way of doing something for the hungry.

At the end of 10 or 15 miles of walking, many have sore feet. They have met some neat people along the way.

Another common fund raiser is a 36-hour fast. The fasters solicit per-hour pledges. It takes an awful lot of guts to deny yourself in our culture 36 hours without anything to eat. The kids live together, play together and learn about hunger together.

These common experiences often influence young people to continue working to ease hunger and other volunteer service. Attitudes are often changed. And, several persons around the world gain more food to stay alive.

Contact your church's state or national offices for names of hunger-relief organizations.

Terry Grove
New Jersey

See also 84) JOGGING FELLOWSHIP, 139) HUNGER IDEAS, 140) BIG DOGS, ARMS SALES AND HUNGER, 142) CAN-A-THON, 143) MONOPOLY MARATHON, 145) ROCK AROUND THE CLOCK, 149) SHARE CROP

142. CAN-A-THON

The youth of our church have developed an exciting project. We call it "can-a-thon." The approach is similar to "bike-a-thons" and "walk-a-thons."

In the "can-a-thon," the youth solicit pledges for every aluminum can they collect and turn in to the church. They receive a receipt for each can turned in. After the campaign ends, the participants collect their pledges. The cans are then sold to a recycling company.

Our campaign lasted about two months. We found aluminum cans along roads, at service stations, at home, at restaurants and many other places. Special arrangements were made with businesses to save cans during our campaign.

The "can-a-thon" was fun, profitable and good for the community. The pledges brought in over $800. We then sold the cans to a recycling company for $200. And special recognition was given to the youth who collected the greatest number of cans.

Sybil McLeese, Rural Hall, North Carolina

See also 71) 2083, 141) WALK FOR HUNGER, 147) CIRCULATION DAY

143. MONOPOLY MARATHON

We used Monopoly to raise funds and to bring youth from different churches together. Our marathon involved two churches, but any number could easily participate.

Each young person solicited pledges for the number of hours his/her church was at the playing board. The money went to the church's hunger program. A group would not get credit for the hours they were out of the game due to bankruptcy.

A single game was played with each church having equal numbers of players at the board. When two players were bankrupt, the game was over and assets tallied. The

144. LIFE-SIZE MONOPOLY

We raised money for missions by playing Life-Size Monopoly. We picked up the idea from another church but added some of our own touches. The high school youth gathered per-hour pledges at our coffee hours after church. Each of the five teams of four persons dressed as representatives of their "token." This included the Wizard of Oz, the Mad Hatter and several other clever ideas. We built a giant Monopoly board by using colored paper and masking tape. The youth moved around the board after "shaking" our huge dice (measuring a foot on each side). We used the 400-square-foot floor of our fellowship hall. We also had speakers, films and other aids to prepare the young people for the missions projects which would receive the money we raised.

We raised over $700 in the 24-hour experience. Church members dropped in to cheer everyone on. It was a great success in terms of raising mission money, learning about mission concerns and building community among the youth.

Joy Edwards, Kingston, Rhode Island

See also 139) HUNGER IDEAS, 143) MONOPOLY MARATHON

---

assets were credited each group's total. A new game then started. The youth group with the most assets over the duration of the games was the winner of the marathon. During the game, spectators were invited to donate to a fish bowl which went to the winning group based on total assets.

Our marathon was 50 hours long. The game began at 6 p.m. on Friday and concluded at 8 p.m. on Sunday.

Some youth stayed at the church for the entire marathon, while others came for shorter periods. Food was pooled and the participants ate in small groups as they wanted throughout the 50-hour period. The most exciting part of the 50 hours was watching two groups of youth (who had never met) become friends.

There was no other structured activity during the 50 hours. One youth brought a television, one a record player, some brought board games. Observers were invited to stop in, especially before and after the Sunday morning worship service.

Ken Scarborough
Townsend, Delaware

See also 139) HUNGER IDEAS, 144) LIFE-SIZE MONOPOLY, 145) ROCK AROUND THE CLOCK, 152) BREAD

145. ROCK AROUND THE CLOCK

Our youth rocked for 25 hours, from Saturday morning till after church on Sunday. (They listened to the service on a speaker system.) The rocking chair marathon—not dance—was the kind of "rock" they employed. As usual, each person solicited pledges with the money going to "One Great Hour of Sharing" and to a local outreach project as well. We had adults discuss with the youth (while they were busy rocking) these various projects. We also played many games and held discussions that were planned as group building activities.

Joy Edwards
Kingston, Rhode Island

See also 139) HUNGER IDEAS, 143) MONOPOLY MARATHON

One Australian group drives around its city looking for down-and-out people to help. Got any down-and-outs in your city?

146. DOWN-AND-OUTS

We have an organization here called the St. Vincent DePaul Society. It attempts to minister to the down-and-out drunks in the city, operating a night shelter for these people. The young people's group within this organization gets together one or two days a week and combs the city in a van, looking for drunks on the streets and in parks. They offer physical and spiritual consolation such as a cup of hot soup, a mug of tea, something to eat, an encouraging word. The young people try to let them know someone cares for them.

Youth groups can learn a lot by simply visiting shelters like the one I've described in their own cities. Simply being there makes quite an impression. Your group may be moved to do something to help the down-and-outs.

Peter Dight
Adelaide, Australia

See also 32) CARING, 61) DISCIPLESHIP, 135) MAGIC BUS, 147) CIRCULATION DAY, 148) APPLES OUTREACH, 161) YOUTH EVANGELISM, 162) YOUTH REACH ADULTS

147. CIRCULATION DAY

Circulation Day is an act of sharing; an event in giving and receiving. It would be unfair to attribute the concept of giving and receiving to any single religion, let alone any one person. But the present idea for Circulation Day began to take form in the 1970s when a local minister suggested that there are plenty of items to go around; we simply need to take the time to give away those items we are not using. Circulation Day is a way our youth helped the needy receive necessary items and helped the congregation to give itself away.

Here are some questions and answers related to Circulation Day:

Q. What kind of items do we give away?

A. Anything (in good condition) which you are not using. At a Circulation Day in Arkansas, one man gave away an automobile. Especially appreciated are items of clothing, toys, books, small appliances.

Q. Can anyone come in and take things?

A. Absolutely.

Q. Will people other than congregational members be bringing items to give away?

A. Yes. People in your neighborhood will catch the spirit of giving and wish to donate items.

Q. Where do we place the clothing, toys and appliances?

A. Most congregations have one large room in which tables may be set up and items can be placed on the tables.

Q. What will be the time schedule for distribution of items?

A. We recommend that people come in from at 8 a.m. to 5 p.m. on a Saturday.

Q. What about crowd control. Don't some people hoard items?

A. There have been no incidents of greed or unruly crowds at any of the numerous Circulation Days held throughout the United States. However, if it appears that someone is acting in a greedy way, simply have a church volunteer ask him or her to leave.

Q. What if we don't give it all away?

A. You need only call one of many service organizations in and they will come and pick up any items left over. The Salvation Army, Goodwill and others are aware of Circulation Day and are ready to respond.

Q. When will people start bringing items to give away?

A. As soon as you begin promoting the event you should receive some calls. We recommend that you begin receiving one or two days before your Circulation Day. With three or four volunteers you can easily sort and stack items in a short time.

Carolyn Rice
Excelsior Springs, Missouri

See also 142) CAN-A-THON, 146) DOWN-AND-OUTS, 148) APPLES OUTREACH, 149) SHARE CROP, 150) BICYCLE SERVICE PROJECT, 151) THANKSGIVING SCAVENGER HUNT

148. APPLES OUTREACH

Imagination is a youth leader's power. We can help people imagine. Creative programming "translates" one thing into something else.

For example, I had a dream one summer that there were an awful lot of elderly people who would love to have real applesauce. Why not prepare a bunch of food and give it to elderly people? Should we sell some to the church members and that would pay the expenses of picking the apples and buying the jars?

It was clear that we could minister to some people by making applesauce. Our group went ahead and picked apples, made applesauce, sold some of it and gave a lot of it to shut-ins.

The successful ministry simply expanded a very simple idea: picking apples. I'm going to continue with very small ideas, broadening them and molding them.

Tiff Bates, Elgin, Illinois

See also 72) CREATIVE CONJURING, 146) DOWN-AND-OUTS, 147) CIRCULATION DAY, 149) SHARE CROP, 162) YOUTH REACH ADULTS

149. SHARE CROP

Our youth group was involved in helping to sell some corn which our church camp had share cropped. A farmer used the church camp property to plant the corn. When the crop was ready, the camp director sent newsletters to church groups in eastern Ohio. He invited the groups to come in and help harvest it. The camp received half of the money from the corn sales to support its program. The church groups could use their part of the money however they chose.

Our group helped with the harvest and sold the corn through a roadside stand. We had about 15 young people working on this project. We gave half of our share to a church-supported hunger project. We used the remaining amount to support our group's program.

John Ballard
Warren, Ohio

See also 141) WALK FOR HUNGER, 147) CIRCULATION DAY, 148) APPLES OUTREACH

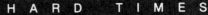 
150. BICYCLE SERVICE PROJECT

We were struggling to find a service project which would help the youth as they helped others. We noticed that bicycling was very important to people in the area. So, we focused our project on reconditioning old bicycles. Church members donated old vehicles. We trained the youth to do the mechanical work. We turned them loose and let them develop their skills. A few skilled adults gave key points of aid as the project developed. The teens were able to care for their own vehicles. We helped find bikes for the youths who had none. This enabled our group to have transportation for other service projects.

Robert Butziger
Deer Lodge, Tennessee

See also 133) PROGRESSIVE DINNERS, 147) CIRCULATION DAY

151. THANKSGIVING SCAVENGER HUNT

Our youth group developed a special pre-Thanksgiving project that combined a lot of fun with an activity that would result in helping others. On the Sunday before Thanksgiving, the youth sponsored a scavenger hunt for a variety of canned goods and staples. These items were needed for the Women's Resource Center (for abused women and children). Teams were given an area of homes to cover. They were supposed to get one item at each house and be back at the church in one hour. People were very responsive. The event concluded with a program led by a representative from the Resource Center.

Joy Edwards
Kingston, Rhode Island

See also 132) GREAT PUMPKIN HUNT, 141) WALK FOR HUNGER, 147) CIRCULATION DAY, 152) BREAD

152. BREAD

We have a very special youth group. You can guess it by our name—SHOK. This stands for the Senior Highs of Kingston. It seems that a group really takes a unique shape when it has a unique name. Well, we are also very much into baking bread. We recently had an all-night bread-baking party at the church on Maundy Thursday to raise money for world hunger. We made a wide variety of bread items—bagels, French bread, cheese bread, etc. While the dough was rising, members made banners, watched films and discussed world hunger.

The bread was sold on our "Bounty Table" on Easter Sunday. The receipts went to our denominational hunger offering. It was a super program.

Dick Hettrick, Kingston, Tennessee

See also 139) HUNGER IDEAS, 143) MONOPOLY MARATHON, 151) THANKSGIVING SCAVENGER HUNT, 169) LOAVES AND FISHES

153. CHRISTMAS OUTREACH

Some of our junior highs attended a youth rally where they were sent out into the streets to do interviews with cassette recorders. One of the ideas which really impressed them was interviewing old people. Eight of the junior highs decided to make this process part of their Christmas contribution to the worship service. They interviewed a number of old people in the congregation. The question which worked the best was "What was your most meaningful Christmas?" This encounter unleashed a flood of moving stories. Sections of these responses were used at the worship service.

We also recycled the torch idea from the Olympics. We took a lantern to an older person's house each week of Advent and had him or her light it. We then took the lantern to the Sunday morning service and lit the advent candle from its flame. Thus the elders of the tribe contributed to the younger members of the community. The youth were the ones who made the connection between these two vital parts of the faith family.

Joan Humphrey
Pittsburgh, Pennsylvania

See also 102) CHRISTMAS NOSTALGIA, 134) OLDER FOLKS IN YOUTH MINISTRY, 136) THE WOOD CARVER'S GIFT, 154) RECIPE CARDS AND KIDS, 162) YOUTH REACH ADULTS, 183) MULTIMEDIA WORSHIP, 207) PARTICIPATORY CHRISTMAS PAGEANT

154. RECIPE CARDS AND KIDS

The Saturday before Christmas was a special time for our senior high group. We sponsored an activity day from 10 a.m. to 4 p.m. for the children of the church and the neighborhood. Children came to the church for recreation, films, cookies, and seven different craft centers where they could make their own gifts with the helping hands of a teenager.

One activity was to decorate the backs of recipe cards that already contained printed recipes that young children could help make. The cards were then stapled and gift-wrapped. We used wallpaper scraps and samples (from large sample books) to wrap their packages. They were quite unique and all creatively and inexpensively done. The youth finished the day exhausted but with a real sense of accomplishment.

Jacqui Birt, Durham, North Carolina

See also 79) HAPPINESS IS . . ., 102) CHRISTMAS NOSTALGIA, 113) "I CARE" VALENTINES, 153) CHRISTMAS OUTREACH, 155) PALM SUNDAY FAIR

155. PALM SUNDAY FAIR

During Lent our senior high class spent each Sunday morning in preparation for our Palm Sunday Fair, an event in which the senior highs provided a learning experience for the church's third through eighth graders on the events of Holy Week.

At the Fair we helped the younger students make collages representing "Crucifixion" and "Resurrection." We showed posters explaining what happened during Holy Week—the highlights of Palm Sunday, Maundy Thursday, Good Friday, etc. We prepared a bingo type game highlighting the Scripture passages associated with the days of Holy Week.

A board game lit up when the children matched the symbol for a particular day of the week with the day (a donkey with Palm Sunday, for example). A picture game used pictures from the line drawings in **Good News for Modern Man**. The pictures had to be put in chronological order to show the order of events during Holy Week.

We had a food booth serving "Food of the Holy Land"—dates, Sahara bread, cheese, etc., and a variety of films and filmstrips on the subject of Holy Week.

We provided prizes for the children when they finished each event—bookmarks with scripture passages on them, balloons with biblical characters, etc. The event was scheduled for the children during the regular Sunday school hour on Palm Sunday, and continued during the fellowship hour for the adults of the congregation.

Monica Brown
Hyattsville, Maryland

See also 113) "I CARE" VALENTINES, 154) RECIPE CARDS AND KIDS, 160) PUPPET MAKING, 211) GOOD FRIDAY SACRED DANCE

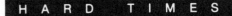 

156. REACH

There were various times when our young people were separated by distance or illness (or other unusual circumstances) from the usual time of study. We have developed a correspondence ministry called REACH (Religious Education and Christian Help).

We send synopses of meetings to youth once every two weeks throughout the school calendar year. In addition, those who were too ill or unable to study received letters written by a team of letter writers. An outgrowth of this special ministry was a newsletter, sharing poems and other contributions from members of this scattered community.

Jan Tully
Victoria, Australia

See also 27) OVER THE RAINBOW, 28) DEAR ME, 52) RETREAT FEEDBACK, 69) SUNDAY SCHOOL PUBLICITY BLITZ, 87) STICKY FLAPS, 100) DEAR TEACHER

157. THE SKATEBOARD OPEN

Our church recently sponsored a "Skateboard Open" that was an outreach to the youth in our community. It was very well received. We used the flyer below to advertise the event.

ENTRY BLANK FOR CHRISTIAN CENTER
SKATEBOARD FIELD DAY DRAWINGS

Name _____ Age _____

Address _____ Phone _____

I am interested in competing in the skateboard race: ☐ Yes ☐ No

I am interested in competing in the skateboard freestyle: ☐ Yes ☐ No

Entry in the Christian Center Skateboard Field Day to be held (time and date), and its contests and drawings is FREE. Winners of the skateboard race and freestyle events will be awarded TROPHIES. All contestants in these events will also be given a certificate good for one free iron-on patch with a skateboard motif. Contestants *and* non-contestants are eligible to register for the Skateboard Field Day drawing. FIRST PRIZE in the drawing will be a HOBIE SKATEBOARD. Other prizes will include arm and knee pads, record albums, and T-shirts. Contestants and registrants for the drawing must be UNDER 18 years of age.

All contestants in the skateboard competitions must secure WRITTEN PERMISSION from their parents or guardian. Skateboard safety equipment (helmet, arm and knee pads) are MANDATORY for all contestants, but will be provided by Blue Sky skateboard park for any contestants who do not own safety equipment.

Every reasonable precaution will be taken to insure the safety of all participants. In the event of an accident requiring emergency care, necessary arrangements will be made by the Christian Center Staff, but parents must assume financial responsibility.

The parents of_____ give permission for him/her to participate in the Christian Center Skateboard Field Day Competitions, to be held on the church grounds (time and date).

Home address

_____

Home phone   Business phone

_____

Signature of parent or guardian

Date

See also 7) PLANNING STRATEGY, 121) PHYSICAL RISK

Paul C. Collins
Albuquerque, New Mexico

158. CLOWNING OUTREACH

Recently we sponsored a "Night of Clowning," a 10 p.m. to 10 a.m. lock-in for our 7th-12th graders. The lock-in included moving out into the community for two hours when we as clowns greeted those participating in Tulsa's "Walk for Mankind."

We invited a guest leader to help us understand clowning as ministry. Prior to the event we had visiting clowns share their experiences in clowning. We also had several pre-planning sessions with adults and the guest leader. Out of this experience we hoped to begin a clown ministry.

This lock-in helped prepare the folks to reach out and touch the lives of others in the community.

Before the lock-in began at 10 p.m., we also sponsored a "Three Hour Spring Fling" at a nearby amusement park.

Here's what our lock-in schedule looked like:

Friday

7:00-10:00 p.m. Meet at church to go to Bell's Amusement Park (bring at least $5.00)

10:00 p.m. Check-in time for lock-in
Doors locked at 10:15 p.m.

10:20 p.m. Gathering time in youth lounge

11:00 p.m. Movie time in Fellowship Hall to see "The Parable"
Reflections led by youth minister
Popcorn and drinks

11:45 p.m. Let's think about our Summer Program
Discussion

Saturday

12:15 a.m. What's clowning all about? What does it have to do with ministry?
Guest leader

1:15 a.m. Chapel service led by guest clown and youth leaders
Movie: "Mark of the Clown"

2:00 a.m. Shut-eye time—Boys in Room 310A, girls in Room 310 C

4:30 a.m. Gathering in Center Youth Lounge for Cheerios and juice and instruction for "makeup" by guest clown

4:45 a.m. Makeup/dressup time to become a clown

6:00 a.m. Picture-making time (individually and as group)

6:30 a.m. Clowns travel to Civic Center to greet "Walkers for Mankind"

8:30 a.m. Return to church

8:45 a.m. Remove makeup and complete evaluation worksheet

9:00 a.m. Big breakfast and Reflection Time

9:30 a.m. Evaluation led by guest clown Decision about future clowning as a ministry

10:00 a.m. Conclusion of lock-in with friendship circle

Richard Ziglar
Tulsa, Oklahoma

See also 115) RETREAT CHECKLIST, 129) COME AS YOU AREN'T LOCK-IN, 159) YOUTH CIRCUS, 161) YOUTH EVANGELISM, 167) CLOWNING, 168) THREE RING CIRCUS WORSHIP

Young people take on a whole new spiritual perspective once they become clowns. Reaching out to others as clowns helps their own faith to grow stronger.

159. YOUTH CIRCUS

Over 2,000 young people gathered together at a local county fairground to hold a fantastic one-day fair. Each youth group representing a different congregation created some kind of booth, display, or ride that seemed fairly typical of what one might find at the "old county fair." Some kids pulled tots around in wagons—charging 25 cents per ride—and using the money collected for their youth service corps.

We had food, games and clowns. The culmination of this one-day event was a full-blown, silent worship event with the clowns. Using some of the youth as my assistants we concluded the event in the afternoon.

The concept underlying the one-day fair was that the church should create an environment in which something can happen. So we took the concept of the fair and created the environment so that the young people who came really were celebrating who they were, what they were, and what their place is in God's kingdom. Clowns don't perform, they create an environment for something to happen. In our worship service that capped off this event the clowns and youth celebrated God's love and the fact of the "good news."

Floyd Shaffer
Detroit, Michigan

See also 158) CLOWNING OUTREACH, 167)
CLOWNING, 168) THREE RING CIRCUS WORSHIP

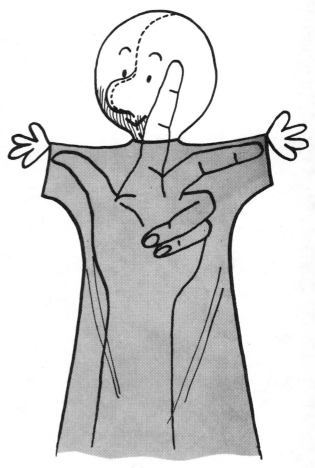

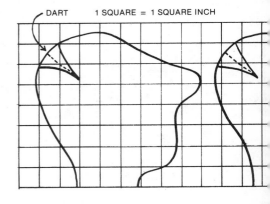

DART   1 SQUARE = 1 SQUARE INCH

160. PUPPET MAKING

Discouraged by the price of puppets? Then make your own! This puppet is inexpensive and a lot of fun to make.

This puppet is one of the more basic types. It is mostly a head in which a finger, usually the index finger, is placed for movement. The thumb and the middle finger are extended into the arms. Puppets of this type are also called "glove puppets" because the hand is concealed within the puppet like a glove.

The head—The head is usually made from a flesh tone of cloth, but other colors are okay, too. The character will determine the color. Features are exaggerated so that they will show up at a distance. Sew the two pieces cut from material of your choice by tracing the pattern below. (This is scaled down and will need to be enlarged.) First sew the dart and then the entire head, leaving the neck open for stuffing and also for your finger. After the halves have been sewn together, stuff until very firm. Leave in the neck a hole for your finger. Or, place in the neck a collar of leather or cardboard and stuff around it. This will give you a comfortable place for your finger.

The hands—Using the pattern, trace around the hand and cut from the same material as the head unless puppet is to be wearing gloves or mittens. It is easier if these pieces are first sewn to the garment and then sewn around when the garment pieces are put together.

The garments—Your imagination is the only limit as to what can be done here. Keep colors bright, patterns small and material more soft and pliable than stiff.

The patterns shown will be of help, but they will not give you detail. Dresses could be cut a bit fuller while suits should be a bit straighter, especially for the front. You will note that the back is slightly larger. This has been done so your hand will have some operating space and not bulge the puppet too much in the front.

Shirts, jackets and blouses will require the long pattern to be cut about the waist mark and pieced together. It is always easier to sew flat pieces than trying to sew around. It can be done but it is harder.

Now go to it. Use your imagination. Bits of lace and fur can change a housewife to a queen. A cape can quickly transform a farmer into a count.

Think about the story you are going to tell or the character you want developed. What type of clothing comes to mind? With that picture in your mind, use the basic pattern and add whatever else is necessary.

Richard Baker
Avonmore, Pennsylvania

See also 155) PALM SUNDAY FAIR, 167) CLOWNING

If any group in the church can spread the good news to the world, it is young people. When they realize the power and love of Christ in their lives, they don't hesitate to tell everyone they meet.

161. YOUTH EVANGELISM

We have been working with our youth in the area of evangelism. It is a fascinating journey together as we work through our own "turning" and our attempts to share that with others.

Here is an outline of our teen evangelism program that we have been putting together.

Acknowledgements:
- We have been transformed from a natural person to a spiritual one.
- The Holy Spirit has been turning us inside out.
- What would have happened to you if you'd never experienced the first turning?
- Christians and non-Christians have something in common: We're both uptight about evangelism. Christians are afraid of offending. Non-Christians are afraid of being assaulted.
- We can *relax!* Relax because we are God's and he lives in us. All we have to do is let him show a little.

Let's Examine
- Our frustrations with evangelism.
- Our fears of evangelism.
- Our motivations for evangelism.
- Our theology of evangelism.
- Our methodology of evangelism.

Let's Have Some Fresh Understandings
- We can learn to expose our faith, not impose it.
- We can learn to relax in the Holy Spirit.
- We need to get rid of God-talk.
- We can learn to ask good questions (non-threatening ones).
- We can learn to listen to them for Christ's sake.
- We can help people to see their needs and the God who satisfies.

Kinds of Teen Evangelism
- One-on-one.
- Two-by-two.
- Group evangelism.
- Service evangelism.

Models of Teen Evangelism

1. **A Conversational Style**
   A. Discover who the person is.
   - Listen first, proclaim second.
   - Listen for commonalities—like interests.
   - Listen for uniqueness—compliment them on a special interest. (If they express a concern and you "blow it," go back later.)
   B. Stimulate interest in the gospel, but don't inundate them.
   - Open their eyes (Acts 26:18).
   - Be vague and intriguing (John 4:1-42).
   - Know or learn something about their interests (Acts 17:28). "Could you explain that or could you teach me?" Don't be afraid to be human.
   C. Learn where they're struggling and share your pilgrimage.
   - Don't confuse the power of the Gospel with the explanation of it.

2. **Incarnational Style—"Christ in you"**
   A. Learn to listen to their story—Jesus did
   - Begin with their needs and agenda, not your own.
   - Every witnessing event is different.
   - Identify felt needs. (John 4, Samaritan woman; John 9, blind man)

continued

YOUTH EVANGELISM

Listen to the stories of Harvey, Linda, and Larry.

Harvey McCoy might tell his story like this: "I live in the inner city with my mother and three sisters. I guess over the last three years I haven't been to church more than 10 times. I used to go, but frankly I was embarrassed being with my sisters. Then about four weeks ago something really crazy happened. Some guy who used to be a gang leader spoke at school. He told us about his early days in Harlem before he was converted to Christ. I'd never heard a man talk like he did about God. I found myself listening and feeling something deep inside me. I guess God has been trying to tell me something for a long time, but for the first time maybe I'm ready to listen."

Linda Henderson explains it this way: "I was baptized when I was four weeks old and confirmed when I was 12 years old. I can't remember a time when I didn't think of myself as a Christian. But I didn't realize how much difference being a Christian makes until recently, when I began to hang around some of my friends' homes where God and Christ are totally unimportant. Four years ago when I was confirmed, I meant everything I said about wanting Jesus to be my Lord and Savior and pledging my allegiance to his kingdom. But now, something new is happening to me. I really want to learn how to begin to experience some of this fantastic love that I've known about for a long time."

Larry Padaka had never been inside a church until he moved to Maryvale a year ago and accompanied his friend Sam to youth fellowship. That same summer he and Sam went to a district church camp. Larry describes his experience this way: "The people there were different! I've never felt so much love in my whole life. But the greatest experience for me was on Thursday night when I responded to the invitation to give my life to Christ. I went forward. I didn't feel anything special right then, but later at the communion service it all hit me. I knew God loved me and had forgiven me. Actually, I waited a long time before going to the communion table. I wanted to be sure I was ready to do what they said: 'Lead a new life following the commandments of God, and walking in his holy ways.' I've sometimes been pretty spastic in my walking since then, but I'm sure I'll never be the same again."

What were the felt needs of Harvey, Linda and Larry?

Harvey _____
Linda _____
Larry _____

Learn to tell your story. What has Christ done in you?

a. Tie your story into their felt need (honestly).
b. Relate how Christ and your relationship have made a difference in your life.
   Learn to tell Jesus' story.
   ● We must know the basics about him: life, teachings, death, resurrection.
   ● We must know him: prayer, sacraments, church, his presence. How do we experience him?
   ● We need to sensitively invite them to open up to him. Can use a prayer, which could go something like this: "Lord Jesus Christ, I acknowledge that I have gone my own way. I have sinned in thought, word and deed. I am sorry for my sins. I turn from them in repentance. I believe you died for me, bearing my sins in your own body. I thank you for your great love. I now open the door. Come in, Lord Jesus. Come in as my Savior and cleanse me. Come in as my Lord, and take control of me. And I will serve as you give me strength, all my life. Amen!"

Randall Scheer
Sterling, Kansas

See also 93) SMALL GROUPS, 146) DOWN-AND-OUTS, 156) REACH, 158) CLOWNING OUTREACH, 162) YOUTH REACH ADULTS, 196) STEP INTO THE OFFERING

162. YOUTH REACH ADULTS

We usually have our minds set to thinking that adults bring young people into the church. Often the opposite is really the case. The children often bring their parents to Christ.

In western Queensland, the kids got together and started their own church services. The rector there got to know the kids through the local school and organized them into clubs. A few youth leaders were recruited. A united effort really got the youth excited. Their parents and other adults around town a few at a time caught the excitement from the youth. The town was more and more revived.

The point of the story is that young people have great influence with their parents. Often parents will follow their child's leading. It's refreshing to know that youth ministry often helps adults come to Christ.

Trevor Smith, Townsville, Australia

See also 57) LET YOUTH TEACH, 134) OLDER FOLKS IN YOUTH MINISTRY, 136) THE WOOD CARVER'S GIFT, 146) DOWN-AND-OUTS, 148) APPLES OUTREACH, 153) CHRISTMAS OUT-REACH, 163) EXTRA! JESUS LIVES, 208) CHRISTMAS STORIES

163. EXTRA! JESUS LIVES

Our junior high group wanted to share the Bible in a contemporary, creative way with the people in our congregation. We ended up, however, sharing the Bible with the whole town! Here's what happened:

We went to our local newspaper folks to see if they would print a one-page sheet of articles written by the group about Jesus' last week on Earth. This one-page sheet would then be passed out on Easter morning after the worship service. The newspaper editor, however, said that it would not be feasible for him to print a single sheet for us. He could, though, publish articles on the religion page of the newspaper prior to Easter. You can imagine our excitement as we began work on this project. Fortunately, we had several months to do our writing.

We chose the highlights of Holy Week. Each youth then volunteered to create a newspaper-like article, a drawing or a poem centering on one of these events. Most of the class members decided to draw some-thing or write an article.

Each young person met individually with me once or twice to work on his/her creation. Most labored hard to create meaningful works. Some even used concordances and background studies. This activity also gave me a chance to find out their strengths and weaknesses in Bible skills and knowledge.

The result of our work was a full-page spread of drawings and articles in our town newspaper the Saturday before Palm Sunday. What a satisfying learning experience this was for all of us!

Holly Burnett
Sandusky, Ohio

Action Strategy . . . Holly's experience was fortunate. Sensitive editors will usually be happy to work with you on such a project. Contact them early, however, in order that the editor will have plenty of time to plan for and edit the articles and art your group produces.

See also 62) THE "AVERAGE" KID, 73) MEDIA PROBING, 183) MULTIMEDIA WORSHIP, 211) GOOD FRIDAY SACRED DANCE

WORSHIP
CELEBRATION

The Book of Acts (2:37-47) shows a vivacious church at work at worship. "And they devoted themselves to the apostles' teaching and fellowship, to the breaking of bread and prayers " (Acts 2:42). It is ironic that worship today often is as vivacious as a soiled athletic sock. This is especially true in the lives of young people. Most regular church worship is focused on adults' interests and concerns. In fact, many congregations intentionally exclude children and youth!

When youth gather for Sunday morning educational class or the evening youth group, they can choose any celebration form. The struggle for the youth advisor or leader is to balance the historical essence of worship with the contemporary forms which are most meaningful to youth. These contemporary forms must be valid, not gimmicky. Simply blessing potato chips and Coke for the Lord's Supper will not make for an authentic and pleasing service.

The contemporary models shared in this section will help you probe a spirit of excitement and possibility for new worship. The friends who share these models sought to share the gospel in exciting new forms. Please don't simply pick up someone's plan without first probing the meaning of worship for you and your tradition. Worship is that unique moment when God's people gather to share a special communication with each other and God. You will want to explore and develop the content of your celebrations to increase this special communication. One of the great results of worship in youth ministry is that young people gain the experience of creating and leading worship. This perspective changes the young worshiper's understanding of worship. Worship becomes more and more relevant.

As you use this section, feel free to let the items stimulate your planning group as you organize worship. Take the order of worship from your Sunday morning service and outline the items which are included. You should probably include most of them in your youth group service. However, you can find creative ways of expressing this content.

It is important to realize that the Christian community has a number of times in its life which permit, indeed, demand something special. The Advent, Lent and Youth Sunday worship times are perfect for releasing the creativity of youth. You are only limited by your imagination and the company you keep.

Young people bring something special to worship by their weakness, their acceptance, their restlessness, their trust, their forgiveness.

164. WORSHIP ENVIRONMENT

It really doesn't make any difference whether you worship in a classy church or a run-down storefront. I am interested in creating a feeling anywhere people worship, where people can begin to feel with their eyes, their ears, their whole beings.

I usually work with a theme, and I am very involved with planning the kinds of programming that will take place in the meetings. Then I deal with visual kinds of things (lights and sound) that will help make the experience happen. I work with colors, music, soft and hard objects. At a recent youth conference we tried to create the experience of power flight, the feeling of God's magnificence.

When we walked into a conference center in Estes Park in the Rockies, I thought, "Why aren't we meeting outdoors? How do you compete with or try to recreate something so beautiful that God has created?"

To make an environment, you first have to think about what you want to do in that particular place. People need to sit down as a group and consider what worship means to that particular community. Then they can begin to think about the symbols, the way a

design or colors can better make that happen.

I think a meeting house or a place where people worship must be able to be changed, because different kinds of experiences happen in worship. When you have everything so nailed down, you say there is only one way anything can happen.

I encourage people to create worship. The worship experience is a special kind of thing that happens in a different way each time. We use visual objects and other things that are different in worship each week. Lots of visual ideas can tell about the Bible, about our faith journey, our experiences in sharing with each other.

People in the faith community should discuss what is going to happen in their church's worship service: What do we want to happen here? What is special about our particular group of people?

Joyce Miller
Elgin, Illinois

See also 3) TEN YOUTH MINISTRY CONCERNS, 15) WONDERS, 42) CAMP PRODUCTIONS, 44) FIRE, 130) PRAYER CHAIR, 193) ROOTED IN WORSHIP

165. WORSHIP TASK FORCE

We've found the "task force" concept an essential help in planning (and defending) contemporary worship. The force's membership should be intergenerational and passionately interested in modern worship.

It is important to start by thinking through the meaning of worship. What does it do? What is it for? How could it better be used? A look at the history of worship is very important because the church for 2,000 years has done all kinds of things. We are just discovering the church's variety of worship styles throughout the ages. If we can say to folks that the church has done this particular thing before, it won't be so upsetting.

After you get in touch with the rich meaning and history of worship, dream of new ways to worship. Then survey the talents within the congregation and try the dream in a worship service. Perhaps the dream is simply a guitarist playing a special hymn. Some slides can be projected on the wall as the hymn is sung.

Contemporary worship requires a lot of prayer, love, patience and caring. Reconciliation needs to take place with the people who get upset with the different worship styles. The best way to bring differing views together is to try to love those who put you down. If possible, exchange feelings about the changes. Let the critics tell their story and share the points where they have problems with the changes. Then make sure they hear the task force. Communicate that the force never meant to hurt anyone. Share your findings concerning the varieties of worship in church history. Explain that worship must be contemporary to enhance relevance. Share your struggles to worship God in ways meaningful to today's culture and issues.

Wes Taylor
Oregon City, Oregon

See also 3) TEN YOUTH MINISTRY CONCERNS, 7) PLANNING STRATEGY, 42) CAMP PRODUCTIONS, 166) GETTING THE WORD OUT, 183) MULTIMEDIA WORSHIP, 191) JEWISH/CHRISTIAN CELEBRATIONS, 207) PARTICIPATORY CHRISTMAS PAGEANT

Worship can take many forms. A worship service that your group prayerfully and sensitively designs can be an unforgettable experience.

166. GETTING THE WORD OUT

Perhaps the best way to avoid communication problems and hard feelings toward alternative forms of worship is to let people know ahead of time that something different will be tried. That way the less-than-enthusiastic folks can choose whether to attend or stay home.

We have a love feast twice a year. There were about eight young people who wanted to work up a movement dance choir for one of these feasts. They developed an interpretation of 1 Corinthians 13, the well-known love chapter. It was a fantastic celebration and creative in the best sense. It quietly invited everyone to reach out and serve one another.

Because the service involved sacred dance, we decided to let the word go out that the upcoming service would involve an art form new to the church. We talked a lot with people and wrote articles for several weeks in the newsletter. We were careful to point out that the movement referred to 1 Corinthians 13.

The anticipation for the service was high. The results were powerful. After the service many had tears in their eyes, saying things like, "How beautiful, what a wonderful experience." Some folks stayed away. That was okay.

Since then, overcoming communication problems has become easier and easier. New worship forms are accepted more readily if adults come expecting the unexpected.

Joyce Miller
Elgin, Illinois

See also 7) PLANNING STRATEGY, 42) CAMP PRODUCTIONS, 69) SUNDAY SCHOOL PUBLICITY BLITZ, 140) BIG DOGS, ARMS SALES AND HUNGER, 156) REACH, 165) WORSHIP TASK FORCE, 191) JEWISH/CHRISTIAN CELEBRATIONS, 197) CHORAL READING, 211) GOOD FRIDAY SACRED DANCE

Your group has untapped imaginative powers. Channel those creative imaginations into a meaningful Christian outreach, such as clowning.

167. CLOWNING

I got very excited about clowns back in the 1960s when I discovered that the word clown came from the ancient word "clod." As you look through the New Testament, you discover the nearest equivalent word for clod is "servant." And I thought to myself, "Wow, that's kind of neat. Jesus must love clowns." That new awareness began to grow into different programs. It took me to colleges, seminaries, retirement homes, hospitals, congregations and shopping centers.

The clown is an unusual symbol. It takes words and turns them into action. It uses exaggeration to describe things. In fact, in the early church there were actually clowns who would occasionally interrupt the service so that people would not take it for granted. They didn't disrupt it because that would be sacrilegious. They interrupted. They surely helped worship come alive.

There are many things happening in our clown groups. We have youth going to nursing homes. We have elderly people and handicapped people who are clowns. Clowning is even being used with the terminally ill and the emotionally impaired.

It's easy to get involved in clown ministry. But first consider the purpose of clowns. A clown takes common things and sets them apart for the uncommon. After all, that is what Jesus did, didn't he? He used spit and dirt in one of his miracles. He set apart bread and wine. He set a child in their midst and said, "Unless you become as a child, you will not know what the Kingdom is all about."

Use this game to begin thinking like a clown. Think like a clown while riding a bus, sitting in school or walking along a road. Look around for common objects. For example, do you have a clean handkerchief? Ask yourself: "How can I play with this handkerchief?" Could you make one of those cat's cradle things? Could you get some other person to hold his or her index fingers up and pretend they are a bull's horns to your cape? Why don't you do clown magic where you put the handkerchief over your hand with one index finger up while you count off "one-two-three" nonverbally? Then pull off the handkerchief. Presto, your index finger is gone! You have pulled it down into your fist. Can you make a mask with it? Or perhaps it becomes a jumping rope in your imaginative hands.

Shoe laces, paper cups or anything in a room could trigger this kind of creativity. This is what clowning is all about: taking the common (what we are as human beings) and setting it apart for the uncommon (which is what Christ has called us to be).

Here's another preparatory exercise for clown ministry. Take a moment in which the group stops talking. In order to use imagination, I believe you need to use nonverbal communication. Take a moment and ask each person to think about some object on his or her person. Maybe it is a loose thread. Maybe it is a Life Saver, stick of gum, key, pencil, belt or shoestring. After that minute or two, play some music. Ask group members to playfully share their common object.

I can tell you what will happen when you first use this kind of game. Some will be reluctant. They will wonder why they came. Others will have an initial idea. However, after three or four minutes, you will see everyone's imagination begin to get better and more complete. Your group will have a great deal of fun as it plays more and more like a clown. Go and do something intentionally foolish for Christ's sake.

Floyd Shaffer
Roseville, Michigan

See also 9) BIBLE EXPLORATIONS, 158) CLOWNING OUTREACH, 159) YOUTH CIRCUS, 160) PUPPET MAKING, 168) THREE RING CIRCUS WORSHIP

168. THREE RING CIRCUS WORSHIP

Several years ago our youth stumbled upon the clown/circus motif and imagery. We were working on a special worship experience for youth and adults. Our theme was "One Circus, Three Rings—Forever and Ever—Hurrah." We held the service in the little theater area of the church. We used a ringmaster as the worship leader. He was dressed to fit the role. We chose the music ("Jesus Christ Superstar"), a film ("The Parable"), balloons, etc., to fit this theme. The response was fantastic. Here is the outline of the service we developed:

ONE CIRCUS   THREE RINGS   FOREVER AND EVER   HURRAH

Think On These Things:

Life is not always meant to be solemn. God meant life to be laughter, singing and praise. Like a circus full of joy. Our circus tent today is meant to be alive with meaning. Feel free to move about and when something speaks to your heart, a poster or a person, find your place in the Sanctuary and think on these things.

Let the Music Begin
- The Overture from Jesus Christ Superstar
- Switched on Bach

An Act of Praise (the people find their seats)

Ringmaster: Make a joyful noise all the lands.

People: Come before his presence with singing.

Ringmaster: Serve the Lord with gladness.

Acts of Singing   The Sons and Daughters
- Hosanna
- Halla lu, Halla lu, Halla lu, Halla lu Yah, Praise Ye the Lord.

Act of Affirmation

Leader: Christians must go where the night is darkest

People: *And be the light.*

Leader: They must go where wrong is strongest

People: *And be the right.*

Leader: They must go where there are cowards

People: *And be courageous.*

Leader: They must go where there are slaves

People: *And be free.*

Leader: Christians must go where there's doubt

People: *And have faith.*

Leader: They must go where there's hate

People: *And be loving.*

Leader: They must go where people are Christless

People: *And be Christian.*

God's First Act

Psalm 23: A scripture from the Old Testament

Act of Praise   The Sons and Daughters
The Swinging Shepherd Blues

God's Second Act   1 Corinthians 13

MC: If I speak with the eloquence of barkers and high-flying angels, but have no love, I become no more than banging drums and crashing symbols. If I have the gift of fortunetelling and mind-reading and hold in my mind all the secrets of God; if I have the body of the strong man, but have not love, I am powerless. If I deliver my body to rest on beds of nails and consume flames; if I have not love, I have given an empty shell. This love of which I speak is patient. It looks for new ways of overcoming difficult tasks. It allows others to use their skills. It does not show off or think itself the most important act.

People: *Love has good manners and does not take advantage of other actors' miscues.*

MC: Love is not touchy.

People: *Love does not count another performer's mistakes to remind him at a later time.*

MC: Love knows no limit to its endurance, no end to its hope for perfection.

People: *Love can outlast anything; love is the one thing that still stands when all else has fallen.*

MC: In this circus we have three great rings: Faith, Hope, Love.

People: *And the greatest of these is LOVE.*

continued

THREE RING CIRCUS WORSHIP

In the Center Ring, The Main Event:
"THE PARABLE"
(An event without words,
except as you supply them)

Who was the clown at the beginning?
What was the meaning of the parade?
What acts of love did the clown perform?
Who was the clown at the end?

An Act of Resolution   Kum Bah Yah
People weary, Lord
People hating, Lord
People dying, Lord
People praying, Lord
People loving, Lord
Come by here, O Lord, Come by here.

An Act of Dedication
MC: See that clown spreading love
around
People: *See people holding hands*

*Beginning to understand
That plain communication
Will end all complication*
MC: Talking about a new direction
Talking about a love infection
Who's that clown spreading love
around?
People: *Where the needs of the world cross
the abilities and gifts that God has
given me:* **There** *is my cross.*
MC: Take up your cross and follow.
People: *Here am I Lord, send me.*

Final Act
Amen. Amen. Amen.

Jo Ann Kirch
Cincinnati, Ohio

*See also 42) CAMP PRODUCTIONS, 158) CLOWN-
ING OUTREACH, 159) YOUTH CIRCUS, 166) GET-
TING THE WORD OUT, 167) CLOWNING, 176)
COMMON OBJECT MEDITATIONS*

169. LOAVES AND FISHES

As I prepared the wor-
ship service, I knew there
would be several ministers
present as part of a visit to
help us evaluate our progress as a church. For that
reason I thought I should
play it safe and do the
usual kind of service. But
when I looked at the lec-
tionary, I found that the
story of the feeding of the
5,000 (John 6:1-15) was the
text. A crazy but appealing
idea came to mind.

I talked it over with my
wife and she urged me to
try my idea. She baked
loaves of rye bread and
wrapped chocolate fish in foil. The only other preparation prior to the service was that
we chose a teenager to act as reporter during the worship. His task was to interview
various people in the worship service like an
on-the-street reporter.

170. FOOTBALL WORSHIP

The quiet roar of a televised football game interspersed with obnoxious beer and tire commercials kept me company as I worked on a sermon. I was churning over Philippians 3:12-14, where Paul exhorts the people to press on to the goals of Christ. Suddenly the natural analogy between football and the passage fumbled into my mind. A game plan for the service was developed. Here's the playbook:

1. *Coming into the stadium* (prelude, call to worship, etc.)
2. *Cheering his presence* (hymn of praise, Gloria Patri, etc.)
3. *Talking with the owner* (prayers)
4. *Halftime* (announcements, greetings, etc.)
5. *You have to sacrifice* (offering)

6. *Words from the coach on playing the game*—This was broken into two parts. The first was "Words from the playbook (Bible)." I read Philippians 3:12-14. Then "Locker Room Talk" (sermon) focused on how we too must "play out our lives." Sometimes we are successful moving down the field of life. At other times, we meet a wall of resistance, or we fumble, or we get our words and dreams intercepted. I then went on and pointed out that God's grace and love enable us to get a new "first and 10."

7. *Invitation to the training table* (communion)—I reminded them that there has been one who was apparently tackled by death and yet appeared in the end zone as a resurrected presence proclaiming victory over what appeared to be defeat. All were invited to this all-pro's table to be part of his winning team.

8. *A song for the team* (closing, hymn, benediction)

The comments following the service were extremely favorable. Everyone understood the metaphor. I believe it could easily be a model for a fall or winter youth service. The response may warrant an instant replay.

Richard M. Hammett
Raymore, Missouri

On Sunday morning we gathered and read the story of feeding of the 5,000. I called for volunteers from the congregation to come forward and take the roles of disciples. I gave them four minutes to prepare to act out the scripture.

After four minutes the disciples came into the service and distributed the food which Jesus blessed.

The interviewer then went into the congregation with a microphone on a long cord and asked for responses. One member shared a simple six-line hymn set to a popular folk tune which told the story. We closed the service with a reading about the feeding of the hungry in the world.

John Roberts
Auckland, New Zealand

See also 17) ENCOUNTER BIBLE CHARACTERS, 54) CHEAP ROLE PLAYS, 139) HUNGER IDEAS, 140) BIG DOGS, ARMS SALES AND HUNGER, 152) BREAD

See also 163) EXTRA! JESUS LIVES, 166) GETTING THE WORD OUT, 192) IDEAS FROM OTHER CULTURES

171. PAPERBAG CONFESSIONS

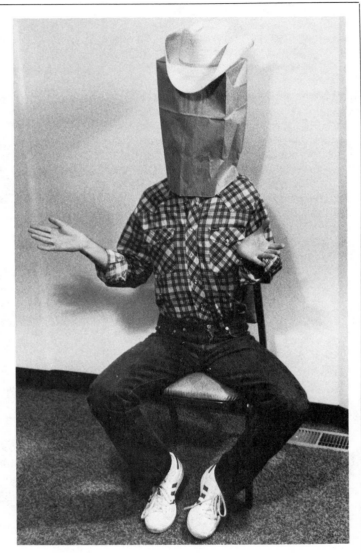

We were working with a large group of high school youth in their school setting where we would be worshiping together. The group desired creative worship. The confession of sin was one part of the service that was especially difficult. The reading of prepared prayers so often does not convey the excitement of spiritual forgiveness known in Jesus Christ. So we wanted to think creatively. And we came up with a real "mind-blowing" idea.

We gave each person a paper bag at confession time. After spending a little time introducing the meaning of confession, we asked each person to put the bag over his or her head and then to reflect on something which was a hidden, sinful part of his/her life.

We were really "playing it by ear," uncertain how we were going to conclude this portion of the service. We took our cues from one of the youth. In typical fashion, after we had removed the bags from our heads, one of the youth pretended that he was going to break the inflated bag. That was it! We asked everyone to inflate the bags. Then we said, "Now let's celebrate the fact that we are forgiven by making a joyful noise." With this announcement the students all broke their paper bags. The noise was joyful!

Warren Smith, Loxton, South Australia

See also 104) SHOPPING BAG VALUES, 176) COMMON OBJECT MEDITATIONS, 178) SIN BURN-OFF

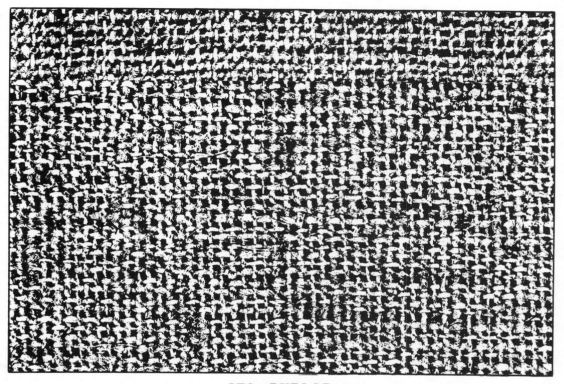

172. BURLAP

Here's a tool I used at a recent retreat for adults and youth. It was well received as everyone worked on feeling the pieces of cloth as they were passed around. People shared their thoughts after each reading. I used the quotes of spiritual brothers and sisters to trigger the thoughts and feelings of the group.

Here are the different items that made the experience:

1. This banner represents the church. It is not finished yet. We hope everyone will become a part of the banner by coloring one square in our design. We are keeping the design a secret until we color as many squares as possible. Much of the banner's message and symbolism is not in the design. It is in the cloth itself. That's what we'd like to tell you about this morning.

2. Bible passages we studied:
● John 13:34-35
● Acts 4:32-34
● Romans 12:3-6
● Romans 14:7-13
● Romans 15:1-7
● Galatians 6:1-2
● Philippians 2:1-7
● Colossians 3:12-17
● Hebrews 10:23-25

3. Burlap is a lot like you and me. Burlap is not uniform. Each piece is unique. A bolt of burlap is supposed to be 36 inches wide, but it's always 35 or 37 inches wide. Each thread (which is really more like small twine) runs across the bolt in an uneven line. Each piece of twine-thread is thick in one spot, but thins to almost nothing in another. Burlap is maddening stuff to work with because the weave is so uneven. A yardstick or tape measure is often of little use. There's no way to draw a straight line on a piece of bur-

continued

BURLAP

lap without violating the integrity of the material. If you're going to mark it, you have to follow the flow of the threads. You have to work with it, not against it. People are a lot like burlap.

4. Burlap is a lot like people. Each piece is unique. Some pieces have strong vertical threads but are weak in the horizontal. Some have strong horizontal threads but are weak in the vertical. Some pieces are tightly woven; others are loosely woven. All from the same bolt, but each piece unique.

5. We have missed the full impact of the Gospel if we have not discovered what it is to be ourselves, loved by God, irreplaceable in his sight, unique among our fellow men. —*Bruce Larson*

6. All burlap is fairly open in its weave, but we're never quite able to see through it. Burlap is coarse and abrasive. If you rub two pieces together, all sorts of irritating, prickly little threads stand up. All burlap has one thing in common: Once a piece is cut out of the original bolt, it tends to unravel at the edges. Each and every piece contains flaws. There are imperfect, woody and discolored pieces woven in with the fabric. People are a lot like burlap.

7. Burlap is a lot like you and me. If you look closely, many of the imperfections have more to do with the strength, than with the weakness of the fabric. And even with the most glaring of flaws, if you try to pull them out, you weaken the whole fabric. You can neatly and easily unravel the threads one by one from an edge, until you get the imperfection out. But then you've destroyed the fabric and have nothing left but a pile of loose threads, without substance or meaning.

8. God does not make the other person as I would have made him. He did not give him to me as a brother for me to dominate and control, but in order that I might find above him the Creator. —*Dietrich Bonhoeffer*

9. Burlap is a lot like you and me. It would take a miracle to make this coarse, dark, imperfect burlap anything other than its natural self. And the subject of this banner, that is, the symbols we will see when it's finished, has much to say about a miracle that changes the coarse, dark, and imperfect part of us.

10. This banner is a lot like the church. When these strips are woven together they begin to form an interesting pattern. Where one piece is weak or imperfect, another is strong and supportive. The woven strips keep one another from coming unraveled.

11. Confess your sins to one another, and pray for one another, that you may be healed. —*James 5:16 (RSV)*

12. God does not comfort us to make us comfortable, but to make us comforters. —*John Henry Jowett*

13. Even though the textures and patterns of the woven banner are interesting, it seems empty and a little drab. There is still

something missing. It is colorless without meaning, without message, without spirit. This woven burlap is only a surface on which to present the message. In the same way, the woven burlap becomes a background for visual symbols. The church, no matter how tightly or interestingly structured, is only a background to reflect the color, spirit, and love of God for others.

14. Merely going to church doesn't make you a Christian any more than going to a garage makes you an automobile. —*Billy Sunday*

15. It would scarcely be necessary to expound doctrine if our lives were radiant enough. If we behaved like true Christians, there would be no pagans. —*Pope John XXIII*

16. No matter how strong the fellowship, unless Jesus is visibly present in our lives, the church is nothing more than empty burlap.

17. Many of today's young people have lit-

tle difficulty believing that God was in Christ. What they find hard to accept is that Christ is in the church. —*Ernest T. Campbell*

18. Jesus prays for his disciples: "I do not pray only for them, but also for those who believe in me because of their message. I pray that they may all be one. O Father! May they be in us, just as you are in me and I am in you. May they be one, so that the world will believe that you sent me. I gave them the same glory you gave me, so that they may be one, just as you and I are one: I in them and you in me, so they may be completely one, in order that the world may know that you sent me and that you love them as you love me"—*John 17:20-23*

19. A prayer: Lord, help us to be the kind of supportive community this banner represents.

Bless the hands and the hearts that are helping create this banner.

As we commit ourselves to be a part of this banner help us to understand what it means to commit ourselves to "being" the church.

We cannot commit ourselves to being part of this banner without coming away with some chalk and lint on ourselves.

Just as surely, we cannot commit ourselves to being the church without having your blessings "rub off" on us.

As we risk being a part of this banner, not knowing its final symbolism and meaning . . . let us commit ourselves to the "risk" of being the church, knowing surely where you have told us that risk will take us.

As we find the spot in the banner that will be ours, help us to find within ourselves the strengths you would have us contribute to the church. Amen.

Adolph Quast
Waukesha, Wisconsin

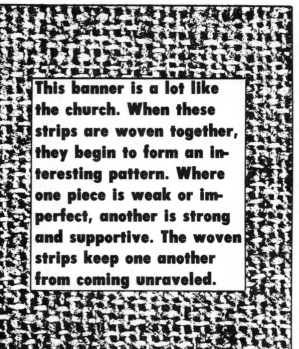

This banner is a lot like the church. When these strips are woven together, they begin to form an interesting pattern. Where one piece is weak or imperfect, another is strong and supportive. The woven strips keep one another from coming unraveled.

See also 47) *LIVING IN TANKS,* 73) *MEDIA PROBING,* 78) *LORD'S PRAYER DANDELIONS,* 116) *GROUP BANNER,* 118) *STOP AND SMELL THE ROSES,* 173) *YARN WEB,* 176) *COMMON OBJECT MEDITATIONS*

173. YARN WEB

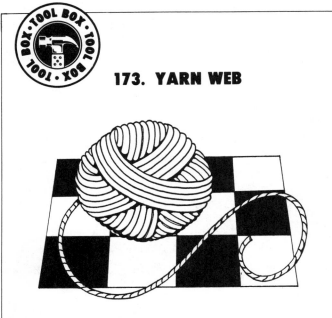

Our theme for our senior high retreat was our need for each other, and ways in which we could reach out to others. To conclude the retreat, we all sat in a circle and gave thanks to other members of the group who in some way had touched our lives that weekend. We all participated, and everyone received thanks for something done during that weekend. Some were thanked for playing a good soccer game, others were appreciated for being good listeners and others were praised for willingly sharing important parts of their lives.

This led into a communion service where the bread and the cup were passed around the circle. We ended with the leader of the group tossing a ball of yarn to a person in the group who was told to pass it on until all of us in the group were connected by the yarn. We used Carole King's record, "You've Got a Friend" as background music for this service.

Monica Brown
Hyattsville, Maryland

See also 49) ALL NIGHT TALK, 51) MOUNTAINTOP TO PLAIN, 105) SPIRITUAL PUZZLE, 130) PRAYER CHAIR, 172) BURLAP, 179) BISQUICK COMMUNION

174. YOUTH AND SOCIAL ISSUES

We attempt to relate contemporary issues into the life of our youth group. The kids appreciate relevance. For example, we did a youth group service on the refugees coming to Australia from Vietnam. Out of the thousands of people who left Vietnam by boat, half died at sea. We got a very small percentage. We found out that no one really knew anything about the refugees. We explored the attitude of the Australian government, how they were helping, hindering or welcoming them.

We put the people in the congregation in a situation where they experienced the conditions that the boat people had to face. So, we put a 6-foot by 10-foot raft in the middle of the altar area with three to four chairs on it. We usually have 25-30 people at the early service. We conducted the whole service with everybody standing on the raft. There were more than 30 people there. Few were able to sit down. Who sits on the chairs? The young people have as much right as the old. Who gets the chairs? We also showed a slide presentation about refugee conditions. An offering was taken for the boat people.

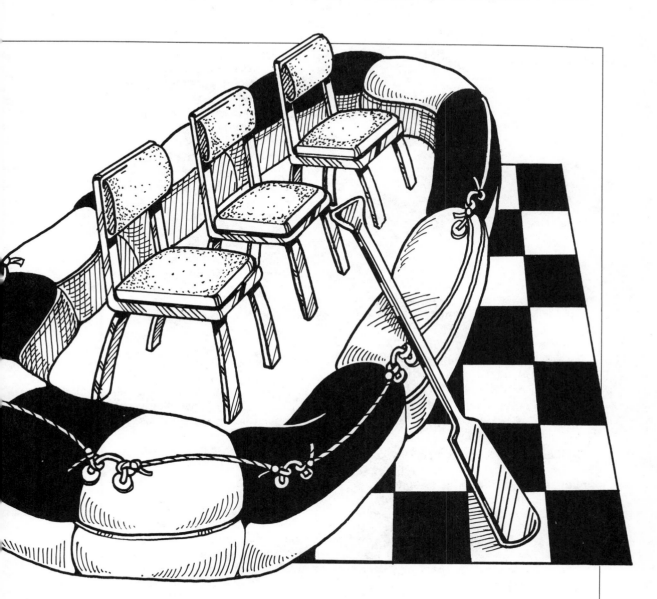

The service raised several issues and revealed how we are responsible to one another.

Ross Gardner
Melbourne, Australia

See also 26) FLIGHT 108, 30) BEING HANDICAPPED, 31) HANDICAPPED RETREAT, 46) HAVES AND HAVE NOTS, 139) HUNGER IDEAS, 140) BIG DOGS, ARMS SALES AND HUNGER, 166) GETTING THE WORD OUT, 200) AMEN!

175. PNEUMA TIME

"Pneuma Time" began a few years back when I developed a meditational booklet for a senior high workcamp. My desire was to have a biblically-oriented journal which would accomplish two things. The first was to help the Bible touch some of the kids' daily concerns. The second was to serve as a discussion starter. The first page of "Pneuma Time" explains the purpose of and tips for using the booklet:

"This booklet is yours to use as you wish. Its purpose is to help you discover new ways of relating to God and other people during this workcamp. It will be most helpful if you take about 15 minutes *alone* each morning, and work on the page for that day. So that you can see your growth during this trip, please *write down* your thoughts and feelings on the back of each page, each morning. At the end of the booklet, there are 3 blank pages to use for notes, a diary or whatever. During the evenings, and at other times when it's convenient, we'll discuss this material. We hope you find it worthwhile to spend some serious time with this booklet. By the way, "pneuma" is the Greek word for 'spirit'."

Here is an example of a meditation from "Pneuma Time":

STRANGERS WITH A GREAT POTENTIAL

Readings
Matthew 9:16-17, Matthew 18:19-20

Meditation on Psalm 142
I direct my cries to the Lord.
Out of the ear-piercing sounds and the ceaseless turmoil of my noisy, busy world,
I speak God's name.
For my heart is deeply troubled and depressed, and I feel weary and faint.
I am confused and lost.
I cannot find my way.
The nameless faces that rush by take no notice of me.
No one knows my name.
And no one cares.
I turn to you, O God.
You have heard me before, and you responded to my cries.
Perhaps even amidst the frustrating activities and busy schedules of my life,
You can hear the cries of me, your lonely child.
O God, deliver me from my prison of loneliness.
Turn my cries of distress into proclamations of joy.
Direct my steps into the fellowship of others who love and serve you. Amen.

To think about . . .
We are a new group of people, gathered in God's name. But we're strangers . . . "no one knows my name and no one cares."
Should we take the effort to care for each other? How can we do it? If each of us is an "old wineskin," what "new wine" could we produce this week?

Andy Rosulek
Madison, Minnesota

See also 9) BIBLE EXPLORATIONS, 28) DEAR ME, 52) RETREAT FEEDBACK, 79) HAPPINESS IS . . .

176. COMMON OBJECT MEDITATIONS

We have found great value in setting aside a few minutes for the group to think, focus and pray together. The meditations below were developed as we focused on common things. These ordinary things of life, however, took on new meanings in our group meditation.

You may wish to expand on these ideas in a variety of ways. There are many other common things around the room. You can find meaning in each common thing as well as relate that meaning to your own experience with God.

"SHOES"
Materials needed:
Shoes of varying sizes

Ideas to develop:
- There are different sizes of shoes
- They are constructed of different materials
- Older shoes are most comfortable

Look carefully at each shoe. Walk in different shoes. Which shoe feels the most comfortable? Other shoes don't feel as comfortable as your own pair, do they? After wearing them several times, they become more comfortable. In much the same way, you grow in the knowledge that God is always with you and is your friend.

Did you ever wear a shoe that was too tight and pinched your foot? Do you think God's love is ever like this? When your conscience tells you to do something or not to do something, could this be God "pinching" you?

Touch the various shoes around you. Some of the construction materials may be imitation and some may be leather. Some people are very genuine and truly live as Christians while others may be like the imitation leather, putting up a good front. Yet within they are not living as God wants them to live. Many times it is difficult for others to tell the difference. But God knows what is in every heart. We cannot fool God.

Think of the different places your shoes have taken you. Name a few of those places. Was God pleased to walk with you?

Did you ever get a stone in your shoe? If so, it prevented you from doing what you had set out to do, at least until the stone was removed. This can happen in our lives. We can be headed in the right direction but something happens to prevent us from going on. Remember that the Bible tells us we can turn to God when we are frustrated and disappointed. He's a good listener!

continued

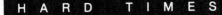

COMMON OBJECT MEDITATIONS

"RUBBER BAND"

Materials needed: A rubber band for each member of the group.

Ideas to develop:
- Rubber bands stretch
- They hold things together
- They are flexible

What can you do with your rubber band? How far can you stretch your rubber band? As you stretch the rubber band think about God's love that will stretch and stretch and stretch! God's love and mercy stretch on forever.

Did you know that some rubber bands have more stretch than others? Search for bands of various degrees of flexibility and experiment with them. People are like rubber bands. Some are more flexible than others.

Find various things that a rubber band can hold together. Put your rubber band around the materials that you have found. Did your rubber band break if you attempted to bundle too many things? When we try to do too many things at one time, we often have difficulty, too. Can you think of a time when this might have happened to you? Are times when we challenge God's love just like when we test the strength of the rubber band? Remember God's love is everlasting. This is God's great gift to us.

"LIGHT BULB"

Materials needed: Three-way light bulb
Night light or small lamp

Ideas to develop:
- Light overcomes darkness
- Brightness varies
- Needs source of power

With all lights off, talk about how you feel in the darkness. Would it be easy to live in a world of darkness? Now plug in your night light. Are you more comfortable? What is the source of power for the light in your life? Remember that Jesus said, "I am the light of the world; he who follows me shall not walk in darkness, but shall have the light of life." Let the night light be a reminder to each of us that God is always near!

Jesus said, "Let your light so shine before men, that they may see your good works, and glorify your Father which is in heaven." Think about this biblical quotation as you view the intensity levels of a three-way bulb, maybe even pretend you are one! Talk about the light bulb as a symbol of God's love shining through you. When are you like a 50 watt bulb? 100 watt? 150 watt? Has your light ever gone totally out? Do you ever turn off your light? Is this necessarily wrong? What causes flickering in a light bulb? The flickering might be compared to crises in our lives. What crises have you encountered in life? Share these personal moments with a group member.

Read carefully and prayerfully to discover more of what is written in the Bible concerning light: Psalms 27:1, Isaiah 2:5, Matthew 5:14-16, John 8:12, John 12:35-36.

"RULER"

Materials needed: Twelve-inch ruler
Ideas to develop. A ruler:

- measures
- is divided into parts
- can be made of different materials

The Beatitudes are standards of measure for the life that God gave us. Read them in Matthew 5:1-11. Think now about the 12-inch ruler as a measuring stick for your life. The ruler is divided into 12 units. How many units is your life divided into? How much time do you give every week to each important unit—church, family, work, etc.? Graph your life showing these segments. Should there be any changes? Think and pray about this.

There are three basic kinds of people in the church . . . wooden, metal, and plastic. The wooden persons, like rulers, are solid, unbendable. The metal ruler persons are flexible, but often cold. Plastic ruler persons are rigid and might break under strain. Think more deeply about each. Decide which you are most like and illustrate or share with a member of the group a time in your life which shows this.

Remember that in the Bible the golden rule is written, "So whatever you wish that men would do to you do so to them; for this is the law of the prophets" (Matthew 7:12).

"SPOON"

Materials needed: An assortment of spoons, including at least one bright silver one.
Ideas to develop:

- Differences in materials
- Differences in function
- Causes of tarnish
- Eliminating tarnish
- Feeding

Spoons, like people, are different in make-up. Some are sterling, some plated, some stainless, some wooden, etc.

How do their different uses speak to us? Tablespoons serve a whole *helping,* teaspoons a *mouthful.* What about the grapefruit spoon with its cutting edge? What is the value of a souvenir spoon? of a spoon which is turned into a piece of jewelry? How are people like spoons?

See if you have any tarnished spoons. How do spoons get that way? Tarnish can be removed. How do we become "tarnished"? How is this tarnish removed?

Look at your reflection in the bowl of a silver spoon. Then look at yourself in the back. Which image do you like better? If your day (or your life) is topsy-turvy, what can you do about it?

A spoon is made for feeding. Much of the world is hungry today. What can you do to help feed it? Jesus said that whenever you have fed "one of the least important brothers of mine, you did it for me!" (Matthew 25:40b). Tom Burdette, Ann Arbor, Michigan

See also 9) BIBLE EXPLORATIONS, 29) A STEP AHEAD, 44) FIRE, 67) AROMA, 72) CREATIVE CONJURING, 73) MEDIA PROBING, 75) A SPOONFUL OF HONEY, 76) TEA TIME, 77) SPONGE BITS, 78) LORD'S PRAYER DANDELIONS, 82) LEMONS, 138) OBJECT-IVE REFLECTIONS, 167) CLOWNING, 172) BURLAP

178. SIN BURN-OFF

177. LIVING WATER

Several young people in our church's confirmation program were mentally handicapped. We chose an unusual prop for the baptism experience to enable these youth to appreciate this special occasion in their lives.

On confirmation Sunday we brought a large fish bowl to the sanctuary, and the youth to be confirmed gathered around it. After focusing my talk on the fish in the bowl, I scooped down into the bowl with my hand and used the water to baptize the confirmands. There was a real sense of awareness about the living quality of this fish tank water.

Ken Kohlmann
Mt. Clemens, Michigan

See also 30) BEING HANDICAPPED, 31) HANDICAPPED RETREAT, 111) MELT THE DEVIL, 210) SNOW WORSHIP

After an evening of fun and Bible study with junior and senior high youth and their parents, we had a worship communion service. As part of the confession, we had a sin burning. All of us wrote our sins on pieces of paper about 2 inches by 3 inches. We stuck these pieces of paper on a nail in the center of a cross (made of scrap lumber, about 18 inches high). After the corporate confession, I went up to the cross, pressed the paper to the wood, fluffed the edges, and lit both lower corners. We sat in silence and watched the paper burn into a black rose. Someone then ended the service with a short talk on how God has forgiven our sins and made us new creatures.

Donna Lenz
Lindsborg, Kansas

Ideas on how to use this idea:
● use as a closing ceremony for a retreat
● have a session on guilt and forgiveness first, then close with this activity.

See also 44) FIRE, 171) PAPERBAG CONFESSIONS, 180) OUT OF THE DARKNESS, 196) STEP INTO THE OFFERING, 210) SNOW WORSHIP

179. BISQUICK COMMUNION

At a group retreat we prepared bread for a communion service by passing around small paper cups half-filled with Bisquick during breakfast. We asked everyone to mix some liquid with the Bisquick to form a dough. People used milk, orange juice, coffee, even maple syrup. Each person placed his or her lump of dough on a greased cookie sheet. Then we pressed the dough together lightly to form a loaf but not enough to mix the individual lumps together. After the dough was allowed to rise, we baked the loaf.

At our communion service later that day, the loaf was broken and passed around. A great discussion followed on how communion symbolizes that we are all individuals, but we become one "mixed up" loaf through Jesus Christ.

Thomas J. Potenza
Barrington, Illinois

See also 105) SPIRITUAL PUZZLE, 118) STOP AND SMELL THE ROSES, 173) YARN WEB, 182) FORTUNE COOKIES

180. OUT OF THE DARKNESS

Our group experienced the meaning of going from darkness into light one evening during our communion service. The young people came into a darkened room with a table in the center. A candle burned brightly on the table. I asked the youth to form a circle around the table, facing away from the center. As we moved through the act of confession (in isolation, facing the darkness), we turned to the center of the room, the light, and into the community of each other and forgiveness.

Lamar L. Imes, Fort Wayne, Indiana

See also 44) FIRE, 109) ROOM DYNAMICS, 178) SIN BURN-OFF, 181) LIGHT AND DARKNESS

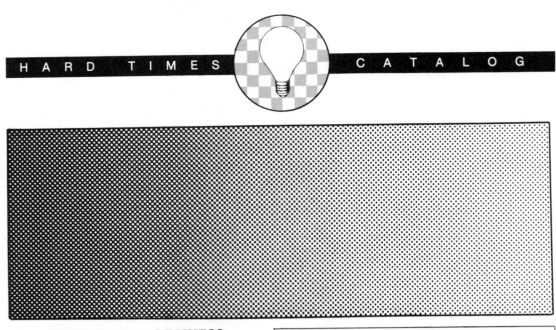

181. LIGHT AND DARKNESS

Time: 2 hours
Comments: Successful model. Intergenerational. Could be used with adults and youth. Minimal talking is necessary to create a reverent atmosphere.
Materials: Bible, newspapers, scissors, communion elements

1. Blind Walk—Pair off with someone you don't usually hang around with. Take your partner on a blind walk through the church. Show them the church through touch. Make it a "religious experience." Then change roles. Return to meeting room and share feelings about being "blind" (30 minutes).

2. Read 1 John 2:7-11 and discuss the meaning of darkness and light in the real world.

3. (Distribute newspapers and scissors.) Each pair finds an article, a word or a picture that symbolizes darkness and another that symbolizes light. The pair keeps their two symbols for later.

4. Confession and Forgiveness—Everyone sits in chairs around a table. On the table are two candles, a cup of wine (or juice) and a loaf of bread. Sit beside your partner. Partners turn chairs to face each other. One says to the other one unlovable thing about himself or herself. The listener responds with one thing about the confessor that he or she finds lovable. Then change roles.

5. Prayers of the People—Each pair shares their newspaper symbol, explaining why it symbolizes darkness or light. One person from the pair offers a prayer of thanks for the light symbol and a prayer asking God to change the dark symbol.

6. Eucharist—The leader informally recounts the gift of Christ as the light of the world and gives thanks for the bread and wine. All say The Lord's Prayer. The communion is shared—one to the other. Each person passes the bread or wine addressing the person by name, e.g., "Jane, the body of Christ, for you" and "Jane, the blood of Christ, for you."

7. Concluding prayer and a sign of farewell—
Leader: "Go forth into the world rejoicing in the light of the Spirit."
People: "Thanks be to God."

Ralph W. Pitman, Jr.
Columbia, Pennsylvania

See also 130) PRAYER CHAIR, 172) BURLAP, 180) OUT OF THE DARKNESS

182. FORTUNE COOKIES

Fortune cookies serve as tasty discussion starters or icebreakers. Our youth group used these at a retreat. During one of our Bible study sessions, we passed out a fortune cookie to each person. They carefully removed the fortune and threw it away. In its place each person wrote a Bible passage, word of wisdom or advice on a similar piece of paper and inserted it into the cookie. We collected all the cookies and kept them until we celebrated communion at the very end of our retreat. The fortune cookies took the place of communion bread. Each person was given a cookie and broke it open, read the message and ate the cookie. After all read their messages, several volunteered to share what the message meant to them. This fortune cookie communion was very moving.

Jan Otto
Gig Harbor, Washington

See also 76) TEA TIME, 133) PROGRESSIVE DINNERS, 169) LOAVES AND FISHES, 179) BISQUICK COMMUNION

183. MULTIMEDIA WORSHIP

Worship should be an experience that relates to life outside the church's walls. Simple audio-visuals help youth worship. You can't do whiz-bang shows all the time. But a simple camera, a little cassette recorder and a microphone can be keys to exciting worship. I am only a student of so many other people who have taught me this.

Here's a multimedia experience that was quite successful. The song, "Love Is in the Air," by John Paul Young was a popular song. At the time I used it, we were hearing it all the time. I love it. I believe that where Jesus walked, love was in the air.

Our group went down to the city square.

continued

MULTIMEDIA WORSHIP

Our city square is where a lot of the people have lunch, browse through shops and that sort of thing. We snapped color slides of different ways "love was in the air" in the square.

We took pictures of young couples eating lunch together, mothers with their children, old couples walking through the square, and a little brother picking up his little sister.

On the night of the presentation to a city-wide youth gathering, I said something like, "Sometimes in our working and study lives we really get bogged down with ourselves. If we look around us, sometimes God speaks to us through the people that we don't know, through the sights and the sounds of the city. We sat in one spot in our city square, and this is what we saw." Then we just played the song and showed the slides. It was powerful. Many young people said to me that whenever they heard that song on the radio, they remembered the slide presentation, and how Jesus' love is indeed "in the air."

Pauline Hubner
Brisbane, Australia

See also 62) THE "AVERAGE" KID, 73) MEDIA PROBING, 80) TV WISDOM, 108) FIVE-PART MEETING DESIGN, 153) CHRISTMAS OUTREACH, 163) EXTRA! JESUS LIVES, 165) WORSHIP TASK FORCE, 184) HUMAN PROJECTION SCREEN, 185) SLIDES AND PRAYERS

184. HUMAN PROJECTION SCREEN

TOOL BOX · TOOL BOX · TOOL BOX · TOOL BOX ·

Dennis Benson, co-author of **Hard Times Catalog,** models his "media robe." He uses the robe as a projection screen for movies and slides.

To conclude a Lenten service, a white-robed figure appeared in the middle of the worship center. He held out his hands in the position of crucifixion. Slides of famous crucifixion paintings were projected on the white robe. It was an extremely effective means of presenting an overview of this historical art of the Holy Week. Projecting images onto a person is certainly a unique way to show slides.

Richard Faris
Danville, Virginia

See also 183) MULTIMEDIA WORSHIP, 185) SLIDES AND PRAYERS, 186) DEAD FILMSTRIPS, 189) SING OUT

185. SLIDES AND PRAYERS

We organized a youth service during the Christmas vacation time. We chose 12 different slides. We also selected the same number of young people. We asked them to reflect on the slide assigned to them and pray until they were moved to approach the mike and share their thoughts with the others. The people on the slides were drawn from many different cultures with many races represented. It was just a wonderful, peaceful and beautiful evening service.

Jerry Duhaine and Bob Black
Lordminister, Canada

See also 62) THE "AVERAGE" KID, 80) TV WISDOM, 130) PRAYER CHAIR, 183) MULTIMEDIA WORSHIP, 184) HUMAN PROJECTION SCREEN, 186) DEAD FILMSTRIPS, 189) SING OUT

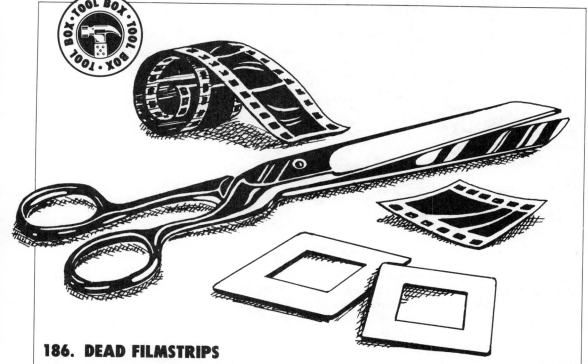

186. DEAD FILMSTRIPS

Most churches have old, outdated and unused filmstrips collecting dust in a closet. Our group transformed these "useless" resources into a neat slide and sound presentation for the church. We bought some slide mounts at a photo supply store. Then we cut up the filmstrips and mounted them into the slide mounts. (The folks at the photo supply store can show you how to mount slides.) Be sure the right people give the group permission as to which filmstrips can be cut up. It was good to see the group create a colorful presentation from filmstrips which had been tucked away in a dark closet.

Jan Otto
Gig Harbor, Washington

See also 80) TV WISDOM, 108) FIVE-PART MEETING DESIGN, 183) MULTIMEDIA WORSHIP, 184) HUMAN PROJECTION SCREEN, 185) SLIDES AND PRAYERS

187. POP MUSIC POSSIBILITIES

We have conducted different surveys with youth and found that almost 95 percent say they are influenced heavily by contemporary music. They also say that they are influenced highly by the church. Finally, they see no connection between pop music and the church.

We have tried in workshops to start out by showing some of the things that are happening with themes. I did a montage of different contemporary music on a certain theme. Five themes are enough to deal with. We look at the implications that those themes have, and we end up talking about some of the themes that are not the most helpful in the world. I come out of that by saying that one of the ways of using contemporary music is to look for what is good in it. If people look each month at several of the most popular albums, they will find some biblical themes and other interesting kinds of subject matter to be used in various places within the life of the church.

I've even used contemporary songs in an evening intercongregational sing-along program. The adults quite often will say that they couldn't hear what those words were. When you flash them up on a screen and the whole crowd sings together all at once, people say that they see a pretty strong Christian statement. Or they will say, "I liked all of it except for this one line." They will spend some time later discussing it. I found that very helpful.

Sing-along slides

I can suggest three or four different ways of making slides for the sing-along process. One very inexpensive way is Panatomic X film. You can use this film with any 35mm camera. The negative is nice; you can color it and the words show up whatever color you used on the slide. The bad thing about Panatomic X film is that it has kind of a greyish effect.

I prefer an offset slide-making process. We take our artwork to a printer and have him reduce it to slide-size negatives. Then we put them into the slide mounts. It has a beautiful black background. Only the words come through and they can be colored different ways. You can do a rainbow or a watercolor effect on the slides. You don't have to have any expertise with a camera to end up with nice slides. All you need is a piece of white paper, a magic marker and a yardstick. Write your lyrics on the white paper. Then take it to a printer. The only expense will be what the printer charges to make that negative. The printer will be kind of slow and hesitant at first, but after a little bit of practice, it will be done in about 3-4 minutes. We have done workshops in which we have turned in about 10-20 of the pages of the lyrics to a printer. By the time the group had finished lunch, the printer had all the slides made. Then you cut them up and mount them.

There is another way to make sing-along slides. I call them glass slides. It might remind you of the old slides that used to be mounted in glass. Take an average size storm window and paint the words on it. Then hold the storm window up over some object that illustrates what the words are about. For instance, we did lyrics to the song "Circles" by Captain and Tenille. I held it up over everything I could see that had a circle in it: wheels, soccer balls, mirror ball—anything that looked like a circle. It

had a terrific effect. Here's how it works: using Kodachrome film and a 35mm camera, shoot through the glass so that the words actually appear on top of whatever you have behind it. It is a neat effect. If you want to copy pictures out of a book you can do the same effect with an 8 x 10 piece of glass from a picture frame. At first, it is hard to get used to writing on glass, but it has a nice effect.

For anything you copy, legally you are required to give credit to the source of the pictures. You are also supposed to give total credit to who recorded the song, the publisher, the date, the writer and the performer.

Bill Wolfe
Nashville, Tennessee

See also 12) DISCOVERY BIBLE STUDY, 22) FILM CRITICISM, 42) CAMP PRODUCTIONS, 62) THE "AVERAGE" KID, 73) MEDIA PROBING, 188) JAZZ UP THE CHURCH, 189) SING OUT, 202) UNITED WE STAND . . .

188. JAZZ UP THE CHURCH

It's interesting and frustrating to be involved in the process of change. For instance, several years ago the thought of using a guitar in church was new. About that same time, I discovered jazz cantatas being written for use in churches. Yet my parishioners told me they would leave if I brought jazz into our church.

I decided not to try anything during the formal Sunday morning worship. But, we decided to have a special evening worship session called the "Night of the Jazz Cantata." Each of the youth and children's choirs presented a jazz cantata. Those who were interested or curious could all come and listen and judge for themselves.

The senior high group presented Rice and Weber's "Joseph and the Amazing Techni-color Dreamcoat." (This was before Rice and Weber wrote "Jesus Christ Superstar.") For the junior high group I discovered a cantata written by the English composer, Michael Heard. I looked around for one for the children's choir, and I couldn't find one. couldn't find one.

I wrote to some publishers. They didn't even respond. So I decided to write my own. Since the senior high group's cantata was based on an Old Testament story, I decided to pull Noah into it.

I mimeographed the sections as I wrote them and the children practiced them. They were having a ball. Each week the children were eager to see the new section of the cantata.

After I'd finished writing the cantata, I titled it "100% Chance of Rain." I put speech in it, added some instruments, and gave a little beat to it.

On the night of the jazz cantata, the children sang "100% Chance of Rain" along with the other jazz presentations. It was well received. Our congregation applauded a little bit more for it than they did the others. Upon request, we repeated it later on a Sunday morning. For the first time in the history of our church, we had applause in a worship service!

Two years later, a close friend of mine, who was on the board of directors of a music publisher, heard about my cantata and asked for a copy of the mimeographed form. He read it through and asked for a tape recording of our cantata. His company decided to publish it.

I have a bulletin where it was in Tokyo—in Japanese. "100% Chance of Rain" has been performed in Africa with an African youth choir. It has been done in England, Canada, and all across the United States.

Walter Horsley
Pittsburgh, Pennsylvania

See also 42) CAMP PRODUCTIONS, 166) GETTING THE WORD OUT, 187) POP MUSIC POSSIBILITIES

189. SING OUT

There is no secret to singing. A lot of people are scared to sing. It is one of the most personal things you can do. Yet, everyone can sing. It is only when people try to sing that they don't sing. They try too hard. How can a group be motivated to sing?

Whoever leads singing must create a non-threatening atmosphere. (When I lead singing, I first check my own attitude.) You have to be relaxed to lead singing. Your relaxed state will then just flow out to the people.

Here is a little vocal exercise to relax your singers. Radio announcers do this: "ahhhhhhhh." Just try it. "Ahhhhhhhh." It is relaxing. Then have the group make the sound of chewing with the mouth open. Exaggerate it. It is a lot of fun. I go to a lot of high schools where kids are kind of cool. They are not going to get involved with any kind of singing. So I get them to "ahhhhhhhh" while chewing with their mouths open.

Use the open mouth chewing sound with a simple song like "Down by the Riverside." Start by singing very slowly. People aren't ready for the speed stuff. Youth are not ready to clap yet. In fact, don't ever ask youth to clap. Ask them to play their hands. It

is a nice musical instrument.

Create the atmosphere and relax. Don't worry about being on pitch. Who cares? They will all get on pitch after a while. Start slow and build it up. Get into the song. Do the first verse many times. Sing songs everybody knows. You will find your group singing is a lot of fun. Keep at it. It takes time to make it safe for folks to sing.

Yohann Anderson
San Diego, California

See also 42) CAMP PRODUCTIONS, 121) PHYSICAL RISK, 184) HUMAN PROJECTION SCREEN, 185) SLIDES AND PRAYERS, 187) POP MUSIC POSSIBILITIES, 202) UNITED WE STAND . . .

 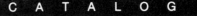

190. A.D. 81

I was involved in an excellent program for high school youth in which we relived the early church. We explained to the young people that they were living in the year A.D. 81. They were to sneak, run or use any other method to leave their "homes" (i.e., the church) and go to worship (i.e., an abandoned building). A basement or parsonage would also work. The youth encountered "Roman soldiers," "Jewish leaders," etc., in the church halls and along the way to the secret meeting place. The "officials" questioned them about where they were going.

When they finally arrived at the place of worship, they found a very worshipful atmosphere. We sang, "They'll Know We Are Christians." Then parts of a letter from Peter were read as if it had been written directly to them (1 Peter 3:13-17). We then discussed problems and persecutions we encounter in our daily lives as Christians.

We shared communion using grape juice and freshly baked bread. We affirmed one another with hugging and sharing. It was an excellent opportunity for worship and biblical application.

Eric L. White
Norcross, Georgia

See also 17) ENCOUNTER BIBLE CHARACTERS, 132) THE GREAT PUMPKIN HUNT

191. JEWISH/CHRISTIAN CELEBRATIONS

Like a lot of good ideas, this one simply evolved from a litttle curiosity. I had heard about the Jewish festivals. Images of Jewish singing, dancing and feasts paraded across my mind. My curiosity led me to a Jewish synagogue, where I requested a couple of books on these festivals, particularly those at Easter-time. The rabbi was most helpful, pleased that a Christian was interested in Jewish festivals.

As I learned more and more about the festivals, the more excited I got. The purpose of a Jewish celebration is to remember God's work with his people. The dancing, feasts and costumes provide the means to celebrate God's historical work, his contemporary presence and his promise that he will never leave us.

Finally, I presented a proposal to our youth group to sponsor an all-church Passover celebration. They liked the idea. So we began working on it.

I called around and found a woman who knew Jewish dances. She was pleased to share her knowledge with the group. The group planned the evening out. We found some Jewish costumes, set the tables in the Jewish tradition and served Jewish food. We led the congregation through simple dances. One dance is more or less a slow shuffle, moving from place to place as a Bible drama is read. An 83-year-old man had no trouble with this dance.

The evening was certainly powerful. Several of the children were wide-eyed. They knew something very special was happening. Several of the people later said the Easter celebration came to life in the dancing, feasting and costumes of the Jewish Passover celebration.

Pauline Hubner
Australia

See also 42) CAMP PRODUCTIONS

192. IDEAS FROM OTHER CULTURES

Worship models from other cultures help us to create new ones for us. For instance, we had a worship service on the river. We got the idea from the deep reverence of the Egyptians for the Nile and the Hindus for the Ganges. In India and Thailand they prepare small boats of banana stocks to offer the gods. We used driftwood, decorated with candles and play money and flower decorations. These driftwood boats were floated away to ask God's forgiveness.

The sea has always evoked immense mysterious awe. The Bible always gives tremendous reverence for the sea. The beach is the border between our familiar world and the mysterious and powerful waters of the sea. We used a beach fire, banners, a tall cross, a dramatic dance and singing to provide the environment for a real celebration.

In Thailand, tissue paper hot air balloons are released at festivals. A string of firecrackers with a long fuse and a load of candies are lifted by the balloon, which is a 3-foot by 4-foot tissue paper cube. Bright squares of tissue are glued together to make the sides. A torch fire is carefully put under it to fill it with hot air. As the hot air rises inside, the hot air balloon puffs out and soon has to be held down to complete the heating. At last, with the kids all dancing around, it is released just as the fuse for the firecrackers is lighted. A streamer trails below and when the firecrackers go off high in the air, a little sack of goodies breaks open and slips of paper with good luck slogans come fluttering down. You can see what a spontaneous celebration it could be.

Turn your attention to the heavens; concentrate upon the forces of God. Make your own hot air balloon for a summer celebration. A church picnic is the perfect setting for a celebration service. If you don't care to make your own, hot air balloons are also sold by scientific supply houses such as Ed-

mund Scientific Company, Barrington, NJ 08007.

Kites also are common in oriental festivals. Kite flying is an art. Youth groups enjoy kite flying. Why not restrict it to homemade kites only? Forewarn everybody to come equipped or come with the equipment to make the kites on the scene.

Feasting was a part of the earliest Christian services. Food is a powerful symbol in itself. Its ramifications are obvious and its appeal to smell, taste, touch and sight are imposing. Why not make soup and serve it hot during services of celebration? Imagine dangling a pot of soup on a tripod over a fire as the service progresses.

These are a few suggestions. As you study other cultures' celebrations, free your mind to dream up creative Christian applications. The fresh ideas will keep your group fresh.

Ken Dobson
Pontiac, Illinois

See also 112) KITE DAY, 170) FOOTBALL WORSHIP, 182) FORTUNE COOKIES, 191) JEWISH/ CHRISTIAN CELEBRATIONS

193. ROOTED IN WORSHIP

I want to share with you one of the best learning programs we have ever tried. Just about any youth group wishing to experience worship in the outdoors could find this useful. It also works well as a retreat.

We called our program, "Rooted in Worship," because we spent the entire time looking at our worship roots. We began by experiencing Old Testament worship and how it affected the tribes of Israel. A Bible study led us to find the answers at how Jesus' death on the cross changed our worship lives. The next morning we looked at the roots of our personal lives and how that affects our worship. Then in the afternoon we studied the roots of our church: baptism, scripture, prayer, and Holy Communion.

We used a 24-hour period, leaving the church on a Friday evening and returning on a Saturday evening. We had a great time.

ROOTED IN WORSHIP

Friday—2:00 p.m. Meet at the church with bicycles and gear for camping. Introduction of the worship weekend:

- Experiencing Old Testament worship in Moses' life.
- Experiencing New Testament worship in relationship to the roots of the Old Testament worship.
- Experiencing worship in the roots of our personal lives.
- Experiencing worship in the roots of our church.

We held a worship service around the cross after a brief discussion of how Moses led his people through the wilderness to the Promised Land. We talked about the hardships Moses faced (thirst, fatigue) and why he was leading his people out of Egypt. Our journey on bicycles was to act out the journey of the Israelites. First, teams were divided into the tribes of Israel. Each team selected a biblical name for their tribe. Sweat bands of varying colors identified the different tribes. "Moses" (our pastor) appeared to lead the worship and also to read the laws of our bike hike. They were placed inside the Ark of the Covenant along with the Ten Commandments. (This was made from a shoe box, decorated with macaroni sprayed gold.)

After a prayer to God for a safe journey, Moses gathered the tribes and led them through the wilderness to the Promised Land. In our case, the trip involved an eight-mile bike ride on gravel roads. As the tribes began to tire, they experienced the fatigue of the Israelites and the thirst. At a predesignated stop, Moses led his people to water and bragged to his people about how wonderful he was to find water for them. God's voice on tape (hidden from their view) admonished Moses for not giving God thanks for the water and told him he could now never enter the Promised Land.

As the tribes continued their journey they complained of fatigue and thirst. At the summit of the hill overlooking our Promised Land, Moses commissioned Joshua to lead his people the rest of the journey. As the tribes reached the bottom of the hill, they looked back and saw Moses was gone.

Joshua then lead his people to the Jordan River. (In our situation, the tribes crossed a creek after removing their shoes and socks. The bikes were also left at this stop and returned for later.) The leaders of the tribes who had carried the Ark of the Covenant waded into the water and waited until Joshua led his people across. As they were crossing, each tribe member gathered a rock

continued

ROOTED IN WORSHIP

to build an altar. One altar was built around the Ark, the other was built around the altar for burnt offerings. (We spent an hour wading in the creek and gathering rocks for the altars. The tribes thought it was great fun to be allowed to do something they are usually restricted from until free time.)

5:00 p.m. We worshiped around the altar for burnt offerings (also used for a campfire). We sacrificed a hot dog to God and prayed for safe journey to our Promised Land (campsite).

GOALS: ● To show the Old Testament forms of worship formed the background for New Testament worship.
● To show how New Testament and Christian worship is different from Old Testament worship.

BASIS: The Israelites' Passover meal to celebrate their release from Egypt is the background for the celebration of Holy Communion

In Old Testament worship the sacrifice was central. In Christian worship Jesus Christ has become the sacrifice once and for all, making it unnecessary for us to make sacrifices.

After a supper of hot dog and marshmallow sandwiches, the tribes set up their tents and had free time to explore.

7:00 p.m. Group recreation.

8:00 p.m. Bible study. Each tribe went with its leader to a quiet spot and used the following Bible study:

Questions and Resources:

1. Discuss the experience of worship that we had when we built the altar and burned the hot dog. Why do you think we did that? Recall the story of the Israelites crossing the desert and entering the Promised Land. Read Joshua 4:19-24. What was the purpose of the 12 stones?

2. Read Genesis 8:20-22. After the flood recedes, what does Noah do? How does Noah worship?

3. Read Hebrews 9:15-22. What does this describe? You may also want to read Exodus 24:1-11. Why did the people sacrifice animals in this way?

4. Why do we no longer practice the sacrificing of animals? See Hebrews 9:23-28.

5. How was the tent of the Lord's pres-

ence set up (Exodus 40:1-33). Where was the curtain? What and who were behind it? Why were they separated?

6. What happens as Jesus is crucified? (Mark 15:38) What do you think this means?

7. Look at the story of the Last Supper (Matthew 26:17-25). What Old Testament festival was Jesus celebrating with the disciples? What was the purpose of this celebration (Exodus 12:43-51) How did Jesus change it?

8:45 p.m. Gather wood for campfire worship.

9:00 p.m. Closing worship around campfire. We reviewed our day and then read the New Testament story of Christ's death on the cross (Matthew 27:45-54). As the part where the curtain is torn from the altar was read, the curtain we had put around our altar was torn. (While the young people were at play we had fastened several old curtains around the Ark of the Covenant.)

The rest of the time was spent singing around the campfire, popping corn and roasting marshmallows.

7:00 a.m. Rise and celebrate!! Breakfast made by the campers.

8:30 a.m. Worship theme: God is the God of our lives. Purpose: To realize each of us is a unique creation of God. We sang about God's creation. We had a period of time for each person to go off alone and meditate.

9:00 a.m. The group divided into their tribes. First of all they hiked into the woods and dug up different types of plants and examined their roots. They then returned to camp and made posters of themselves. (Poster boards had been made with an outline of a youth's body and roots leading down.) The campers dressed their body outlines with scraps of material and filled in the roots of their lives with felt-tip markers.

10:15 a.m. Break. Juice and Rice Krispies treats.

10:30 a.m. Tribes again went on a hike and looked at God's creation. Why did God create a tree? a bird? an insect? a snake? Each person received a piece of paper and

was asked to think about an object they just observed. Their leaders asked them to write five reasons why God created the object they chose. After this was completed, they went on another hike and looked for signs of pollution. While they were hiking, they were asked to think of a slogan on caring for God's creation that could be made into a bumper sticker. When we returned to camp, each person made a bumper sticker (contact paper, scissors, etc.).

Noon. Lunch break: cold cuts, cheese, chips, cookies and fruit.

12:30-1:30 p.m. Free time.

1:30-2:00 p.m. Group recreation.

2:00 p.m. Worship: The tribes gathered and displayed what they had made in their morning sessions: posters, reasons for God's creation and bumper stickers. This was a good time of sharing our personal thoughts on the roots of our lives.

Ahead of time, we made a poster of a church building with roots coming down. We discussed the roots of worship in the church: baptism, scripture, prayer, and communion. Each tribe then studied one of the church roots and discussed what they mean in our personal lives. The tribes were responsible for preparing worship on the root they studied for our evening session, which parents attended. We used the following guide for this study:

BAPTISM. Baptism is remembering the basics of our personal roots. We remember in baptism how God brought each one of us into his family. We are brought into a family only once. However, when we worship we remember God's great act of love that allowed us to become a member of his family.

We asked the youth to compose and share statements of what baptism meant in their lives.

SCRIPTURE. We find our roots in the Bible, in the story of God's love for his people. We usually look for three parts of that story to read during worship. First, we read a portion

continued

ROOTED IN WORSHIP

of the story that tells of God's love for his people in the Old Testament. Second, we read a portion of how God continues to work in his church in the New Testament. Third, we read about God's love for us through Jesus Christ from one of the gospels. All three lessons may have a similar theme.

This group's task was to pick the scriptures and act out one of the stories.

PRAYER. Prayer is special communication with God. Just as roots need frequent rain to live, we need to communicate clearly with God to keep us alive. Although we pray for our own needs, we also pray for others, for the church, for the sick and for the lonely.

It was this group's task to write the prayers for our worship.

HOLY COMMUNION. We remember Jesus Christ through the Lord's Supper. Jesus said, "Do this to remember me." In communion we remember Jesus' death and resurrection. We remember how he died for our sins. We do this not only by hearing but also by tasting, touching, smelling, and seeing.

This group was responsible for the prayers of thanksgiving, the Lord's Prayer and serving the communion.

3:30 p.m. Break: pop and snacks.

4:00 p.m. Take down tents, clean up area and prepare for return trip.

5:00 p.m. Parents arrive with food.

6:00 p.m. Worship service led by the campers around the campfire. Worship was based on their afternoon study of the roots of the church.

7:00 p.m. Homeward bound.

Carol Anderson
Duncombe, Iowa

See also 13) HOW-WE-GOT-OUR-BIBLE GAME, 12) DISCOVERY BIBLE STUDY, 15) WONDERS, 51) MOUNTAINTOP TO PLAIN, 52) RETREAT FEEDBACK, 43) BLUE TASSELS, 115) RETREAT FEED-CHECKLIST, 164) WORSHIP ENVIRONMENT, 165) WORSHIP TASK FORCE, 191) JEWISH/CHRISTIAN CELEBRATIONS

194. ON THIS ROCK

The youth group was on a camping trip for the weekend. Wanting to use the environment and the beauty of all that surrounded us as we worshiped, I happened upon a very large rock or boulder. The rock had many small pockets or holes all over it. I filled these indentations with water. We gathered around the rock for our confessions of sin. After a period of time members of the circle took turns washing the hands of the person next to them. The boulder experience helped us learn about this purification rite in a fresh, new way.

Earl Sires
Cleveland, Ohio

See also 15) WONDERS, 111) MELT THE DEVIL, 164) WORSHIP ENVIRONMENT, 171) PAPERBAG CONFESSIONS

195. FA-LO-PE WORSHIP

It was a super retreat with our junior highs. At one point, they pushed me to the perfect question, "What makes up a worship service?" I threw it back to them. We spread huge sheets of paper on the ground. I gave them markers. They were asked to list the ingredients for the worship service. We soon had all kinds of word lists and even pictures. The lists included terms like prayer, singing, sermon and the offering. However, some of the kids used terms like faith, love and hope. The group decided that worship was both nuts-and-bolts and feelings. How could we include them all in the worship service?

The kids decided on their own term for the ingredients: fa-lo-pe. It is the combination of faith, love and hope. A list of available objects to represent faith, love and hope was created. The list included sunflower seeds, apples, bananas, oranges, lemonade, grape juice, water, the Bible and pine cones. The group agreed to use sunflower seeds to represent the concept of faith, lemonade to represent the concept of love, and a pine cone to represent the concept of hope.

The concluding worship experience featured a time of individual sharing about what the retreat meant to each person. After this moving experience, the group began the fa-lo-pe. A cup containing sunflower seeds was passed to each person with the words, "Have faith in God." Each individual took a seed and ate it. He or she then passed the cup to the next person. In a similar manner a cup filled with lemonade was passed with the words, "Enjoy the love of God." The service ended with a blessing for peace and was followed by a 10-minute quiet period in which participants individually and silently reflected on the worship service in the out-of-doors. All were given a pine cone as a symbol of hope as they returned to the retreat center.

Wayne A. Knight
Billings, Montana

See also 52) RETREAT FEEDBACK, 72) CREATIVE CONJURING, 115) RETREAT CHECKLIST, 193) ROOTED IN WORSHIP, 197) CHORAL READING

196. STEP INTO THE OFFERING

We recently had a retreat which featured a very moving worship experience. The young people were asked at one point during the worship service to make an offering of themselves. The planners for the retreat had built a large offering plate which was placed on the floor. Each person was invited to step into the plate and offer his or her life for Christ, if ready to make the commitment.

Charles Martin, Pittsburgh, Pennsylvania

See also 130) PRAYER CHAIR, 161) YOUTH EVANGELISM, 178) SIN BURN-OFF, 198) THE "CALL," 199) "I WILL SERVE THE CHURCH . . ."

197. CHORAL READING

I have developed a choral reading of 1 Corinthians 13. Young people seem to appreciate this kind of opportunity to get close to the biblical material. I believe in good literary form. However, it should be based on a solid relationship to the text.

This choral reading provides a wonderful opportunity to explore the meanings of love with your young people. The results of the youths' presentations of the choral reading on Sunday morning will deeply move the congregation.

1 Corinthians, Chapter 13:
A Choral Reading

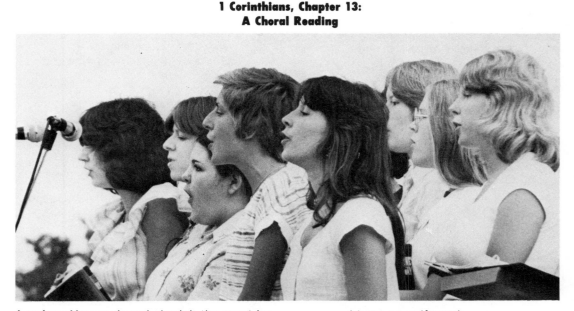

Leader: You seek and cherish the most important spiritual gifts.
But still, I will point out a way beyond all comparisons
To get all your gifts together.

Women: If I speak with the tongues of humans or even of angels,
But do not receive and give love;
I am like someone who rings a bell in the middle of the night;
A brassy cymbal, just making noise.

Men: And if I have gifts of prophecy, and can explain all mysteries, and comprehend all knowledge;
And if I have miracle-working faith, strong enough to tear up mountains,
But am not loved or loving;

I have no self-worth.

All: And if I give away all my possessions; bit by bit, each time I am asked;
And burn out my body in church activities,
But do not give and receive love;
There is no benefit to me or others.
Love stretches out patience, affirms where it can.

Solo voices:
1. Love doesn't envy, does not have to brag.
2. Love simply is, and does not have to prove itself.
3. Love does not act inappropriately.
4. Love does not have to have its own way.

continued

CHORAL READING

5. Love does not easily get upset.
6. Love does not maintain a museum of wrongs.
7. Love does not rejoice in wrong-doing, ever.

All: But joins in the rejoicing when people become real.
Love covers all situations.
Love trusts in all circumstances.
Love hopes under all conditions.
Love endures; whatever comes,
Love keeps on giving, and never gives up or gives out.

Men: But prophecies will pass away, and tongues will cease,
And knowledge becomes obsolete.
For we know only in part, and prophesy only in part.
But when the whole truth of God comes, what is only in part will be put away.

Women: When I was a child, or lived with a child,

I chattered like a child, I thought like a child,
I manipulated like a child.
But when I became full-grown, mature,
I kept childlike ways in their proper place.

All: Now we see through a dim looking-glass, darkly.
Then we will see Christ face-to-face.
Now I know only in part.
But then I will know and be known completely,
As God already knows me.
When all has been said and done, what will remain?
Faith, hope, love—these three.
And the greatest of these is love.

Paul M. Wright
Santa Clara, California

See also 166) GETTING THE WORD OUT, 195) FA-LO-PE WORSHIP

198. THE "CALL"

We put a great deal of emphasis on the preparation and support of the youth advisors and the youth officers. As we work with a new group of advisors and/or youth officers, we study and discuss the sense of "call" that each person feels.

To undergird the important role that these persons were assuming, we made them the focal point of our morning liturgy. Using a sense of celebration through banners, etc., the new leaders took active roles in the worship service, participated in the music, and at the handshake of peace they were com-

missioned. The congregation responded by pledging their support for the new youth officers and leaders. Each new officer was given a cross as a sign of his/her new office.

Terri Jones
Scott Township, Pennsylvania

See also 8) RECRUITING TEACHERS, 124) YOUNG PEOPLE AS LEADERS, 196) STEP INTO THE OFFERING, 199) "I WILL SERVE THE CHURCH . . ."

199. "I WILL SERVE THE CHURCH"

The confirmation class was in charge of the worship on the Sunday the church publicly welcomed them into the body. Members of the class shared in presenting the prayers, scripture and sermon. Each young person drew by lot a question such as "I intend to serve this church by . . .," or "My experience in confirmation class has taught me . . ." The answers to these questions formed the sermon.

Roger Kemp
Crittenden, New York

See also 56) CONFIRMATION RING, 125) LET THEM LEAD, 196) STEP INTO THE OFFERING, 198) THE "CALL"

200. AMEN!

Our junior high confirmation class was discussing how Christians can respond to the world's hunger, poverty and deprivation. After our discussion I asked each student to write a sentence prayer about a particular world concern.

Using my cassette tape recorder, I recorded each student reading his/her prayer. After each sentence prayer, the group responded by saying, "Amen." The group's response was weak at first. But after two or three prayers, the class really began to get into it and the "Amens" got louder and louder. The following Sunday morning the recorded sentence prayers by the junior high youth for the concerns of the world were used in the place of the usual pastoral prayer. At the end of the tape, the congregation responded with a resounding, "Amen." The choir then led the congregation in the familiar "A-men, A-men . . ."

Neil H. Cross, Mt. Pleasant, Iowa

See also 130) PRAYER CHAIR, 139) HUNGER IDEAS, 174) YOUTH AND SOCIAL ISSUES

201. WORSHIP INTERVIEWS

There are many ways youth can be encouraged to minister to adults. So often they feel that everything is being done "to" and "for" them as youth. They appreciate the opportunity to give some of what is special about themselves to others.

For one particular Sunday, we designed a worship service which was to be led by one person from each different grade. They conducted the entire worship service and shared their faith with the congregation in many different ways. Here are some of the questions they asked the congregation:

1. If Christ hadn't come, what would be different?

2. What are the things most important about your life in this church?

3. What are the five things you like about this church?

4. What does God do all day?

5. If Jesus Christ were minister in our church today, what would he be doing?

6. What would your life be like if you skipped church all the time?

Kit Schooley
Fayetteville, North Carolina

See also 153) CHRISTMAS OUTREACH

202. UNITED WE STAND

"Celebration" is a youth group composed of young people from the Presbyterian and Episcopal churches here. It started out as an experiment. The experiment was successful.

Celebration meets every Wednesday evening. It includes children and youth from the first grade through high school. The meeting place is rotated among the churches. The Wednesday session may include crafts, Bible lessons, field trips, recreation, a common meal and a choir program.

One of the unexpected outcomes of this program has been the emergence of three youth choirs. These choirs make the rounds to the various churches on Sunday mornings.

The youth remain active in their own churches. Celebration simply helps them unite in a common body of Christ.

Bruce Allison and Jerry Miller
Lincoln, Illinois

See also 187) POP MUSIC POSSIBILITIES, 189) SING OUT

203. PEANUTS AND BACCALAUREATE

To celebrate baccalaureate Sunday, we passed out peanuts to the worshipers as they entered the sanctuary. To begin the sermon, I went into the congregation and asked the following questions:

"Look at your peanut closely. Is it large or small? light or heavy? rough or smooth to the touch? Are there rib lines on it? Does it smell?

"Now crack open the peanut. What do you see? Is there a red skin on the meat of the peanut? What color is the peanut's meat? How many peanuts are in your shell? Is the inside of the shell different from the outside?

"Now you may eat the meat of the peanut if you wish. How does it taste?"

At this time, I passed brown paper bags to gather the peanut shells. At the same time (I was still among the congregation) I mentioned that we probably associate peanuts with sporting events: football, baseball and basketball. I asked for other ways peanuts are used in the world. Some responses: peanut oil, peanut butter, candy, cookies, a child said that elephants enjoy peanuts. The purpose of this part of the sermon was to enlarge their thinking about peanuts.

I returned to the pulpit and began the rest of the sermon with a brief summary of the life of George Washington Carver. I stopped at the point when Carver went to Tuskegee Institute with the challenge to help the black farmer. Carver saw the peanut as the way to diversify cotton-dependent farmers.

"What could George do with a peanut?" I asked. "In a makeshift laboratory at Tuskegee, Dr. Carver took in his hand a lowly peanut. 'Tell me, great Creator, why did you make the peanut?' he prayed to God."

I then shared with the congregation a list of over 300 items that George made from the peanut.

I stressed in the rest of the service the words: "Tell me, great Creator, why did you make me?" I encouraged graduating high school seniors to follow God's will and to be of service to others.

I concluded with: "If God can take a peanut, and through one person, create over 300 products for the service of others, think what God can do with the life of one person who prays, 'Tell me, great Creator, why did you make me?' . . . and then follows the will of the Creator."

Dick VanSkike
Longmont, Colorado

See also 103) GRADUATION DINNER, 204) SENIOR SHEET, 205) BACCALAUREATE

204. SENIOR SHEET

We were concerned about the lack of "rites of passage" in our culture, especially from childhood to adulthood. There are not very many times in young persons' lives when attention is focused on their accomplishments. We decided that graduating from high school was an appropriate time for the church to not only "recognize" the graduating seniors but also treat this special rite of passage as a unique experience in the life of the youth.

While each senior received a special gift during the worship service, ushers handed out sheets containing a picture of each senior (most seniors have one readily available), the name of the person, and some information regarding future plans (very brief). Our graduates and congregation realized that they were passing from children to adults.

Joel Baker
Lebanon, Ohio

See also 41) SENIORITIS, 88) YOUTH DIREC-TORY, 103) GRADUATION DINNER, 203) PEA-NUTS AND BACCALAUREATE, 205) BACCA-LAUREATE

205. BACCALAUREATE

Baccalaureate services are sometimes seen as old-fashioned, but our youth seem to appreciate them more each year. Since its inception 15 years ago, our annual baccalaureate service has seen increased attendance each year. Even youth from other churches come with our own seniors.

Members of the senior class plan and conduct this festive occasion. Each dons his/her cap and gown regalia. Following the service, each graduate stands in a receiving line. This encourages individuals to express best wishes to each senior. Then a reception is held in the fellowship hall.

David Shaheen
Silver Spring, Maryland

See also 196) STEP INTO THE OFFERING, 203) PEANUTS AND BACCALAUREATE

206. WEDDING CASSETTE

It is a special time for me when youth I've worked with decide to be married. I like to give a special gift. I record the wedding service on a reel-to-reel recorder. Then I interview the family and the guests at the wedding, using my cassette tape recorder. Guests and family are encouraged to offer prayers, wishes, and blessings to the couple. The tapes are then edited onto a cassette, featuring the wedding service on one side. The wishes, greetings, prayers and blessings to the couple and to their parents are on the other side.

Ivan Jacobs
San Jose, California

See also 123) CAMP TAPES

207. PARTICIPATORY CHRISTMAS PAGEANT

In late November last year several people began to wish aloud for an old-fashioned Christmas pageant, not the kind with parts to learn, but a chance to stand near the manger and witness the birth of our savior again. Late November is hardly the time to begin planning a full-blown pageant in the traditional sense. So, we staged a pageant of the "unusual" variety.

We decided to include people of all ages—the whole Sunday school in fact—on the Sunday before Christmas in an unrehearsed pageant. One person would take the role of storyteller while everyone else would walk through the story in the role of one of the characters. There would be costumes for everyone. They would be improvised that morning. Each member of the committee took responsibility for gathering props for one group of characters and planned to be in that costume area on Sunday to help with costume creations. The props we used were as follows:

- Shepherds—about 20 walking sticks, a pile of logs arranged as a campfire, and twine for tying up costumes.
- Wise men—three crowns or fancy headgear; three pretty boxes or jugs as gifts; twine for tying up costumes.
- Angels—about 20 white candles, some matches and twine for tying up costumes.
- Family—a manger and leaves of straw.
- Taxpayers—twine for tying up costumes.

For two Sundays before the pageant, we took time in classes and in worship to explain what was to occur and to ask people to bring old sheets, curtains, cloth remnants, towels and anything else they could see being made into no-cut, no-sew costumes when they came. We promised that whatever they brought would be returned undamaged.

continued

PARTICIPATORY CHRISTMAS PAGEANT

An infant and her mother were recruited to be Mary and Jesus so we'd be sure to have a live Jesus. An older member was also recruited to be the head angel and was given advance instructions on his role.

The rest happened on Sunday morning. Everyone (about 40 people of all ages) gathered in the fellowship hall. Members of the committee spread their costume makings around so that the area for each set of characters had what was needed.

Without any introduction, the storyteller (dressed in a simple peasant costume) entered clapping her hands over her head to get attention and launched into her story and direction as she walked among the people. During the pageant she spoke without a script and improvised some to respond to what was happening:

"I am Miriam, and I am in a long line of women who have told people stories they already knew so that they would forever be relearning who they are. My many-times-great-grandmother crossed the Red Sea with Moses and the Hebrew slaves." Then she burst into song telling the story of what had just happened as God's story.

"Today I come to tell you again the story about the day Jesus, our Lord, was born on this earth as a tiny baby just like you were _____ (fill in name of adult in group) and just like you are _____ (fill in name of infant in group). But I shall not simply tell my story alone because it is not my story but our story. We must tell it together. We must live it together. So come let us take parts. We shall all be shepherds or angels or wise men or among the host of taxpayers and citizens who found themselves in Bethlehem on that most extraordinary night.

"_____ and _____ have already offered their services as Jesus and Mary. Is there one who will stand with them as Joseph?" (Get a volunteer and send them to the person to help the family make costumes and get in place.)

"Who will volunteer to walk in the shoes of the three wise men and their three ser-vants who carried their treasures?" (Get volunteers and send them to wise men costuming area.)

"And the night requires angels. A note is necessary to remind you that angels are simply messengers from God. We really do not know what they look like. Most often we think of them with two wings, a white gown and a halo, but the Bible describes them in a variety of ways. Today our angels will wear pure white and will carry a candle as a symbol of the message they bring to light up our world. _____ has agreed to be the lead angel and has special instructions for you who will be the angelic hosts. Who will be an angel?" (Send volunteers to the angel costuming area.)

"And now we need some shepherds. Who will take on the job of caring for the sheep in the cool, dangerous night on the hills outside of Bethlehem? The shepherds were of all ages and both sexes. They were simply people who did a hard job." (Send volunteers to shepherd costuming area.)

"We who remain are the taxpayers and the unnamed numbers of people living quietly in the unusually quiet town of Bethlehem. You are the everyday people of all generations whom the Lord God loves and sent his son for. So go put on some of the costumes of the common folk."

We checked individual groups to be sure everyone was ready and found their places. It took 10 minutes for the costuming. When everyone was about ready, we helped them form into a long line. A few people were asked to lead. Wise men went at the end.

"Follow me to join the journey of thousands. It is the year when Caesar Augustus decreed that a census be taken of the entire Roman Empire for the purpose of taxation. That was when Quirinius was governor of Syria. So it was his job to carry out Caesar's census in Syria. Each man was required to appear with his wife and children before the registrar in his home town. There were no exceptions. An elderly grandfather or a sick

continued

PARTICIPATORY CHRISTMAS PAGEANT

child or a lame beggar or a pregnant woman must stand in person to register—no matter the incovenience, or pain, or even loss of life. To resist was unthinkable, but to grumble and gripe and even swear about it was common. How would you like to walk for two straight days, maybe 10 miles each day, down dusty, dull roads? How would you like to keep up with your children on such a trip? And what could you rig up to carry your elderly father or mother on the trip if he or she were simply too frail to travel?

"It was in times like this that one remembered the promises of a Messiah, Son of God, who would put all these injustices aright and bring in an age of decency and peace. Yes, we all need a hope, a dream to hold on to in the bad times. But we cling to them, little expecting to see them become a reality. And so it was with those weary, taxed travelers who crowded into Bethlehem." (Bring the group to a stop at the place where the shepherds are sitting around their campfire.)

"But stop and be aware of those around you, travelers. You are not the only folks in town tonight. Indeed, on the edge of the town are people who will spend the night out-of-doors with senses alert to dangers. This is not the only night these shepherds will spend trying to keep warm while keeping a constant watch over the quiet ways of the sheep and the even quieter wolves and bears. It's a hard life. Tomorrow you, too, shepherds, will have to take turns going in to register and pay taxes you cannot afford to pay. At least tonight it is not raining and there is a certain peace out here away from the crowds. But it is in such an ordinary time that the night is literally shattered and an angel appears." (Angels are facing away from the group and behind the shepherds. They turn around at this point.)

Lead Angel: "Don't be afraid. I come from God to give you good news. Today in Bethlehem a baby is born who is the savior of the world. This is the way you people will know him. He will be wrapped in soft clothes and lying in a manger in a stable. Glory to God in the highest." (Other angels reply to each of the following by saying, "Glory to God.") "Praise God, you shepherds. Praise him, you taxpaying men and women. Praise him, you little children. Praise him, young and old people. Praise him, rich and poor people. Praise him, powerful and powerless people. Praise him. Glory to God in the highest and on earth peace among all people."

Storyteller: "What will you do, shepherds? Come let's go. Let's see if it's true. Let's see what a baby savior looks like. Let's see what God has told the shepherds about. Hurry, shepherds. Run to see it. To see if anyone else knows. Where will we go? To a stable? A savior in a manger?" (While saying this, start coaxing and leading the shepherds and following taxpayers to the place the family is. We placed our family under a stairwell in a back hall.)

"It is true, shepherds! There is a baby in a manger. And a mother is there to care for him and love him and wonder about your presence. So stand or sit and watch. Simply be here. Is it possible that in that baby the hopes of the whole world will be answered? Born in a stable? It is all you can do to believe you are here. But do sit and take it all in so you can remember every detail.

"Shepherds, taxpayers, there are still others in Bethlehem today. Three foreigners and their servants. These men caused a real scene this morning when they showed up at the palace looking for the new king. Herod called in all the professors from the temple to find out what was going on. 'Who was this king? Where would he be born? What about this star they had followed across half a continent?' After some discussion Herod sent them to Bethlehem where the scriptures said a great Jewish leader would be born. So they came and are even now among us. Make way for them. Have you ever seen such cool power? These are men who know what it means to command. So come forward wise men. You, who are smart and rich and powerful. Come greet the king whose birth you saw in the star. You know how to treat a king. Bow. Turn to your servant to bring your precious gifts. Offer the king gold and frankincense and myrrh. Then, like the rest of us, stay a moment in the quiet stable and take it all in. Let's sing together." (Storyteller starts singing of one verse each of "Away in a Manger," and "Silent Night.")

"But we cannot stay long in the stable. There are sheep to tend and the return trip to consider. There are taxes to pay, and for the small family, a frantic trip to Egypt to avoid Herod's death order. And there is a world out there to tell our story to, a world that aches to meet Jesus in a manger, to know that God loves them enough to send his son that they might have life. So, go." (Storyteller begins one verse of "Go Tell It On the Mountain," and follows with one round of "Amen.")

Carolyn Brown
Hillsborough, North Carolina

See also 17) ENCOUNTER BIBLE CHARACTERS, 20) STORYTELLING, 42) CAMP PRODUCTIONS, 102) CHRISTMAS NOSTALGIA, 153) CHRISTMAS OUTREACH, 165) WORSHIP TASK FORCE, 166) GETTING THE WORD OUT

208. CHRISTMAS STORIES

During worship on one of the Sundays of Advent, we decided to feature an intergenerational exchange between the youth of the church and the older adults. Before the worship time, each young person had been paired with an older adult. Using a portable microphone, each youth asked an older adult to tell the congregation the memory of a Christmas when the older adult was a child. There were some fantastic memories and stories.

Sue Rueben
Pittsburgh, Pennsylvania

See also 20) STORYTELLING, 102) CHRISTMAS NOSTALGIA, 153) CHRISTMAS OUTREACH, 162) YOUTH REACH ADULTS

209. THE MESSAGE OF THE CAROLS

We would like to share the following Christmas program which Edith wrote and has used successfully a number of times. It requires a relatively small cast and minimal production. It is simple, and yet the message is very direct. Our youth enjoyed presenting it for the church.

The Message of the Carols

(Suggested backdrop: Windows might be made yellow, door red, church gray with white trim for snow. Place small green trees and white sheets in front of church backdrop.)

Characters:

Bob Stewart, young pastor; Beth Stewart, pastor's wife; Danny Palmer, blind boy; Mrs. Palmer, Danny's grandmother; Mr. Blackwell, wealthy, hard-hearted man; Sis, girl in early teens; Mike, about 9; Mary, about 7; Mrs. Todd, middle-aged lady, a social climber; Cliff Sanders, college boy; Jessie Miller, tired, worn mother; five young children for last scene only; narrator.

Props:

Church backdrop (heavy cardboard propped so door may be opened), two small evergreen trees, sheets to represent snow, cotton for snow on tree branches, artificial snow sparkle, wreath for door of church, sign to announce Christmas service (lettered so may be read from a distance), floodlight, mike for narrator, white cane, outdoor clothing for participants, rocking chair, two straight chairs, box wrapped as Christmas gift, sack of groceries, curtains or sheets (if needed for curtain), wire on which to hang curtains.

SCENE 1

(Young pastor and wife are placing sign on church door which announces special Christmas service.)

Bob: If only we'd have some response to our efforts! It seems no matter what we do, no more than a half dozen children show up!

Beth: Oh, Bob, surely the Lord will hear our prayers! All our visitation hasn't been in vain. This is perfect Christmas weather. The snow on the trees and roof is so beautiful! It's just right for our Christmas service. Let's pray once more before we go home that the Lord will bring some people to the church for the service—people who really need help.

Bob: Right! Let's ask him to cause folks to read this notice of our service and be drawn by the Holy Spirit to come. But we still need someone to play that organ. I tell you, the Christmas carols played on that old organ would just set off our Christmas service!

(Bob and Beth stand with bowed heads in front of church, then turn and walk to right, out of sight.)

Narrator: The next evening a box came from home for Bob and Beth containing a large fruit cake and other gifts. Beth had an idea. "Let's take part of the cake to Mrs. Palmer. She's been sick all week and this will give her a little feel of Christmas." And so they started out to visit Mrs. Palmer with the Christmas gift they wished to share.

(Beth and Bob walk past church from right, carrying Christmas package.)

Note: This part, which takes place in Mrs. Palmer's house, may just be related by narrator as the light on the church is dimmed. Or it might be presented by closing curtains from both sides of platform to leave an opening several feet wide. The light will be off the church and a rocking chair and two straight chairs will be placed in the opening. After Mrs. Palmer is seated in the rocker and Bob and Beth in the straight chairs, a floodlight might be turned on them.

SCENE 2

(Organ or record softly playing in background, "O, Little Town of Bethlehem")

Narrator: As Bob and Beth reached Mrs. Palmer's, they could hear Christmas carols being played on an organ! The carol was played beautifully—"O, Little Town of Bethlehem, how still we see thee lie—" *(Pause to listen to music.)*

Bob: Mrs. Palmer, where is that music coming from? It's beautiful! I must see . . . *(starts to rise from seat)*

Mrs. Palmer: No, Pastor Stewart. Wait till I tell you. You see, my grandson has just moved in with me. Danny's blind and very timid. It's hard for him to meet folks. He spends all his time at that old organ in my back room. It's the only comfort he has. He seems to forget himself when he's playing, and I love to hear him. He's getting better every day, I do believe.

Bob: He plays wonderfully! Say, Mrs. Palmer, I must see Danny. I believe he's part of the answer to our prayers! Do you suppose we could get him to play for the Christmas service at church?

(Lights out while chairs are removed and Bob, Beth, and Mrs. Palmer leave.)

continued

MESSAGE OF THE CAROLS

Narrator: Bob, the young pastor, was able to win Danny's confidence and told him of his plan. Danny never thought he could serve the Lord. But now here was a way. He promised to go to the church the next evening and try the carols on the church organ.

SCENE 3

(Floodlight on church as Bob, Beth and Danny come from left and enter church door.)

Bob: *(As they near door)* You see, Danny, the carols you'll play at the Christmas service will bring blessings to many. I've borrowed a loud speaker from the pastor in Hazelton so we can pipe the carols out to the street. As you play, those who pass will hear the Christmas music, too. *(The three enter the church.)*

Narrator: As Danny practiced on the church organ, Beth and Bob prayed that those passing would somehow be touched by the music. Little did they realize that right then their prayer was being answered outside the church door.

(Carol: "It Came Upon a Midnight Clear," played softly on the organ or record.) When the words are mentioned, a singer (out of sight) might sing the appropriate verse. The words should be clearly yet simply sung, as if the person standing in front of the church listening is recalling them. Enter from right: Man—well-dressed with hat, perhaps cane, walking along slowly.)

Narrator: As Mr. Blackwell, one of the noted hard-hearted misers of town, was out for "some air," he passed the little church just as the carol, "It Came Upon a Midnight Clear" was being played. He paused and listened. Unaccustomed tears came to his eyes. That carol had been his mother's favorite. How well he remembered those words!

(Carol is sung off stage as Mr. Blackwell stands with hat in hand, listening.)

Narrator: "Peace on earth, good will to men, from heaven's all-gracious King!" Then the words, "And still celestial music floats o'er all the weary world." How weary he was of life! And Christ had come to bring peace, but Mr. Blackwell had found no peace. Tonight it seemed as if that peace longed to enter his life as he stood in front of the little chapel. Perhaps he'd do something he'd not done in years. He'd come to the Christmas service announced on the door. Maybe he could find the peace the old carol spoke of! *(He moves closer to sign as if reading, then leaves on left of platform. Music fades.)*

(Carol: "Away in a Manger," played softly on organ or record.)

Narrator: Other young folk rushed by the church, minds set on parties. But the Holy Spirit saw three youngsters who had no Christmas party to attend. The music reached them.

(Enter from left: Sis, girl about 14, with little brother Mike and sister Mary. They skip along, bundled in winter clothes. As they hear the music, they stop.)

Mike: Sis, listen! Isn't that pretty? I know the words to that song. *(These children or three children off stage could sing the carol.)*

Mary: Sis, it says, "Be near me, Lord Jesus." Can he be near us now? I think we need him now that we're alone.

Sis: I don't know, Mary, but I'd like him to be near me, too. It seems like we ought to go to church somewhere this Christmas. Don't you think this would be a nice one? Look, that sign says they're having a special Christmas service tomorrow night. Let's plan to come. But come on, we've got to hurry home now. *(They leave on right of stage; music fades.)*

(Carol: "O Come, All Ye Faithful," played softly on record or organ.)

(Enter from right: Mrs. Todd, well-dressed lady with hat, walks briskly across platform, then stops, listening to music. Play carol through.)

Narrator: "O Come, All Ye Faithful . . . Come and behold him . . . O come, let us adore him . . . Yea, Lord we greet thee . . . Jesus to thee be all glory given." Mrs. Todd stopped and listened. "O come, all ye faithful." Hadn't she been a faithful churchgoer for years? Yet, she felt a stabbing pain when she thought of the words "adore him." She had never adored or really worshiped him. She knew the empty, useless feeling that engulfed her was because she had only been concerned with herself. She peered cautiously at the sign on the door, looking both ways to be sure no one saw her. Something about that music seemed to draw her. Do you suppose she could slip over for the service tomorrow night? Just to hear those carols again—that surely would help her to forget herself. Maybe she could find out how to worship him. *(Mrs. Todd leaves platform, music fades.)*

(Carol: "Hark! The Herald Angels Sing," played softly on record or organ.)

(Enter from right: Young college boy with hands in pockets, walking buoyantly. He whistles with the carol being played, goes almost past church, then turns and comes back, listening.)

Narrator: Cliff Sanders, home from college for Christmas, was enjoying every minute. He'd just come from a high school buddy's house and was on his way home. Down deep he knew several reasons why he was glad to be home, here in peaceful little Greenville. Everything seemed to speak of the Christmas he'd always known— the Christmas "they" were trying to rob him of at the college he attended. Hadn't his professors openly made fun of Christ's birth? It was so good to get away from those confusing thoughts for a

continued

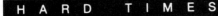
while. The words of the carol he'd often sung at this time of the year were ringing out so clearly: *(Carol may be sung here by a soloist out of sight.)*

Narrator: "God and sinners reconciled . . . Light and life to all he brings; Risen with healing in his wings . . . Born that man no more may die."
That's what the professors were making fun of—eternal life, salvation. But Cliff knew they were wrong! He'd go on believing as he had as a boy, regardless of what they said. Why, he'd come to the service announced on the door and make it final. He'd ask the Lord to help him be a true Christian regardless of influences around him. *(Cliff exits; music fades.)*

(Carol: "Silent Night! Holy Night!" played softly on record or organ.)

(Enter from left: Jessie Miller with sack of groceries. She walks slowly, tiredly.)

Narrator: Jessie Miller trudged the long way home with the groceries. True, she was but one of many weary folk that had passed that way. But tonight Jessie realized she needed help! It seemed her work was never ended. Providing and caring for those five youngsters seemed to take every minute of the day and half the night, too. If only she could get a good long rest—maybe a rest for her mind and soul even more than for her body. If only she didn't have to worry so about the future and how to make ends meet now that Frank was gone! And then, saturating the air and bearing in upon her thoughts were the glorious strains of "Silent Night, Holy Night." She stopped

and set down her bag, enraptured with the serenity of the scene and the carol played so beautifully. *(She sets down her bag and stands with folded hands, listening. Play song through, then have words sung softly, perhaps by a group of voices in unison.)*

Narrator: "Silent night. Peaceful night. Darkness flies, all is light . . . Christ the Savior is born, Jesus the Savior is born!" The familiar words rang through Mrs. Miller's tired mind. Yes, Jesus had come to bring peace and rest to the weary. Why, how had she neglected his house and the reading of the Word and prayer for so long? She'd become so busy that she'd forgotten to draw upon him for strength! Well, this would be the turning point.) She'd come to this little church and bring the children, too. *(She picks up bag and moves out of scene as music fades.)*

SCENE 4

(Bob, Beth, Danny enter church. If platform is so arranged that they could not leave after Scene 3, omit this entry. (Carol: "O Come, All Ye Faithful," played joyfully on organ or record. From different directions, with only a short space of time between, all who stopped by the church in Scene 3 come and enter door. After all have entered, entire group or a number of voices off the platform sing the carol heartily. If there is no way to fit the larger number of people behind church scene, you may simply want them to gather in front of the church and sing. At the end of the carol, draw curtains or dim lights as all leave except Bob, Beth and Danny.)

Narrator: And so, the first Christmas service at the chapel in Greenville was held. There was not a large crowd, yet it was a glorious service. Not only did the people whose hearts had been touched the night before come, but as they heard the Word of God proclaimed by Bob, and as Beth sang at the close of the service, the song became their prayer: "Thou didst leave thy throne and thy kingly crown, When thou camest to earth for me; But in Bethlehem's home was there found no room . . . O come to my heart, Lord Jesus. There is room in my heart for Thee." *(This song might be sung by a soloist or the person playing Beth might sing it.)* The hearts of those who listened were touched. They responded to the simple invitation to ask Christ into their hearts. And the angels in heaven rejoiced to see not one, but a number make their peace with God. *(Music fades.)*

(Bob, Beth, Danny come out door. Or, if all have stood at door in group, they may simply bow their heads in prayer now.)

Narrator: After all others had left, Bob, Beth, and Danny closed up the little church with rejoicing hearts, anxious to tell Grandma Palmer about the glorious service they'd had. Standing there in front of the church, they again bowed and thanked the Lord for the answers to their prayers, and for this, the best Christmas they had ever known. *(Bob appears to lock door, takes down sign and the three move off the platform to the left.)*

Edith Armstrong and Sylvia Lee
Springfield, Missouri

See also 102) CHRISTMAS NOSTALGIA

210. SNOW WORSHIP

We decided to ask the 100 young people on a weekend retreat to create the closing worship experience. The worship session they created was a one hour and 40 minute celebration which featured many exciting and meaningful items.

For instance, the group which led the confession portion of the service introduced a large, tightly packed snowball. As it was passed around, the young people read passages from the Bible which featured the purifying aspects of water. Some people put the snowball to their foreheads. Everyone experienced the cleansing of God's love as they rubbed their hands over the snowball's cold surface.

Jim Kramer
Mt. Lebanon, Pennsylvania

See also 72) CREATIVE CONJURING, 104) SHOPPING BAG VALUES, 111) MELT THE DEVIL, 177) LIVING WATER, 178) SIN BURN-OFF

211. GOOD FRIDAY SACRED DANCE

I am a quiet person and pretty shy. That's why I was hesitant to try sacred dance in the church. I didn't know much about it. I had seen a limited amount and hadn't liked what I saw. Yet, I still thought it would be interesting to try it.

I asked our pastor if he would allow me to develop music and mime for our Good Friday service. He readily agreed.

I chose eight people. They were of all ages: teens, older adults, and the rest of us between. We worked with the choir. I showed them what I wanted, and they put together an 11-minute medley of Easter songs to begin the service.

After the choir finished and left the altar area, singers in the balcony began "Were You There?" The reverent mood was suddenly interrupted by a bang of the sanctuary door. The singers stopped. The people started, turned, and Christ was there dressed in conventional clothes of today. He had on jeans. He staggered down the aisle carrying his cross. The cross was a human being with arms outstretched and in a stiff cross-like stance. If you have ever carried someone like that, you will know what a burden it is. The person was actually being dragged.

When Jesus got three pews from the front, he staggered and fell. The rest of the mimes came from the stage area, passing him. Each had his or her own movement which was his or her ego and personality. I took the role of a hard woman, a vamp type. I smiled at him and mocked him. Then I spat on him. (People in the audience were

shocked!) Other mimes came to him and related to him. No one really offered to help. Some were just curious. Others were insulting. Someone kicked him.

Three of us picked up the cross (person) and dragged her onto the stage. We planted her on a box so that the cross would be higher than Christ. Those three individuals then swooped down on Christ and picked him up and dragged him up and "nailed" him to the cross.

Then those of us who were hostile circled him with "Kung Fu" chopping movements. Then we went away momentarily and the three friendlies came up and wept and swooned under his feet as he looked down on us. The friendlies and hostiles then flowed together, maintaining the same movements. The friendlies, of course, had soft compassionate movements, while the hostiles did this "Kung Fu" movement.

Finally, one of the hostiles took his hand and thrust it into Jesus' side—and Christ screamed and slumped over. The friendlies removed Jesus and carried him away. The congregation then sang "Were You There?" This was a pretty down note to end on. After all, it was Good Friday.

Jane Small, Elgin, Illinois

See also 17) ENCOUNTER BIBLE CHARACTERS, 40) GOOD SAMARITAN MIME, 42) CAMP PRODUCTIONS, 155) PALM SUNDAY FAIR, 163) EXTRA! JESUS LIVES, 166) GETTING THE WORD OUT, 191) JEWISH/CHRISTIAN CELEBRATIONS, 213) THE FIFTH GOSPEL

212. "ARCHIE'S SONSHINE"

"Archie's Sonshine" was written one evening by Patty Sprain, a young mother of four small children as she sat up with her teething baby. She wrote for three hours as the ideas came together. Her creation served as our Easter sunrise service.

"Archie's Sonshine"

An Easter Sunrise Service

Props:

1. Large box marked "Archie's Sonshine."
2. Banner with J-E-S-U-S on it.
3. Helium-filled balloons
4. Cards light enough to be carried by the balloons. The cards read as follows: "This card contains a little 'Sonshine' from the West Salem, Wisconsin Presbyterian Church in commemoration of their Easter 'Sonrise' service: 'Follow Jesus and you will pass from death to life.' "

Costumes:

Archie, Reggie and Betty—white T-shirts, new jeans, clean tennis shoes
Ethel—red T-shirt, jeans
Veronica—dressy blouse and slacks
Jughead—vest loaded with food in the pockets
Dilton—suit and tie
Everyone has name pinned on back except Reggie—Reggie's on front.

(Minister welcomes congregation, followed by a moment of silence.)

Speaker I: Surely the presence of the Lord is in this place. For he said if two or more of you are gathered in my name, there I am in the midst of you. Let us lift our hearts to him as we sing this song of praise. *("Morning Has Broken" is sung.)*

Speaker II: Have you seen Jesus, my Lord? Lord? He's here in plain view. Take a look. Open your eyes. He'll show it to you. For the heavens declare the glory of God and the firmament shows his handiwork. *("Have You Seen Jesus, My Lord" is sung.)*

Archie: Hi! My name is Archie and these kids are the Archie Gang. You remember us don't you? Here's Veronica, the rich girl *(Veronica stands)*; Dilton, who's the brain *(Dilton stands)*; here's Reggie, who thinks only of Reggie *(Reggie stands)*; Betty, who knows the way *(Betty stands)*; Ethel, who's always suffering from shortcomings *(Ethel stands)*; and of course here's Jughead, who never refuses to eat *(Jughead stands)*. We're here to make your Easter service special by presenting my story, "Archie's Sonshine." *(All except Archie sit.)*

Archie: Like I said before, my name is Archie and I've got a twinkle in my eye, a spring in my walk, and a smile on my face. It's all because I've accepted the Easter

continued

ARCHIE'S SONSHINE

message and discovered a whole new kind of sonshine. That's spelled S-O-N-S-H-I-N-E. It's not the sun that shines from above but the son that shines from inside of me. And that kind of son gives me everything I need. I am even able to grow stronger and rid myself of all my hang-ups.

Reggie: Ahhh, don't let 'em kid ya, folks! I've heard all that song-and-dance before. Everybody knows that the only way to get anywhere in this world is by using your muscles *(flex muscles)* and good looks. Take me, for instance, Reggie; that's spelled R-E-G-G-I-E and I shine everywhere. I don't have any hang-ups. I just think of me.

Archie: As I was saying folks, I don't have any more hang-ups since I've accepted the Sonshine. I've found a whole new reason for living.

Jughead: Speaking of living, I'm going to die if I don't get something to eat around here!

Reggie: You just had breakfast!

Jughead: But it seems I just can't get full. The more I eat, the hungrier I get. Of course, my motto has always been "I live to eat." Sorry, Archie, what were you saying?

Archie: I was saying, I've found the full joy. The Sonshine fills me up in the way your food, Jughead, never could. Why, I never have to be depressed again.

Ethel: Depressed, he says. What does he know about depression? Look at me. I've got buck teeth, freckles, bozo hair, and everybody makes fun of my clumsy ways. I feel so unloved. Why was I ever born?

Archie: Ethel, you have to live for that special Sonshine I've been talking about.

Ethel: But how do I get it, Archie?

Archie: Hey, Betty, come here. We've got another fish on the hook.

Betty: Hi, Gang!

Archie: Ethel here, wants to know how to get that certain Sonshine in her life.

Dilton: Did I hear someone say they wanted to know something? Well, I've just completed my 10th reading of the total volume of the last edition of the Encyclopedia Britannica. What is it you need to know? I've got all the educated answers to everything.

Betty: Don't be hurt Dilton, but all the knowledge and education in the world can't help with the answers when it comes to the Sonshine. In fact, we have to let the whole world go in order to find the answer within.

Veronica: What's that you say, Betty? Let the world go? What! Give up all my furs, cars, houses and money? I'd break out in hives, I'd get ulcers; why I'd have anxiety attacks. Give up all my riches? Over my dead body!

Betty: And that's just what you'll be—dead, Veronica, unless you accept the Sonshine. The Sonshine came to give you life. If you don't let him inside of you, you'll die forever. The Sonshine gives you eternal life. But the world gives you death.

Veronica: But can't I have just a little bit of the Sonshine and keep part of the world?

Betty: No way. The Sonshine says you must die to the world to find eternal life. That means it's all of your heart or nothing. If you do it'll mean a whole new life.

Ethel: That sounds good to me. Anything's better than being depressed in this life. If I know I have eternity to look forward to, I'll never be lonely again *(puts hanky in box marked Sonshine).*

Dilton: Well, I guess it's beginning to make sense to my intellectual mind. I can let the world's knowledge go as long as I know I'll discover new and even more exciting things in the next world. *(drops a bunch of books into box).*

Veronica: Well, I never liked to be a party-pooper, so goodbye my long lost friends *(drops furs and car keys into the box).* Gee, I feel free! That wasn't as bad as I thought it would be.

Reggie: Well, this hurts more than you'll ever know *(takes off name and puts it in box).*

Jughead: All of a sudden I've lost my appetite *(drops sandwiches, fruit, candy, etc. that he had stuffed in his clothes into the box).*

Betty: We have them all in the net, Archie. Let's give them the Easter message and show them the Sonshine. Seeing that they gave the Sonshine their life, let them receive him now. *(All reach in the box and pull out banner and hold it up so congregation can see—large letters spell J-E-S-U-S).*

Gang: Now gang, let's sing a song to tell the congregation exactly what we're going to do now that we've accepted the Sonshine *("Love Him in the Morning" is sung. Gang starts passing out balloons.)*

Archie & Betty: To close the Sonshine service—that's spelled S-O-N-S-H-I-N-E—we pass out these balloons to you. Please hang onto them until all have received balloons and recite the closing prayer. *(Archie's gang sings "Pass It On" while balloons are being passed out.)*

Gang: *(In unison)* Will you please join in the closing prayer.

Congregation: These balloons are filled with helium. Because of this, if I let one go, it will rise without hesitation. All these balloons were filled from the same can of helium and even though each one is individually different, they are in unity and will go heavenward. I hold this balloon as a symbol of myself. As I let the world go and accept the Easter message "Nobody comes to the Father except through me," just like this balloon, the Lord will fill my heart with his Spirit. My old life will pass away and I will be new. Because of his power within me, I will be able to face every trial in this life. And just like this balloon, I will rise heavenward when his plan for me is completed on this earth. Until that time I will let him live through me. I will work hard in union with others, always watching for his triumphant return. In a moment as I let this balloon go, just as I let my life go to him, I will watch it rise heavenward and remember: By the cross he has saved me. By his power he has raised me! To God be the glory. *(All release balloons. Congregation is invited to breakfast in fellowship hall.)*

Helen Harold
West Salem, Wisconsin

213. THE FIFTH GOSPEL

I am a storyteller, whether I do it in writing, on the stage or wherever. Several years ago, I struggled through a period of extreme doubt about my faith. I knew doubt could be good for me, but I still felt something was wrong with me for having doubts.

I attended a two-day seminar led by a friend on the topic of doubt. What I learned there changed my life. I learned that the opposite of faith isn't doubt; the enemy of our faith is not caring. I knew that I cared. I knew that caring was at the heart of my doubt.

I began to improvise stories about such topics as Jesus having an argument with his mom about what time to get up in the morning. Or Jesus asking his dad: "I have a date tomorrow. Can I borrow the reins to the donkey?" Imagine a water fight between the disciples and Jesus on a hot day.

I reread the scriptures. I sat down one day with a youth minister in my church. I told him my stories and he loved them. He asked me to tell them to the youth group. I did. But I just improvised—no script. I ended up telling stories for two solid hours. I was exhausted. The young people were exhausted.

Before the evening was over, several young people became Christians. It was thrilling. I knew I had something there, though I didn't know quite what.

The next couple of months, I told my stories as a 90-minute one-man piece of drama. (I called my act the "Fifth Gospel.") After 25 performances of the "Fifth Gospel," it began to jell. People were responding to God through this unique media, not only to one-man drama, but to drama in the church.

The "Fifth Gospel" has now become my reality. It is the title for that whole area of my life where I explore new creative means to talk to God through my art. I am discovering that God speaks my language and I should talk back and teach others that language.

I find non-Christian young people especially responsive, not just to the "Fifth Gospel," but to the fact that a Christian is following his creative urges. My act is sometimes offensive to the church, and it is sometimes deliciously surprising to the world. It is exciting for me to have those two kinds of identities.

As Jesus exemplified, you must risk being misunderstood in many things you do. Some of your conscious efforts will simply rub people the wrong way. To survive the criticism, you have to believe in yourself. You have to know that at the heart of what you are doing is a deep love for God and a desire for people to love him the way you do. If you are doing creative worship, drama, or music in the church just to offend people, just to show them they are wrong, God won't bless it. But if you are doing it because it is your unique and loving expression toward God, he will use whatever you have to offer.

If you are satisfied in yourself before God, and no one accepts what you offer, it isn't your problem anymore.

Craig Wilson
San Diego, California

See also 18) THE PRODIGAL DAUGHTER/SON, 20) STORYTELLING, 21) ECHO PANTOMIMES, 42) CAMP PRODUCTIONS, 140) BIG DOGS, ARM SALES AND HUNGER, 211) GOOD FRIDAY SACRED DANCE

214. "THE LOST SON"

This chancel play is best done when actors improvise their lines. The lines and directions are given to aid in the direction of the play.

(Father and son walk out together. Son is dressed in overalls; father in sport shirt and slacks.)

Father: There was once a man who had two sons.

Son: And the younger of them said to his father: *(turns to father)* Father, give me my share of the property because I've decided to leave the farm and set out on my own to seek my fortune.

Father: I wish you'd stay son, but I will not stand in your way. *(Hands over a wad of play money.)* Here is your share—good luck to you. *(Father exits.)*

Son: And so the son set out to see the world. *(Walks in large figure eight depicting a long trip. After about 20 seconds he stops, places his hands on his hips and looks around.)* Wow! Look at the beautiful city! *(A woman, dressed attractively, approaches the son.)*

Woman: Say, tall, dark and handsome, what are you looking for?

Son: I'm looking for a good time.

Woman: Well, you'll have to have money for that.

Son: I've got plenty of money *(shows her his wad of bills and places them in back pocket).*

Woman: In that case let's go and paint the town red!

Son: And so they went and ate dinners at the finest restaurants. *(The two sit on chairs placed to the rear of center stage and pantomime eating and drinking; he throws some money around.)*

Woman: And they danced. *(The two get up after dinner and dance.)*

Son: And they bet on horses. *(Pantomime watching a horse race—he puts down money for the bets.)*

Woman: And gambled. *(Pantomime gambling—slot machines, poker, etc.—he paying the bill.)*

Son: Well, what shall we do next? Hey! I'm all out of money! *(pulls front pockets inside out).*

Woman: Well, it's been nice knowing you, take care of yourself. *(She walks away.)*

Son: Now what do I do? *(thinks for a moment)* I'm sure getting hungry. I think I better find a job. *(He begins his figure eight walking again. Old man enters stage right; son bumps into him.)*

Son: Excuse me, sir.

Old man: Look where you're walking next time, kid.

Son: Please sir, I'm hungry and broke. Do you have any work I can do?

Old man: Work!? Work!? We're in the midst of a recession here; there is no work.

Son: *(on bended knee)* Oh please, sir, I'll do anything.

continued

LOST SON

Old man: Well, I do have a pig farm outside of town and I could use a hand feeding the pigs. Follow this road till it ends and you'll find my farm.

Son: Thank you sir! *(begins again to walk a figure eight)* I wonder where that farm is? *(stops suddenly and makes a face as if he were smelling something terrible)* I think I've found it *(pantomimes feeding pigs)*. Here piggy, piggy; here piggy, piggy (stops and considers eating the pigs' food—thinks for a moment, and then throws it down). I think I'll go back to my father's farm—at least there I'd have enough to eat. I will go back to my father and beg him to take me back, not as his son but as a hired hand, for I am not worthy to be his son. *(Begins another figure eight walk for 20 seconds or so.)*

Father: *(Enters stage right)* But the father saw the son while he was still a long way off and ran up to him and hugged him *(runs up to son and hugs him)*.

Son: Father, I am a disgrace and I am no longer fit to be called your son.

Father: Forget it son. You are back, you are alive, it's great to see you!! *(calls out to servant)* Servant, servant!

Servant: *(Enters stage right)* Yes, sir?

Father: Bring my best robe and my son's slippers and call our friends, for my son is back. My son who was dead is now alive. He was lost and now is found!!

Servant: Yes, sir! *(Servant exits stage right, with father and son behind him. Older son enters stage left.)*

Older son: Just then the older son came home from work and heard the commotion in the house. He called for the servant. Servant!

Servant: *(Enters stage right)* Yes, sir?

Older son: What's going on inside?

Servant: Your good-for-nothing younger brother is home and your father is throwing a big party for him.

Older son: He is?! Get my father at once, please. *(Servant exits stage right.)*

Father: *(Enters stage right)* Yes son, what is it you want?

Older son: John tells me that my good-for-nothing brother is home and you're throwing a party for him. Father, how could you?!

Father: But son, he was lost but now he has found himself. I wanted to celebrate his return.

Older son: Dad, how could you? After all, I've been with you for years. I've worked for you night and day and you never gave me a party.

Father: But son, everything that is mine is yours, but your brother who was dead is now alive. Come in the house. Let's celebrate together.

Older son: Never! Never! Never! *(He struts off in a huff, stage left.)*

Father: *(To audience)* I love both my sons. I wish they could love each other *(shrugs his shoulders and walks off slowly stage right shouting into the house)*. On with the celebration!

Kenneth Gruebel
East Williston, New York

See also 14) JURY BIBLE STUDY, 18) THE PRODIGAL DAUGHTER/SON, 58) PARENT/YOUTH ENCOUNTER, 59) THE WEEKEND PARTY

215. THE UNFORGIVING BROTHER

(Matthew 18:21-35)

Narrator: Sometimes the parables of Jesus are a little difficult for us to understand. Our play this morning is our attempt to update the Parable of the Unforgiving Servant as it appears in Matthew 18:21-35. We've entitled it "The Parable of the Unforgiving Brother." *(Narrator exits.)*

Peter: Jesus! Jesus! *(runs across the stage)* Jesus, how many times should I forgive my friend—three times, five times, seven times!?!

Jesus: No, Peter, not seven times *(shaking his head),* but 70 times seven.

Peter: I don't think he's that good a friend.

Jesus: Perhaps not, Peter, but you will be treated by God the way you treat others. Let me tell you the story about a father who had two children. *(Center stage—man in an easy chair reading the evening paper—his young son runs up to him.)*

Bob: *(Breathless)* Sis said you wanted to see me, Dad.

Father: Yes, I did, Son, but you didn't have to run. Do you remember when I gave you that $20 bill last week to buy me the Sunday paper?

Bob: Sure, Dad.

Father: Well, Bob, I'd like my change back, please.

Bob: Gee, Dad, I gave it to Mom.

Father: I checked with your mother first, and she said you didn't give it to her.

Bob: *(Looking worried)* Uh, well, umm . . .

Father: *(Becoming angry)* I'd like my money back, Son.

Bob: Dad, I don't have it. I used it to buy that neat-looking race car set I wanted for Christmas but didn't get *(somewhat sarcastically).*

Father: First you lied to me, now you tell me you spent my money without my permission on a race car set. That does it! You're grounded for the next two months, and besides that I'm cutting off your allowance.

continued

THE UNFORGIVING BROTHER

Bob: Dad, you can't. Look, I'm sorry. I realize I was wrong. Please don't ground me. I'll never do it again . . . Please . . . I promise, Dad . . . please? I've learned my lesson. Please don't punish me.

Father: All right, Bob, maybe you have learned your lesson. Just don't ever let me catch you doing it again.

Bob: Thanks, Dad. You're great. (He walks away—Father resumes reading his paper.)

Alice: (Bob's younger and smaller sister enters the scene stage right.) Hi, Bob!

Bob: (Angry and hostile) You're gonna get it now, you little squealer. Give me back that dollar you owe me or I'm going to let you have it.

Alice: Bob, I don't have a dollar right now—here, take this quarter and I'll pay you the rest in a couple of days.

Bob: I want it now or you're going to get it.

Alice: Bob, please don't. I'd give it to you if I had it.

Father: What are you kids fighting about now?

Bob: (Self-righteously) Alice owes me a dollar and won't pay me back.

Father: Bob, you'll never learn, will you? I forgave you for lying and taking $20 that didn't belong to you, and you couldn't even forgive your sister for one measly dollar. That does it. Get to your room. I'm grounding you for four months or until you learn how to behave.

Jesus: That is how my Father in heaven will treat you if you do not forgive one another from your heart.

Kenneth Gruebel
East Williston, New York

See also 59) THE WEEKEND PARTY

216. THE GOOD SAMARITAN
(Luke 10:25-37)

This chancel play is best done when actors improvise their lines. The lines and directions given are to aid in the direction of the play.

(Jesus, dressed in robe and sandals, and a lawyer, dressed in a suit, enter and stand stage right. A crowd is sitting center stage which watches entire play.)

Lawyer: (To congregation) There once was a very smart lawyer who confronted Jesus to test him. (to Jesus) Teacher, what shall I do to inherit eternal life?

Jesus: What is written in the law?

Lawyer: You shall love the Lord your God with all your heart, soul, strength and mind; and your neighbor as yourself.

Jesus: That's right, do this, and you will live.

Lawyer: But, Teacher, who is my neighbor?

Jesus: A man was going down from Jerusalem to Jericho . . . *(A man dressed in street clothes enters stage left whistling. Jesus and Lawyer slowly move out of the scene.)*

Traveler: *(When he reaches center stage)* . . . suddenly robbers came upon him and beat him and stole all his money. *(As he is saying this two masked robbers dressed in black rush toward him, beat him to the ground and take his money. They leave counting the money as they go. Traveler lies on the ground moaning.)*

Minister: *(Enters stage left dressed in liturgical garb)* A minister happened to pass by on his way to a committee meeting. *(Minister stops, looks at the Traveler, joins his hands together as if to pray.)* Be filled and warmed my son and go in peace. *(The minister then continues on his way).*

Traveler: Groan . . .

Levite: *(Enters stage right dressed in a leisure suit)* A liberal Levite also happened to pass by on his way to a town council meeting *(stops and looks at the man, shakes his head and looks up at the congregation).* No-good drunks should be locked up in prison where they belong. I'm going to bring this up at our council meeting *(exits stage left).*

Samaritan: *(Enters stage left dressed rather poorly)* A Samaritan going nowhere in particular saw the man and said, 'Hey man, what's happening?'

Traveler: *(Groans)*

Samaritan: Say, you're not doing too well *(helps the Traveler up).* I think I better get you to the Holiday Inn down the street *(places a bandage stained partially red around the Traveler's head and helps him over to the first pew, where he knocks on the wood).*

Innkeeper: *(Stands up from behind first pew dressed in appropriate garb)* Whatta ya want?

Samaritan: I'd like you to put my friend here up for the night.

Innkeeper: *(Excitedly)* He's bleeding all over my new carpeting—get him out of here!

Samaritan: But the man is hurt and needs attention.

Innkeeper: All right, follow me. *(They exit stage left. Jesus and Lawyer re-enter stage right during the exit of the Innkeeper, Traveler and Samaritan.)*

Jesus: Now which one was a neighbor to the Traveler? *(With that, the Minister, Levite and Samaritan run back on center stage and stand facing the congregation. Jesus then runs behind them and places his hand over the Levite's head.)* Number one? *(then over the Minister's head)* . . . or number two? *(then over the Samaritan's head)* . . . or number three?

(The crowd members boo and hiss when number one and two are called and cheer when number three is called. All exit stage left.)

Kenneth Gruebel
East Williston, New York

See also 34) NEIGHBORS AND FRIENDS, 40) GOOD SAMARITAN MIME

217. THE SOWER
(Mark 4:2-32)

Narrator: *(Dressed in farm clothes)* Jesus taught the people many things during his earthly pilgrimage, but the ordinary people like you and me remember the stories that he told most of all. We'd like to share with you this morning our own version of "The Parable of the Sower." *(Takes a cloth bag from his side and begins to toss out rice, representing seeds.)* Once upon a time there was a farmer who went out to do his spring planting. And as he was sowing his seeds . . .

Seed 1: *(Dressed in brown, pops up from behind 1st pew)* Some fell upon the old farm path. *(aside to audience)* Hey, this is no place for a seed to grow. I could get stepped on. *(imagining a giant foot is coming down on him).* Hey, hey, watch where you're walking—who do you think you are, the Jolly Green Giant? *(Suddenly falls to the ground. Gets up very wearily as if he'd been stepped on.)* I'm never going to grow up to be a big plant like my dad. I'm probably just going to be bird seed. Oh no, here he comes again. Hey, watch it! *(falls out of sight).*

Narrator: *(Pauses from his sowing seeds)* I guess that's the way it is sometimes—some folks hear God's word, but they're so busy watching out for themselves they never get a chance to grow. Well, back to work *(tosses more rice).*

Seed 2: *(Dressed in green, jumps up from behind a pew)* Boy, this rocky ground is great. Look how fast I grew *(looking around).* Looks like I've got the place all to myself. That's what I like—privacy!!

Sun: *(Dressed in yellow, carrying a great big cardboard cutout of the sun)* But since the seed fell on rocky ground there was no depth in its roots, so when I came out, I scorched the plant, and it soon withered and died. *(draws close to the plant)* Scorch!! Scorch!! Scorch!!

Seed 2: It's getting hot out here. I could use a drink of water *(begins to weave in place).* I think I'm going to faint *(falls over).*

Sun: Ta . . . DAAAAAAH!! *(bows to the audience)*

Narrator: Be careful now; don't be like the plants on the rocks, for their roots have no depth, and when trouble comes, they soon wither and fade away. Think I'd better get back to my planting. Excuse me, please . . .

Seed 3: *(Dressed in green, surrounded by actors dressed in black)* Some of us fell among the weeds. Hi, fellas, how are you? It's good to be with you. I hope we can become good friends.

A black weed: Okay boys, let's get him. *(They beat the green seed down.)*

Seed 3: Help! Help! Help! *(falls)*

Narrator: One should choose one's friends carefully. Oh well, easy come, easy go *(walks slowly away).*

Seeds 4 & 5: *(Popping up from the center)* Hey, don't forget us!! We're the heroes of this parable!! We're the seeds that fell on good soil and produce a lot of fruit. *(They pass out apples, oranges, bananas to those in the first few pews.)*

Narrator: Sorry, fellas, I almost forgot. Sometimes God's seeds fall upon good soil—listening and understanding ears—and they are the ones that really do bear much fruit.

We hope all of you are like the seeds that fell on the good soil. *(Narrator bows with rest of the cast.)*

Kenneth Gruebel
East Williston, New York

See also 17) ENCOUNTER BIBLE CHARACTERS

218. "GOIN' TO NINEVAH"

Here is a play I have written entitled "Goin' to Ninevah." The play is a sometimes humorous look at the story of Jonah. Five of our high school youth presented it recently at a variety show sponsored by our youth group. The congregation responded to it very well. It lasts about 20 minutes and the only equipment required consists of a few simple props and a speaker system for God's voice.

**"GOIN' TO NINEVAH:
The Story of Jonah and the Lord"**

(A Dramatic Reading for Five Voices)

SCENE 1

(As the scene opens, Jonah, an itinerant peddler, is packing up his bags for his next round of visits to the surrounding villages. He is humming away to himself, muttering about how this item or that will make a big sell and about how he may be able to retire in a few more years if his business holds up. As he is working away, the phone rings.)

JONAH: Jonah Jones, peddler, purchaser, and preacher! I peddle pans at portentiously puny prices!

LORD: Knock it off, Jones! This is the Lord and I haven't got time for that!

JONAH: Oh yeah!? Well, I haven't got time for you either! Not now! Not ever again! I remember the last time you called me just as I was about to leave on a business trip! That one cost me 600 bucks, my new suit, and four nights in that lousy jailhouse in Jerusalem and if you think I'm going through that again you're crazy!

LORD: Look Jones, you know as well as I that all of that was your fault! Now I happen to know that you are going to be in the vicinity of Ninevah on this trip and I have a special mission for you! I want you to stop off there and tell those fools that their wickedness stares me in the face and that I'm not going to tolerate it any longer! Got that? I want you to tell them to shape up or else!!!

JONAH: Well, it just so happens that I won't have time! No, one of my donkeys is lame and I'll be late for my appointments as it is!

LORD: I can take care of that!

JONAH: No! I don't want any more of your help! I'm not going! And I'm particularly not going anywhere near Ninevah! Those crummy Assyrians don't deserve any warning! After what they did to my brother, I say, "Let 'em burn!"

LORD: Jonah, I insist!

JONAH: Please Lord, don't make me do it! I hate those smelly Assyrians! Yuch! They're so dirty! And you know you can't trust one farther than you can throw him! I know, Lord! Let's wipe 'em out! Just you and me, Lord! I'll go over to Ninevah and set fire to a couple of their buildings and then you make a great big wind come up and we'll burn down the whole city! What about that, Lord? *(silence)* Not even a little fire???

LORD: No, Jonah, not even a little fire.

JONAH: Okay, Lord. You win. I'll do whatever you say.

LORD: Thanks, Jones. I knew I could count on you.

JONAH: *(Dejectedly)* Bye, Lord. *(Jonah is thinking.)* Oh, man! He did it to me again! Why *ME!?* Why do I always get stuck with the dirty work!? Ninevah! Those rotten Assyrians! . . . You know what? I'm not gonna do it! Nope! Old Jonah is no fool! I've been working hard and I deserve a little vacation! Hmmm . . . A little trip to sunny Greece is just what the doctor ordered! A little vacation cruise to Tarshish! I'm gonna call my travel agent . . .

SCENE 2

(As the second scene opens Jonah is sitting huddled up in a blanket on the deck of an old steamer. The ship is rocking heavily and Jonah is miserable. In the background can be heard storm noises.)

JONAH: Burrr!!! Some vacation cruise this is! That rascal of a travel agent! I bet he was in cahoots with the Lord! Ohhh! What a ship! This old steamer shouldn't sail in a bathtub! And this storm! *(Crash)* This storm! I have the feeling that somebody's trying to tell me something!

SAILOR 1: *(Talking to another sailor as they enter from the side)* O gods of Babylon, have mercy on us! I've never been in a storm like this!

SAILOR 2: DDDo yyyou ththink we have a chance? *(Shaking with fright.)*

SAILOR 1: Not unless we find out what's causing this storm!

SAILOR 2: WWWhat dddo yyyou mean?

SAILOR 1: Get a grip on yourself, man! This is no ordinary storm! Something on this ship is putting us under a bad omen! We've got to find it and get rid of it! *(They begin to look around. Jonah, who has been cowering lower and lower attempts to crawl away unnoticed.)*

SAILOR 2: Hey! What's that! *(They run over to Jonah. Sailor 1 pulls him up to his feet.)*

SAILOR 1: Who are you? And what are you doing on this ship?

JONAH: My name is Jonah Jones. And I am on this barge because I am trying to escape from Yahweh, the Lord of Israel who created the heavens, the Earth, and this wretched sea! You have no idea how cantankerous he is! Last year he sent me on a mission to Jerusalem in which I wound up broke and in jail, and now he wants me to go preach to those heathens in Ninevah! Well, I'm not having any of it, I tell you! I'd rather feed the fishes than go preach to those low-down Assyrians!

SAILOR 1: Aha! What'd I tell you! I knew there was a reason for this storm! *(To Jonah)* You have angered Yahweh and if we don't get you off this ship, we'll all go down together!

JONAH: You mean . . . *(Jonah gestures to the side of the deck.)*

SAILOR 1: I'm afraid so!

JONAH: Alas!!! This looks like the end of me! I should have known the Lord would find out about this.

continued

GOIN' TO NINEVAH

I'll bet he's bugged my phone! All right! Throw me over into the raging sea to meet my untimely fate! *(The two sailors pick Jonah up and throw him over the side of the deck)* GERONIMOOO!!! *(Jonah emerges center stage paddling desperately.)* Help! Ooooff! Help! Ooooff! I'm sinking! I'm going to drown! *(Still paddling)* What's that?!! Up ahead! Oh, no! It's a gigantic whale! Sure hope he's not hungry! Oh, no! He's coming this way and he sure looks hungry! Get away you old whale! Ooooooooo . . . *(Jonah does a front somersault, lies quietly for a time, then stands up and begins to feel his way around in the dark.)* Hey! Who turned out the lights in here? What's going on??? Where am I anyway?!! *(Jonah strikes a match, yells, quickly blows it out)* Good heavens! I've been kidnapped by The Blob! No, wait! Was that a nightmare I had or could it really be . . . I think it was, I think I am, I think I'm in the belly of a whale . . . How long have I been here? *(Consults his watch.)* Three days! Three days? That's a good sign! Maybe the Lord hasn't forgotten me after all! *(Gets down on his knees.)*
I called to the Lord in my distress and he answered me;
out of the belly of this whale I cried for help, and he has heard my cry.
You cast me into the depths, Lord, far out at sea, and the flood closed around me;
all your waves, all your foam, passed over me,
I thought I was banished from your sight and would never see your holy temple again.
I was sinking into a world whose bars would hold me fast forever. But you brought me up alive from the pit, O Lord.
As my sense failed me I remembered the Lord, and my prayer reached you in your holy temple.
Men who worship false gods may abandon their loyalty, but I will offer you a sacrifice with my words of praise;
I will fulfill my promise; victory is the Lord's.
(With this Jonah sits back and begins to rock around as the whale begins to shake.)

JONAH: Whoa! I think this whale is getting an upset stomach! This ride is worse than my old Ford's! I think I'm going to be leaving soon and I just hope we're near something dry and firm! Whoooa! *(Jonah does a backwards somersault and rolls out onto dry land.)* Land! Oh boy! Land! Oh, I thought I'd never feel the earth or see the sun again! Praise the Lord!

LORD: *(As a voice from the sky)* Jonah!

JONAH: *(Looking around)* What? Who called me?

LORD: All right Jones, you know who this is!

JONAH: Ma!?

LORD: This is the Lord! And while you're down there praising me, don't forget the promise you just made!

JONAH: Forget! How could I forget? You think I want to go through that again? Jail was bad enough, but a whale! Who could even believe that I would be swallowed by a whale! No Lord, I'm on my way!

(Jonah starts walking in place facing the audience.) Oh, boy! Sure is a long way to Ninevah. Sure is hot! Those crummy Assyrians! Who'd believe that Jonah Jones was . . . Oh well, got to keep walkin'. I don't know what might happen to me if I don't. The Lord sure drives a hard bargain! . . . Aha! *(peering ahead at the audience)* There it is! There's Ninevah, that monster of a city! *(Walks down directly in front of the audience.)* Ninevah! Hear the word of the Lord! Your wickedness stares me in the face! Shame on you who lie in bed planning evil and wicked deeds and rise at daybreak to do them, knowing that you have power! You covet land and take it by force. Your houses are full of fraud as a cage is full of birds. You grow rich and grand but refuse to do justice. The claims of the orphan you do not put right nor do you grant justice to the poor. "Shall I not punish you for this?" says the Lord. "Shall I not take vengeance on such a people? I have told you what is good and what it is that I ask of you: Only to act justly, to love loyally, and to walk humbly with your God." Behold, Ninevah, in 40 days you shall be overthrown! *(Jonah moves offstage.)*

KING: *(The King of Ninevah stands up in the middle of the audience and begins to read his proclamation.)* This is a decree from I, the King, and my Royal Court. No man or beast, herd or flock, is to taste food, to graze, or to drink water. They are to clothe themselves in sackcloth and call on God with all their might. Let every man abandon his wicked ways and his habitual violence. It may be that the Lord will repent and turn away from his anger so we will not perish.

LORD: Oh Ninevah, I am well pleased with your repentance. I shall spare you from the disaster which I threatened.

SCENE 3

(The third and final scene takes place out in the countryside where Jonah goes to sit and see what will happen to Ninevah.)

JONAH: *(Walking slowly out from the side to center stage)* I knew it! I just knew this was going to happen! Of all the luck! Those crummy Assyrians! How could they repent—they're too dumb to repent! But they did! And all because old Jonah told them to! Oh, my! If this ever gets around back home—
that old Jonah helped the Assyrians—I'll be ruined! No one will have anything to do with me! No one will buy any of my . . .

LORD: What's the matter Jones, feeling sorry for yourself again?

JONAH: Oh, Lord, don't you see? This is what I said would happen in the first place? I knew you were a gracious God, merciful, slow to anger, full of steadfast love, and willing to repent of the disaster. But it makes me so mad, I could just die! In fact, that's what I'm gonna do. I'm gonna march right on out to the desert and sit in the sun until I die! *(Jonah turns and marches in place for awhile, slowly moving toward the back of the stage. He stops, turns,*

continued

GOIN' TO NINEVAH

looks around, then sits down dejectedly.) What a place! What a place to die! Nothing in sight but that old bush over there. *(Jonah gestures to one side.)* But oh, sure is hot . . . no water, no breeze, no nothing! . . . Maybe I'll just, maybe I'll just move over a little into the shade of that old bush. *(Jonah crawls over.)* No sense making this more painful than it has to be. *(Jonah sits for awhile, then is aware that he is feeling even more heat. He begins to fan himself rapidly, then looks around to see what the problem is.)* My bush! My bush! It's withering away right before my eyes! *(Turns back to audience.)* This must be the Lord's doing! Even here he has followed me! I should be better off dead than alive!

LORD: Are you so angry over the bush?

JONAH: Yes, Lord, mortally angry!

LORD: You are sorry for the bush, though you did not have the trouble of growing it, a plant which came up in a few nights and withered in a day. And should I not be sorry for the great city of Ninevah, which I created, and which is filled with children who do not know their right hand from their left? Come, Jonah! Sulk out here no longer, but do what I require of you: act justly; love loyalty; and walk humbly with me—home! *(Jonah lingers a moment absorbing what the Lord has said. Then he gets up and slowly walks off stage.)*

Dan.Schifeling
Oak Lawn, Illinois

See also 17) ENCOUNTER BIBLE CHARACTERS

219. JESUS MEETS THE ELDERS

The chancel play has been one of our favorite means of reaching an audience/congregation with a message. Jesus encounters some elders of a congregation and an interesting conversation goes on from there.

Jesus Meets the Elders

J—Jesus
1—Elder 1
2—Elder 2
3—Elder 3

1   Good afternoon, we're here to evaluate several of the candidates coming before us, the pulpit nominating committee, for evaluating persons for our pulpit. Our first young man is a recent graduate of Nazareth Seminary and his name is Jesus. Is that right?

J   Yes, that's right.

2   Do you have a last name?

J   No, but I do have some nicknames . . .

2   Oh?

J   Like Son of Man, Christ, the Annointed One, Suffering Servant, Messiah . . .

1   Okay, okay. In flipping through your dossier, Jesus, we haven't had a chance to look over everything, but my goodness it seems just fascinating; you seem to have had a wide variety of experience and certainly some marvelous training in the ministry. I wonder if you could tell us a little of your background. You didn't say much about that here.

J   Well, what specifically would you like me to relate to you?

3   Could you tell us where you're from? What part of the country?

J   I was born in Bethlehem.

3   Oh, Bethlehem, Pennsylvania. There's a wonderful *(your denomination)* Church there. Do you know it?

J   Well, no.

3 It's a fabulous congregation, doing some wonderful things. I'm surprised you weren't in touch with them.

J It wasn't Bethlehem, Pennsylvania.

3 Oh, in Ohio?

J No, it was Bethlehem of Judea.

3 Judea, is that a . . . ?

J . . . on the Mediterranean.

3 Oh, you're a foreign student.

J Yes (laughs).

3 I understand. That's interesting. I didn't know we had any foreign students coming before us.

J You see, I was born in Bethlehem, but we didn't spend much time there. My father had a vision, a dream, and we spent some time in Egypt and then in my hometown, Nazareth. My father, you could say was a carpenter; well, he wasn't exactly my father . . . My mother was a virgin . . .

2 My goodness! That's highly irregular, isn't it?

J I spent pretty much all my life in Nazareth until this time. It was time for me to begin my ministry, so I thought I'd come to (name of church).

2 Now Jesus, regarding your field work requirement. We believe this is an essential part of seminary education. Did you do your two years in a local parish?

J Well, no, to answer you quite frankly, I wasn't in a parish.

2 I see. Then you must have been ministering to hospital patients. We know that's popular.

J Well, no, not in a hospital either, though I do heal the sick.

1 In a home for boys and girls?

J No, not in that kind of place either, though I do believe that children are essential to the Christian community.

2 Well, most definitely it was a prison then; that's as in as you can get these days.

J No, it wasn't in a prison either, although I do believe we should visit prisoners. Basically, it was in the hills and valleys surrounding the villages and towns that I did my ministering.

1 Oh, you were a street minister! That certainly clarifies a few things. Did you have any extra-curricular activities while in seminary . . . any sports . . . intramural ball?

J Well, no, not really intramural ball . . . but I really took a liking to fishing. You should have seen some of the catches . . . unbelievable. The boats almost sank and of course boating and fishing go together.

1 To what do you attribute your success in fishing, any particular reason . . . good solid bait?

J No, not good solid bait so much as good solid prayer; the Holy Spirit led to our fishing success. My other hobbies include mountain climbing and water-walking!!!

2 Oh, where, back in Judea?

J Yes, and then there was the time I had a hiking experience in the wilderness for 40 days . . . kind of a survival school. It was a great spiritual awakening. Fantastic.

1 Backpacking with young people?

J No, I did it on my own. I didn't take any supplies or water or anything.

1 You know, Jesus, one of the basic reasons for going to seminary is to learn how to preach; preaching is really the center of our service in the (your denomination) tradition and I wonder . . . would your sermons correspond with our tradition of using the basic three-point plan?

J Well, not really, in fact, I don't write out

continued

JESUS MEETS THE ELDERS

my sermons at all. I let the Holy Spirit direct my thoughts when I get up to preach. In fact, I don't usually even preach in churches. My best sermon—just to give you an idea—was on a hillside and there were multitudes surrounding me and I sat down to talk . . .

1 Aren't you exaggerating—multitudes don't come to hear a (*your denomination*) preach on a typical Sunday.

J As I remember, it wasn't even a Sunday.

2 They took time off from work?

J Yes. Well, I'd been gaining popularity as a preacher and healer and miracle worker—but that's another story. The text of my sermon was:
•Blessed are the poor in spirit, for theirs is the kingdom of heaven.
•Blessed are those who mourn for they shall be comforted.
•Blessed are the meek, for they shall inherit the earth.
•Blessed are those who hunger and thirst for righteousness, for they shall be satisfied . . . and it goes on and on from there. That was probably my most moving sermon. As you can see, it was considerably more than three points.

1 Now what I'm wondering, however, is . . . do you outline your sermons according to the introductory sheet; that's very important you know.

J Yes, I suppose it is, but the only thing I had for it was a title.

1 What was the title?

J I called it "Sermon on the Mount."

2 No theme at all? . . . I see.

1 Do you have any particular thoughts on salary expectations you'd be looking for in your first call?

J No, I don't really worry about such things.

1 That's typical among seminarians—idealism and so on. Financial matters are really of the utmost importance to clergy

types, and I feel that after a few years in the parish you'll realize that finances and salary are pretty important. After all, if you're going to do the Lord's work you might as well get paid for it.

J It seems to me that if we seek first his kingdom, all these other things should be ours as well and will be.

2 That's a good point, but in practice it still takes hard cold cash to bring home the bacon. Certainly the Lord isn't going to provide food, clothing and shelter. The Lord helps those who help themselves.

J Yes, that may be true, but consider the ravens; they neither plant nor harvest, they have neither storehouse nor barn, and yet God feeds them. Of how much more value are we than the birds?

1 We're more important than ravens . . . but that's an isolated case.

J Consider the lilies of the field, how they grow, they neither spin nor weave, yet I tell you not even Solomon in all his glory was decked out like one of these.

3 But do you think the Lord's going to take care of you, pay your taxes . . . ?

J Render to the IRS the things that are the IRS's and to God the things that are God's.

3 Jesus, we are middle of the road on the view of consuming alcohol, but we feel a young man should take a position, so when confronted he'll have an answer. Do you feel it's okay for a Christian to take a drink?

J I really can't see anything wrong with drinking a little wine; in fact, I attended a wedding in Cana and it was quite an affair. About halfway through they ran out of wine and my mother . . . I don't know if you know my mother Mary . . .

3 I don't believe so, we don't usually go into personal family ties.

J . . . she asked me to help, so I performed a small miracle and changed the vats of water into wine. It was exquisite.

2 Jesus, we're at that point in our interview when we examine you on the form and content of the English Bible. I presume you're prepared for that?

J You mean the Torah and the Prophets? I know them cold.

2 Well good, if we could . . .

J Even the wisdom books I have down pretty pat.

2 Good, good. I think that takes care of the Old Testament; what about the New Testament?

J The New Testament . . . well, you might say that my friends and I created it.

2 Now, Jesus, we were wondering about social involvement in the community, you know, how you translate your faith into concrete action.

J I don't quite understand the intent of the question.

2 In other words, do you feel the Christian church ought to be involved in the community in project, to help our fellow man or should we remain within the walls of the church building?

J Oh, no. I definitely feel we should go outside the walls of the church. In fact there was a time when I had a little trouble with a church. They were having a bazaar in the church.

1 Like a Christmas bazaar? We always have a Christmas bazaar to beef up our budget, so we'd expect you to participate in it. How do you feel about that?

J You know what I do when I see that? Not in my father's house . . . it was a mess! I couldn't stand it!

1 Now, young man, I should like to point out that our church has had bazaars for years and they have been a good thing. I can't understand why you're against it.

J Because my father's house is a house of prayer. Bazaars make it a den of thieves and robbers.

3 Maybe we'd better give this man another example. In our society . . . in the cities, especially, there are people whose moral standards are not exactly what ours would be like . . . prostitutes abound there. Should the church take some action to clean up this moral depravity, get them punished?

J I always thought we should take out the log in our own eye before we removed the splinter from someone else's eye.

3 What's your point?

J I always thought that we had better look at our own lives and clean them up before we try to clean up someone else's.

2 Oh, we don't have any prostitutes in our church.

J We should love all people even if they don't go to our church.

2 But don't you feel adultery should be punished because it is morally wrong? That's the real issue. Just last week a young girl approached me and I told her I was going to have to report her to her church for censure and tell the police to keep an eye on her activity.

J It seems to me, sir, that those of us without sin should cast the first stone, so to speak.

1 Let's move on. Some of us have been disturbed with the way our church has been spending its money on people who don't really deserve it.

J I don't know. Seems to me that the church should be involved with those who need help most whether we think they deserve it or not.

1 Well, yes. Another area of importance is that of personal theology. What do you think of the Second Coming?

J I'm glad to be here.

1 Are you born again, Jesus?

J I guess you might say so.

2 You do believe in a literal interpretation of scripture?

continued

JESUS MEETS THE ELDERS

J Could you be more specific?

2 That Christ was crucified, put in a tomb . . .

J It was really lonely.

1 That he rose from the dead, walked through doors . . . you do believe that?

J Yes, it's an historical reality.

1 Our final concern is the results of your ordination exams. The results show that you failed all four.

J Well, I wasn't familiar with the proper forms of worship. I had always gone off and kneeled and prayed.

1 How could we justify ordaining you if you don't take worship seriously?

J I believe.

2 What? But you failed theology, too.

J What does it matter as long as I believe in God?

3 Jesus, these exams are graded by good Christian people who are aware of what's needed in parish work. How will you relate to people if you can't pass these exams?

J Do you really think that failing exams means a person can't relate to people?

2 Of course.

J Oh, the fun exam was the church govern-ment one. It's amazing how many ways you can zap your brother and make it look legal . . . censure, complaint, excommunication.

1 But those rules are for our protection so the church has only people who are worthy of belonging. Do you have a better plan?

J You should love the Lord your God with all your heart and with all your mind and with all your strength and you should love your neighbor as yourself.

3 What about exegesis, the proclamation of God's word. Surely you should've passed that.

J I guess I failed because I didn't use any commentaries.

2 Jesus, do you have any final comments before we vote on your fitness for the Christian ministry?

J Just one. Do you think you'd recognize your Lord if he walked in right now? (Turns to audience.) Would you?

Kenneth Gruebel
East Williston, New York

See also 17) ENCOUNTER BIBLE CHARACTERS

JUNK YARD SORTER: THE INDEX

The purpose of this index is to help you find entries according to themes, issues and happenings in youth ministry. Each entry is listed by its number and title, not by page number.

bow, 29) A Step Ahead

HARD TIMES HOBOS: CONTRIBUTORS

(Contributions are listed by entry numbers, not page numbers)

Roger Kemp
57, 125, 129, 199

Jo Ann Kirch
168

Wayne A. Knight
195

Steve Knox
108

Ken Kohlmann
177

Jim Kramer
210

Paul Krupinski
83, 93

Milan Lambertson
140

Donna Lenz
178

Gary Logan
111

Willard McCown
8

Sybil McLeese
142

E. Jane Mall
72, 76

Charles Martin
85, 123, 196

Roland Martinson
96

Joyce Miller
164, 166

Michael F. Miller
122

Tim Morrison
48, 102

Michael Moynahan
73

Virgil Nelson
4, 7

Grant & Wendy Nichol
5, 90, 91, 94

Jan Otto
131, 182, 186

William R. Pennock
27

Paul Perry
75

Ralph Pitman Jr.
181

Marcy Posner & Terry Caywood
92

Thomas J. Potenza
179

Lynn Potter
118

Jim Powell
45

Adolph Quast
58, 172

John & Bobbie Rankin
28, 67

John Rawlinson
1, 81

Dan Reed
86

Beverly W. Rice
80

Carolyn Rice
147

Ron Rich
55

John Roberts
169

Andy Rosulek
175

Sue Rueben
208

Henry Sawatzky
14

Ken Scarborough
26, 59, 71, 104, 143

John Scherer
17

Randall R. Scheer
9, 66, 120, 161

Dan Schifeling
218

Dr. Christopher Schooley
24

Kit Schooley
201

Thom Schultz
51, 126

Carol Seibert
101

Floyd Shaffer
159, 167

David Shaheen
88, 205

Mike Shaughnessy
77

Chris Shiber
138

Margaret Simpson
37

Earl Sires
121, 194

Jane Small
211

Trevor Smith
44, 162

Warren Smith
171

Steve Sonnenberg
70

Jesse J. Sowell Jr.
10

Harold Steindam
13

Wesley Taylor
3, 30, 115, 165

Richard Teaford
47

Jan Tully
156

Oscar F. Twedt
89, 139

Dick VanSkike
203

Karen Walisch
33

Larry K. Waltz
31

Phineas A. Washer
103

Gary Weaver
61

Eric L. White
190

Doug Whiting
56

D. Ray Wiggins
128, 133

Craig Wilson
213

Leigh Wilson
16, 19, 40

Bill Wolfe
60, 187

Paul M. Wright
197

Ken & Cathy Yost
79

Richard Ziglar
158

THE
BENSON FAMILY
Bottom, from left: Jill and Amy
Standing: Marilyn and Dennis

THE HEAD HOBOS: ABOUT THE COMPILERS

Marilyn J. Benson is a professional teacher, workshop leader, planning consultant and curriculum specialist. She has been chairperson of several regional and national agencies, such as the North American Broadcast section of the World Association for Christian Communication.

Marilyn is past chairperson of the South Hills Inter-faith Ministry, a large interdenominational service agency. She is involved with a consortium of home health agencies and hospitals with the South Hills Hospice Division, helping those agencies learn how to care better for the terminally ill.

Marilyn is co-author of the book, **Promises to Keep.**

Dennis C. Benson is a Christian media consultant, minister, creator of the "Recycle Youth" tape series and author of 15 books, including **The Basic Encyclopedia for Youth Ministry, The Ministry of the Child, Making Tracks, Recycle Catalogue** (Volumes 1 and 2) and **The Rock Generation.**

He has served in the past as a seminary instructor in New Testament Greek and exegesis, suburban pastor, college chaplain, producer of award-winning radio and television shows for interdenominational agencies, and youth director for many churches.

Marilyn and Dennis are publishers of **Recycle** and **Scan** newsletters. They are veteran youth workers and pioneers in "recycle theology," a creative process of finding new communication uses for existing resources.

Together, they form the centerpoint of a network of thousands of youth workers who recycle creative ministry ideas and techniques.

Through their recycle cottage ministry, they have sold over 300,000 cassette tapes on topics ranging from drugs to mime to experiential Bible study.

Marilyn and Dennis have two teenage daughters, Amy and Jill. They live in Pittsburgh, Pennsylvania.

OTHER YOUTH MINISTRY BOOKS FROM GROUP BOOKS:

The Basic Encyclopedia for Youth Ministry—Answers, ideas, encouragement, and inspiration for 230 youth ministry questions and problems. By Dennis C. Benson and Bill Wolfe. Hardbound. $15.95.

The Youth Group How-to Book—Detailed instructions and models for 66 practical projects and programs to help you build a better group. $14.95.

Youth Group Travel Directory—A nationwide listing of churches that will offer lodging and fellowship to your group at little or no cost. $7.95.

The Best of Try This One—A fun collection of games, crowd breakers and programs. $5.95.

More . . . Try This One—More games, fund raisers, crowd breakers, discussions and projects. $5.95.

Try This One . . . Too—The latest in the "Try This One" series of discussions, games, fund raisers, crowd breakers and projects. $5.95.

Available at your Christian bookstore or from the publisher

____The Basic Encyclopedia for Youth Ministry. $15.95.
____Hard Times Catalog for Youth Ministry. $14.95.
____The Youth Group How-to Book. $14.95.
____Youth Group Travel Directory. $7.95.
____The Best of Try This One. $5.95.
____More . . . Try This One. $5.95.
____Try This One . . . Too. $5.95.

Subtotal	$ _____
Postage and handling	$ ___2.00
Total enclosed	$ _____

NAME _____
ADDRESS_____
CITY _____ STATE _____ ZIP _____

SEND TO:
Group Books, Box 481, Loveland, CO 80539

105330